VIETNAM VETERANS
The Road to Recovery

VIETNAM VETERANS

The Road to Recovery

Joel Osler Brende
and
Erwin Randolph Parson

PLENUM PRESS • NEW YORK AND LONDON

Library of Congress Cataloging in Publication Data

Brende, Joel Osler.
  Vietnam veterans.

  Bibliography: p.
  Includes index.
    1. Veterans — United States — Psychology — Addresses,
essays, lectures. 2. Vietnamese Conflict, 1961–1975 — United
States — Addresses, essays, lectures. I. Parson, Erwin Ran-
dolph. II. Title.
  UB357.B74   1985   355.1′156′0973   84-26396
  ISBN 0-306-41966-1

First Printing — March 1985
Second Printing — July 1986

Plenum Press is a division of
Plenum Publishing Corporation
233 Spring Street, New York, N.Y. 10013

Printed in the United States of America

FOREWORD

What does it mean today to be a Vietnam veteran? Indeed, what does it mean to be an American in the post-Vietnam era? These are but two questions many thoughtful Americans are seeking to answer while attempting to understand the much broader picture. How has our involvement in Southeast Asia affected our yesterdays, our living of today, our planning for tomorrows?

We are in a period of transition in this country. A time when public attitudes change—when our perceptions of ourselves and the world in which we live swing wildly from one end of the scale to the other. For some this may be a quiet time in which international events seem immersed beneath immediate cares of family and finances. For others the present may be very unsettling, a time when our past overwhelms our ability to place ourselves in the present and to chart a course for the future.

Where are we going, America? What does losing a war portend? Do we as a society have repressed feelings of guilt and vulnerability that manifest themselves in national policy and voting patterns? Might we fall into the snare of anger, recrimination, and bitterness that consumned Germany after World War I? Might we react by blindly following a charismatic leader down a poorly illuminated path to future disaster? In this nuclear age, America, can any superpower afford to suffer the prolonged psychological after-shocks of a "lost war" syndrome? What do we still believe in, America? Indeed, do we maintain any of the values we once held sacred?

It should be noted here, at the beginning, that independent research by Dr. Parson ". . . indicates that not only have most Vietnam veterans adjusted well, but some men are now better adjusted than before going to Vietnam." America is a multifaced conglomeration of individuals, families, races, of social, religious, financial, governmental, and business groupings all diverse yet interconnected. Like Vietnam veterans, nothing said using the collective term holds for all the individuals. Like Vietnam veterans, most of America has adjusted to the trauma of the events of the '60s and early '70s. And like Vietnam veterans who feel they cannot rest until all their brothers are healthy, America will not be able to rest until all Americans have returned to the fold.

I wish I could take you on a trip back in time and place—back to the old imperial capital at Hue and the surrounding area in 1970 and 1971. My own experiences there came at this time, a time when American and South Vietnamese military efforts had finally produced a mostly safe and secure country. It was my feeling then, as it is now, that given our limited military objectives, we reached those objectives during this period. To understand what it means to be a Vietnam veteran today it is imperative that we understand who we were then and what we accomplished.

The military situation in the mid and late '60s was one of continually expanding areas of U.S. and ARVN control with the "light at the end of the tunnel." That tunnel seemed to collapse with TET of '68 and our confidence and perspective changed.

Yet in cities like Hue, where the North Vietnamese massacred 6,000 civilians during their month-long occupation in 1968, the NVA incurred the hatred of the local population. The communist loss during the TET

'68 counter-offensive, along with the battle for Khe Sanh, their loss in Cambodia in 1970, and the ill-fated 1971 disruption of the Ho Chi Minh Trail in Laos, set the stage for the period from 1969 to 1972.

Each month more and more refugees returned to the land from which they had either fled or been forced. By the end of 1970, 97% of the refugees had been resettled on their own land and another 2% were in new villages that they had agreed to accept. The regional and popular forces, who for years had been the brunt of many jokes [even though they accounted for 37% of all enemy combat deaths while sustaining 28% of all southern casualties and spent only two to four percent of the war budget] had become very effective in protecting their home villages.

In areas like "The Street Without Joy," resettlement was accomplished through the combined efforts of the villagers, the ARVN, and American forces—particularly U.S. combat engineers. Roads were constructed tying historically isolated and poor hamlets to central market places, schools and hospitals were built with soldiers laboring beside villagers—Peace Corps style. American medics went beyond the point of simply treating villagers for common skin diseases and other tropical maladies. They established programs and trained Vietnamese health care workers.

There was one major reason for the success of the resettlement and the education and medical programs, for the increase in rice production and in the fishing industry catch, and for the bustling market places—the population centers were secure.

Vietnam has not been that peaceful since. Never again will as many people live on the land that their ancestors farmed, that hold the remains of their family past. The '72 and '75 offensives produced millions of refugees. In 1977 more than half a million people were forced into "new economic zones." In 1983 there were guerrilla actions in every province of I Corps and throughout most of the rest of the country. Buddhist and Catholic rites were restricted. There are now no opposition radio broadcasts, no opposition newspapers, and no freedom of movement. So many people are hungry that nearly five percent of the population has attempted to flee the country with one third dying at sea. Upwards of half a million old regime soldiers have been shipped to the Soviet Union where they are virtual slaves in some of the 2000 camps east of the Urals. And 43% of "independent" Vietnam's national budget goes to a military that maintains a police state in the north and the south while at the same time attempts to colonize Cambodia and Laos—a military surpassed in man-power by only China and India.

Most of the people of South Vietnam, especially in the northern half of the country, lived within a narrow coastal strip. By 1970, almost all the fighting had moved away from these centers and was concentrated in the mountainous jungles of I Corps.

"The New Vietnam Scholarship," an article by Fox Butterfield which appeared in the New York Times Magazine, stated, "After TET [68]— though most Americans at home had given up on the war—the cumulative weight of American firepower and spending in Vietnam [and I would add, the sacrifice and labor of American troops] dramatically undercut support for the communists. As a result, the United States was probably in a stronger position in Vietnam in 1972, just prior to the Paris Peace Accords, than at any previous point in the War."

In the Spring of '72 the NVA launched a conventional tank-led blitz-krieg across the DMZ which captured the city of Quang Tri and much of the two northern-most provinces. The ARVN halted the thrust, counter-attacked, and retained virtually all lost territory. The NVA offensive was front page news in the U.S., the counter-offensive, other than the U.S. bombings, slipped to the middle and back of our papers. This led many Americans to believe that the South Vietnamese would not or could not fight for their own country. This was a critical period. Most of the populated areas of the country were enjoying unprecedented peace and freedom, while the military was fighting exhausting battles from which they need time for recouperation. This is also the period of the Kissinger–Tho ne-gotiations in Paris. The North, like the South was militarily exhausted, and, internationally, the U.S., USSR, and The People's Republic of China were working out a new world order in which the Vietnams were becoming irrelevant.

The 1973–75 situation also found Nixon and Watergate obscuring and tainting the Vietnam picture. Watergate became the final blow to our support of the South Vietnamese. Immense pressure for withdrawl of troops, aid and moral support, combined with negotiations that were kept secret from our ally. We withdrew our ground forces from combat by March 1972, and all American forces by the end of January 1973—a time when the South Vietnamese were just establishing themselves.

We cut our support and left the South Vietnamese to fend for themselves. Our aid to Vietnam in 1973 was 3½% of the budget for the year 1969. Adjusted for inflation in the wake of the oil-embargoes, the 1974 budget equalled 1%. The result of the 1975 NVA assault is well known. Reasons for that success are obliterated from our social conscious by the results. America, sick with Watergate and tired of paying for the war in Vietnam, simply closed its eyes and backed out. The loss was entirely political. Saigon fell in April of 1975.

The Vietnam Era as defined by the Veterans Administration extended from August 5, 1964 to May 7, 1975. During that period 9,087,000 men and women served in our armed forces. Three and a half million served in the Southeast Asian theater and 2,586,152 men and 7,848 women served within the boarders of South Vietnam. The government estimates that approximately 800,000 war veterans are suffering from varying degrees of post-traumatic stress disorders, disorders that are significantly intrusive enough to rob their lives of fulfillment and meaning.

And what of the rest of our society? Let us assume that each era-veteran has one living parent, that three-quarters are married, that each has one sibling and one child. That equals over 43 million people—nearly twenty percent of our population—with a direct personal link to the military during the Vietnam era. If we add to that number the active protestors and their direct families the total probably runs over thirty percent. Seen another way, sixty million Americans came of age during U.S. involvement in Southeast Asia and the Vietnam War was and is the single most significant international event in their lives.

At times I feel it is a shame that diagnostic categories for societies and professional services do not exist to help heal the emotional wounds from which not only combat veterans suffer, but which our society suffers.

In this book by Doctors Brende and Parson, we come to understand the processes and phases of post-traumatic stress disorders, beginning with the traumatic event, through the initial phenomenon of denial/numbing/intrusion, the manifestations of repressed fear and guilt, and the phases of recovery. If one were to read only a single book dealing with veterans and post-traumatic stress, this should be the book for it is unsurpassed in depth and breadth of subject—historically, theoretically, and practically.

Note the parallel construction of the opinions below. Drs. Brende and

Parson write, ". . . a victim . . . would likely experience immediate denial of the memory of the traumatic event as well as a 'numbing' of the associated fear, emotional pain, and sometimes even physical pain. The victim would then be unexpectedly overwhelmed with the fear and pain when re-experiencing the traumatic event in the form of intrusive memories, images, or nightmares."

Jack Fuller in his article, "The War in Words" (Chicago Tribune Magazine 9/19/82), had been speaking about veterans not being able to forget Vietnam. "The rest of the country can't seem to forget, either," he writes, "but it doesn't know what exactly to remember. It sees Vietnam everywhere, a ghost in every conflict. Vietnam in Angola. Vietnam in Nicaragua. Vietnam in El Salvador, in Guatemala, in Beirut. The ghost whispers contradictory messages. To some it says, "Stay out." To others it says, "Fight this one to win." The ghost is a moralist, a tactician, an oracle of national will. And it is a hearty spirit. It is always there. From time to time, politicians have proclaimed that we have finally put the war behind us. But we have always proven them wrong. They flaunt the deep feelings at their peril; to deny the ghost is folly. The country may at times seem to be sleeping, but the sleep is troubled."

During the period of denial, subconscious fears of vulnerability and repressed feelings of guilt, along with learned and conditioned responses, have caused veterans suffering from PTSD to strike out irrationally, exhibiting at times depressive, at times dissociative behavior. Drs. Brende and Parson note that "Combat veterans have been conditioned to fight, be courageous, and not admit defeat." They continue, "This has made it hard for them to accept their problems and ask for help."

As a nationalistic people, have we not also been conditioned to fight, be courageous, and deny defeat? Does America suffer from fears of vulnerability and repressed feelings of guilt—guilt over involvement in Southeast Asia, guilt over our eventual political forfeiture? Like some Vietnam veterans, when the nation is triggered by a cold war probe, perhaps we strike out too quickly, too forcefully. And like Vietnam veterans who fear their powers and their ability to control them, perhaps there are times when we avoid taking a stand.

Treating an individual who suffers from symptoms of PTSD, therapists attempt to have the patient return to and relive the stressful occurrence, to analyze the event and his feelings both at the time of the occurence and in the present. Paraphrasing Drs. Brende and Parson's words about the treatment process, one might say, "The abreaction of the traumatic experience is not the final destiny—we do not simply wish to relive the event. The destiny will be reached when the nation can traverse the path further in order to understand the causal relationship between the event and the present state of affairs—and then to find in the event a new meaning so that the nation can make the emotionally charged experience an acceptable memory."

Time magazine columnist Lance Morrow had an insight to understanding when he wrote, "The nation will not recover from it (the war), or learn from all that slaughter and guilt, until it acknowledges that the men who fought the nation's first teen-age war (average age = 19.2 years), did not cook up the war by themselves in a mischievous moment."

Psychologist Arthur Egendorf, a Vietnam veteran and coauthor of "Legacies of Vietnam" was more direct in his comments. ". . . factionalism rooted in the Vietnam era still seethes, though now it is mostly beneath the surface. Americans have yet to see that veteran's problems, while serious in their own right, are symptomatic of a historic dilemma that faces the country as a whole . . . the nation must begin to recognize that along with the dead and wounded, our sense of common purpose was a major casualty. . . .

"In disowning our past, we blind ourselves to its hold on us. We fail to note that each new third-world trouble-spot automatically triggers a replay of the drama of the Vietnam years . . . .We divide ourselves between people who advocate muscle and those who respond from the heart. And again we forget that a body functions well only when its organs work in concert."

To understand our political and cultural behavior today, as well as the behavior of individual veterans, it is imperative to know the what, why, and how of our involvement in Vietnam. Chapter One of this book is a brief, balanced review of that history, a balance we've seen in few written or televised historical accounts. Allow me here to repeat some subjective feelings I had written in a column in 1976, a column that, at that time, no one was interested in publishing.

> Once we decided to withdraw we rejected the entire package, the war as immoral, the GVN as illegitimate, and our own political leaders as corrupt. And we came home.

Veterans, including in-service veterans, suffered a period of cultural crucifixion, partially self-imposed, for their role in this war. Most had no reason to feel personal guilt, though within America there exists a socially-induced repression of the Vietnam experience. A general public opinion against the war generalized to an aggressive negative opinion of the individual soldier.

For many young men to whom the experience was the pinnacle of their adolescence, their final rite of passage, this repression has caused intangible identity crises. They successfully vaulted the ultimate obstacle but were denied or denied themselves manhood.

In the past several years I have spoken to thousands of veterans. Almost all have expressed a feeling that we were doing something good in Vietnam. We were not there to kill but were there to save lives. We were there to help preserve freedom, to give a new nation a chance to grow.

I have many of the same emotions today that I had in 1970 and in 1976. If I killed someone in Vietnam, I believe that action saved the lives of other Americans and, more importantly, saved the lives of many South Vietnamese citizens. It also provided them with security during the period I was there and assisted them in their move toward a free and independent country. The fact that South Vietnam is not free today, that it is a virtual colony of the North exploited for the good of a four-family oligarchy (as is Laos, Cambodia, and indeed even North Vietnam), does not negate the fact that I and most of my American combat brothers served there honorably, indeed heroically.

I am today, as I have always been, of the opinion that killing should hurt the killer—that, thank God, it does indeed cause lasting emotional scars—even if that killing is considered justified. If it did not hurt, we would not be human. It is of note, that if the act is a gruesome atrocity, the suffering is far more severe. But even if a killing is completely in line with the rules of war, the killing of another human does and should hurt. It should not be so tragic as to incapacitate a man for life, cripple him emotionally for life, but it must make one ABHOR WAR. It must make one say, "I've seen war, now I must be, even if it seems impossible, a force for peace—a person who speaks out for peace and whose actions promote peace."

The personal cost of liberty and freedom remain personal sacrifice and responsibility directed by a strong set of personal values and principles. The same can be said of a civilization. The cost of national freedom is responsible action and vigilance guided by a set of moral principles.

For the freedoms we have in this country, the benefits of our birthright, there is a price. The price for freedom of speech includes the responsibility to speak along with the responsibility to defend the rights of others to speak. The freedom to own property includes the responsibility to respect the property of others.

Our responsibilities do not stop at our borders. We are 4% of the human population of this single eco-sphere, earth. We can not, and should not, impose ourselves and our views on everyone else. Yet we still must feel responsible for the human rights of every human being and do what we can in order to insure freedoms and liberities that we, as Americans, demand are inalienable, *not* because we are Americans, but because we are humans.

On the road to recovery, again to paraphrase Drs. Parson and Brende, perhaps one of the most difficult barriers for the nation to surmount is to eventually give up the desire for revenge . . . to stop harboring resentment (at the North Vietnamese, the South Vietnamese, the doves, or the hawks). This will eventually pave the way for America to analyze threats objectively, to become comfortable with normal feelings of anger, and to express this anger safely.

What does it mean today to be a Vietnam veteran? It means one participated in the most significant international event of our generation. It means suffering the scorn of our country for a political forfeiture not of our making nor under our control. It means watching a country and a people to whom we gave a year of our lives, some much more, suffer the humiliation of exploitive colonialization and the absence of human rights to a degree that has not been known in that land in the modern era. It means to know, that despite the tactical blunders we committed, despite the economic havoc wreacked upon South Vietnam, despite the errors in judgment made by some that led to atrocities and American deaths, we fought hard, generally honorably, generally effectively, as freedom fighters against one of the world's best equipped and best trained military forces.

And it means that today, we are at the vanguard of those coming to grips with the meaning of the Vietnam experience.

What does it mean today to be an American in the post-Vietnam era?

Where are we as a nation going? It is important to dive into our past, to feel it, to know who we were then, if we are to know who we are now, and where we are going. We are at a point in history where we can take a step toward the most wonderful future for mankind or where we can end human, and perhaps all, life on earth. Vietnam is something to reflect on, to learn from, to face—but it is not something to refight. We do not have enough energy or time to refight Vietnam. We are at a crossroad and the decisions we, America, mankind, collectively, actively make or passively allow to be made for us by a handful of "experts and leaders," these decisions will determine the course of our future. We must be very careful about the way we think and about the decisions we make and it is not possible to make clear decisions for the future without first coming to terms with our past.

JOHN M. DEL VECCHIO

PREFACE

War brings about so deep and profound an alteration of its "survivors" that many of them are troubled by a sense of having lived two lives. When soldiers return back home, particularly those who entered the war as teenagers, they have difficulty resolving the contradictions within themselves as well as their sense of identity.

Severe problems with identity are most prevalent within a society whose forces have been defeated. The American Indians were defeated and deprived of their native lands and customs. But almost as significant, they suffered through years of shame, for having lost the lands they had long inhabited. Only recently have they found the self-respect to stand up for their rights as a people.

The South has not forgotten the Civil War. Tourists driving through the South are often struck by the many memorials and other reminders of that war, referred to in some cities in the South as the War of Northern

Aggression. One can get the sense, within certain Southern communities, that the South feels somewhat disparate from the country as a whole, that it still has not fully recovered from its defeat.

The aftermath of World War I found the vanquished Germans consumed by national anger and bitterness. Many of their veterans suffered psychological wounds because of the national humiliation of defeat and because of Germany's consequential ostracism by the rest of the world. This set the stage for the groundswell of support for Hitler's aggressive actions propelling Germany into World War II.

America fared far better than Germany following World War II. Even though there was a moderately high psychiatric casualty rate of 23%, veterans proudly felt they had participated in winning a war of profound significance. Our national commitment had given great meaning to the war and made victory possible. Individual soldiers were thus rarely burdened by the postwar guilt and isolation associated with heavy combat.

In contrast, combatants in the Vietnam War, the costliest and longest war ever fought by the United States, were considered losers. The war polarized the country into camps of "hawks" and "doves." One was either pro or anti war. And the burning match held to draft cards inflamed our college campuses for years. The war left in its wake a vast wasteland of its survivors' devastated dreams and foiled plans. Americans killed in combat numbered 57,931 men and 8 women, with an additional 2,488 either missing in action or prisoners of war. And many are still suffering from post-war symptoms. Investigators have conservatively estimated that 20% of all Vietnam veterans and 60% of combat veterans[1] are psychiatric casualties. Based on earlier reports that 2,800,000 American soldiers served in the Vietnam theatre, 1,000,000 of which saw combat,[2] 560,000 to 700,000 were estimated to be post-war psychiatric casualties. These estimates have been recently revised, however, based on a 1980 report that 3,780,000 Americans served in the Vietnam theatre rather than 2,800,000.[3] Using these higher figures and the results of recent research studies, [3,4,5] National Vietnam Veterans Outreach Program Officials now believe that as many as 750,000 to 950,000 Vietnam veterans need counseling or readjustment services because of posttraumatic symptoms. The round figure commonly used is 800,000, and even this may be too low. As early as 1977, research psychologist John Wilson predicted that the psychiatric casualty figures would peak to an unspecified amount during the mid-1980s.[6] An estimate in 1981 suggested that it would eventually reach a staggering 1,500,000.[7] We find ourselves faced, then, with an estimated 39% of all Vietnam veterans who still suffer from posttraumatic symptoms.

Why so many? Guilt is the issue—a pervasive individual and collective guilt about the nature of the war and the means by which it was fought, even the means by which it was lost; guilt about measuring the war's success in numbers of dead bodies. Guilt tainted our armed forces, like black sheep among the white sheep of America. Guilt sealed the lips of thousands who still keep secret the enormity of their dehumanizing acts committed in Vietnam. A reconnaissance officer has said about being able finally to face responsibility for his actions in the war: "I hated what I did, and I hated the war because it made me do those things. But most of all, I hated myself for doing them. Only when I could forgive myself and my leaders who sent me there, did I start getting better."

It is not hard to understand why Vietnam veterans have remained isolated from the society that sent them to war. Suffering from a pervasive sense of shame and unspoken guilt, they may still be suffering from deep emotional wounds that have not healed. They continue to punish themselves in angry, self-destructive ways. This, in turn, discourages most Americans from wanting to help. But a growing minority of Vietnam veterans and their supporters continue to speak out. And the results have been positive. The media now give increasing attention to the nature of the Vietnam War so that we may better understand why so many veterans have so often felt that their efforts were futile. Perhaps most important, Congress and the Veterans Administration, since 1979, have come to recognize the needs Vietnam veterans have for specialized psychiatric care and readjustment counseling.

There is, nonetheless, a large segment of our society that remains relatively unaware, unconcerned, or helpless to do much for our forgotten warriors. This may be seen most clearly by many of our veterans' very recent history of repeated employment changes or continuing unemployment. Rarely do employers make an effort to understand the special nature of the problems veterans have in keeping jobs; nor do many grant temporary "sick leave" for the veterans to receive help. Considering the Vietnam veterans' history of unpredictability, perhaps it is understandable. Unfortunately, most Vietnam veterans with "posttraumatic stress disorder" have yet to band together and find a common path toward recovery. However, we can all walk the path to recovery together if we acknowledge that the Vietnam War was our war, and each of us contributed something—family, friends, protest or support, and of course tax dollars needed to pay the bill for 18 years—$120 billion.[8] As much as we would rather forget, it is our mutual responsibility to understand and to shoulder a part of every Vietnam veteran's burden, because, in a way, we are all recovering Vietnam veterans.

ACKNOWLEDGMENTS

To our editor, Linda Greenspan Regan, we owe the continuity of this book. Her skills of editing, encouragement, and thoughtfulness provided us with the creative incentive necessary to produce it.

And to our families who stood by us during this long, hot, and seemingly endless summer of rewrites, frustration, forgotten meals, and constant deadlines.

I (J.O.B.) would like to dedicate my efforts to my wife Jacqueline, whose love, editing, and sense of humor gave me the inspiration to write it.

I (E.R.P.) would like to dedicate this book to my loving wife Jane and our children, Marlena Marie and Erwin Randolph II.

And most importantly, we dedicate this book to the Vietnam veterans who have allowed us to share their grief, their sadness, their courage, and their very souls to help bring us all closer to closing the open wounds of war.

CONTENTS

Chapter 1 / AMERICA IN VIETNAM: PROTECTORS, AGGRESSORS, AND VICTIMS

Years after the Vietnam "Conflict," as our nation's leaders chose to call it, veterans are slowly streaming into mental health facilities, Veterans Administration hospitals and counseling centers because their lives lack meaning and purpose. At the same time, they reveal deep emotional wounds that are as yet only partially healed.

Approximately 800,000 Vietnam veterans remain, to various degrees, depressed, confused, ashamed, grieving, or enraged,[1] including an estimated 33%[2] to 60%[3] of all combat veterans. Six out of ten Vietnam veterans either opposed or did not understand their mission.[2] No wonder they became disillusioned and depressed because the country that sent them off to "save the world from Communism" rejected them on their return, calling them, among other things, losers. Feeling like pawns of Washington politics, they resent having been told that their country lost the war and they are to blame for it.

1

Many thousands, who still suffer unending grief, remember their buddies who fought and died there without a seeming purpose. Thousands of others feel alienated and rejected by the America that never embraced them on their return from battle and even called them "baby killers." Thousands remain confused because of the many South Vietnamese peasants who were unreceptive to Americans sent there to "help them fight for their independence." Thousands more are haunted by memories of atrocities and still feel shame for burning villages, defoliating vast areas of fertile fields and bountiful jungle, and participating in a war that left 4 million Vietnamese people killed or wounded.[1]

Americans who were in Vietnam during the idealism of the mid-1960s believed they were fighting Communism in Vietnam to prevent, via the "domino theory," its eventual encroachment on American shores. But as the war went on and on, the struggle to free the South Vietnamese people from Communist domination lost the support of the Americans back home who erroneously perceived it to be a civil war between the North and South Vietnamese. American soldiers—and civilians alike—became confused as to whether the war had anything to do with either Communism or democracy. It became perceived as a war without valid meaning or objective, a nucleus for civil unrest on American shores, and a cross to bear for America's returning warriors.

Although many Americans eventually believed themselves to be losers in a misconceived war, others have come to believe that the war was not misconceived, nor lost. Recent evidence provided by Vietnamese who have fled the country, supports the view that North Vietnamese Communists were indeed more interested in a takeover of the South than in liberating their countrymen from foreign domination. Truong Nhu Tang, a former member of the National Liberation Front (NLF), also called the Vietcong, now living in Paris, has revealed that "Vietnam is now practically an instrument of Soviet expansionism in Southeast Asia. . . . North Vietnamese Communists had engaged in a deliberate deception to achieve what had been their true goal from the start, the destruction of South Vietnam as a political or social entity in any way separate from the North. They succeeded in their deception by portraying themselves as brothers [of South Vietnamese members of the NLF] who had fought the same battles we were fighting and by exploiting our patriotism in the most cynical fashion."[4]

It has also been frequently overlooked that in many ways our military effort in Vietnam was successful. For example, the TET Offensive has been perceived by many Americans as a loss. Yet, Mr. Tang says, "It is a major irony of the Vietnamese war that our propaganda transformed this military debacle [of the NLF and the North Vietnamese] into a brilliant victory, giving us new leverage in our diplomatic efforts, inciting the American antiwar movement to even stronger and more optimistic resistance, and disheartening the Washington planners. The truth was that TET cost us half of our forces. Our losses were so immense that we were simply unable to replace them with new recruits."[4]

Furthermore, after the TET Offensive, the balance of power shifted toward the South Vietnamese government's favor as NLF forces lost their image of invulnerability and fewer South Vietnamese youth entered their army as recruits. It is true, however, that the United States did not take military advantage of its "victory" as President Johnson discovered that his military advisors had no clear-cut plan for winning. Instead, he soon began to deescalate. But in spite of American deescalation and cessation of military efforts, Vietcong and North Vietnamese troops had lost much of their previous impact after the TET Offensive.[5] Despite this military success, our eventual withdrawal in 1975 contributed to the fall of South Vietnam, the subsequent tragedy of the Communist invasion elimination of the liberation forces in the south, and imprisonment of hundreds of thousands of former South Vietnamese army officers and officials, and the massive genocide within Laos and Cambodia. The hasty departure of Saigon leaders, together with the abandonment of support by Americans, resulted also in the fleeing of hundred of thousands of "boat people"[4] and the forcing of a half million Vietnamese into labor camps in the Soviet Union.[6]

Thus, in spite of the fact that America was not defeated militarily, we failed to achieve our primary objective—to keep Communism out of South Vietnam. There are a number of reasons for this, one of which is that the administration in Washington did not develop a clear policy as to how they intended to protect the South Vietnamese from Communist aggression. Second, before becoming militarily involved, they were uncertain about a general strategy, perhaps because President Johnson failed to get a congressional declaration of war before committing troops there. Third, once militarily involved, American military leaders in the Pentagon failed to develop a military strategy that would achieve their desired purpose. In his analysis of the war, Colonel Summers, a Vietnam veteran, believes that we should have established an expanded blockade, using both the Navy and the Army, to form a demilitarized zone across Vietnam and Laos, similar to what was done in Korea. This would have been the basis for a defensive war against the North Vietnamese military efforts while the South Vietnamese troops fought the NLF (Vietcong) guerrillas.[7]

It cannot be denied that America's failure was also partly related to the frequently changing political climates and presidents, each of whom inherited from his predecessor a policy that he may not have agreed with. The failure of American policymakers was, in large part, the reason that many American soldiers became victims of the war effort. Their resulting individual problems often began shortly after returning from Vietnam. In others, their problems were individual manifestations of a national humiliation, and didn't develop until after the United States was perceived as having been driven out by North Vietnamese Communists in April 1975. For many other American soldiers leaving Vietnam in the late 1960s, believing that they had left their war memories behind, their problems did not emerge until 10 or 15 years later; occurring so frequently in the late 1970s that the "delayed stress syndrome" became a trademark for Vietnam veterans' problems.[8]

There are increasing numbers of books, movies, and television documentaries that are finally enlightening the American people about the complex basis for our involvement and eventual "loss" in Vietnam. To understand the plight of the Vietnam veteran, it is first necessary to have some knowledge of events leading to the war. For without comprehending the forces of history at that time, it is impossible to understand the Vietnam veteran. For this reason—and because of the time that has elapsed—Americans may now be able to take an objective view of the war to understand its occurrence as well as accept its unpleasant outcome.

American policymakers in the late 1950s and early 1960s were concerned about the welfare of Vietnam. In the early 1960s the American public had little information about Vietnam and slowly received bits and pieces from national leaders who didn't seem to know much more than they. American intelligence personnel reported that "democratic" South Vietnamese leaders were struggling to defend Saigon and neighboring villages from terrorist attacks by North Vietnamese Communists who had infiltrated into the South. The efforts by American advisors during President Kennedy's administration took on the role of protectors, and they often appeared helpful indeed. In 1962, American advisors supported a plan to protect the South Vietnamese villagers from "Communist" attack and provide them with medical care and education. This plan, called the "strategic hamlet" program, transplanted villagers to compounds protected by South Vietnamese soldiers and provided them with a school, medical clinic, and food. Although the villagers disliked the hamlets, which were very restrictive, the South Vietnamese government enticed their participation with the promise of a $21 bounty for each cooperating family and a free daily ration of dried fish for the first few months.[9]

This program appeared initially to be a successful pacification plan for unprotected native people. The South Vietnamese president at that time, Ngo Dinh Diem, hoped that it might also become a plan for fortifying his own ideological revolution, which he called "personalism": that is, communal living featuring private ownership of land, personal morality, strong sense of family, and the merging of individual goals into a common purpose. Our advisors, who participated in setting up the hamlets, were enthusiastic and hopeful about the potential success of this program although they viewed the plan as merely one of defense. Secretary of Defense Robert McNamara, making on-site inspections in 1962, announced that it was the backbone of a new program to counter subversion against the South Vietnamese government.[9]

In 1962, an elite counterguerrilla group of American Army personnel, called the Special Forces or Green Berets, developed 26 "Special Forces Camps"—training camps for the Civilian Irregular Defense Group Program (CIDG) to teach self-defense, improve the standard of living, and win the loyalty of primitive Montagnard villagers (the mountain people from the Central Highlands of Vietnam). When the Green Berets' work was finished, they had trained a staff of 280 Montagnard nurses and medics and 10,000 armed defenders in 129 fortified villages.[9]

A number of Americans participated in this program. A physician friend of ours, for example, spent 13 months in Vietnam in 1967–1968, providing medical care and education, at great personal risk, to these Montagnard natives who were enemies of the North Vietnamese and Vietcong guerrillas.

After he returned to this country, although having many terrifying nightmares related to the dangers he experienced,* he had good feelings about his medical work and his efforts to improve their basic hygienic condition. To this day he remains proud of what he contributed, what he learned about Vietnamese people, and of being an American.

His effort was typical of a number of fulfilling missions reported by many Americans who went to Vietnam. William J. Lederer has described another meaningful experience reported by a group of American Marines. After spending some time studying the Vietnamese language, culture, and a favorite game called Co Tuong (something like chess), the Marines proceeded to apply this knowledge in such a way as to advise the South Vietnamese. A villager whom Lederer interviewed explained[10.]

> The Marines put notices in all the hamlets in our area. These notices were that the Marines were sponsoring a Co Tuong tournament to see who was the best player. The announcement said that the winner in each hamlet could come to Phong Bac on the night of the Harvest Festival and there play each other to see who was the best man of all . . . maybe 1,500 people came to Phong Bac to watch the Co Tuong tournament to see who was the champion. I [Nguyen] won the tournament. My father taught me the game when I was about four years old. Perhaps that's why I am the hamlet [village] chief, because I play Co Tuong well. After I had won, and the people were still congratulating me, [the Marine colonel] came through the crowd and spoke to me in Vietnamese. It was not fluent Vietnamese, but I could see he had studied hard and practiced a lot. . . . A few days later, about fifteen Marines went through the hamlets and played Co Tuong with my people. Naturally, everyone in the village would watch the game. At first I was suspicious. But after several weeks I saw that the Marines enjoyed the game. They did not interfere with us in any way. They did not resume giving us free presents and making us look like beggars.

Nguyen and his villagers developed a trusting relationship with the Marines, who were able to prevent the Vietcong from interfering with the people's lives in the village, and as a result, their casualties were limited to only a few. In addition, the Marines were able to help the villagers improve their agricultural productivity and thus achieve the goal of American policymakers in the first place, namely to help the Vietnamese become

* This physician's postwar experiences are further described in Chapter 9.

more independent, without massive military action against the Vietcong. The unfortunate outcome of their plan was its discontinuance because of lack of support from military officials who saw it as being too simplistic for large efforts at "Vietnamizing" the military effort.[10]

John Del Vecchio, a combat reporter in Vietnam assigned to the 101st Airborne Division in 1970, has reported that many soldiers in Vietnam had meaningful experiences. He has talked to between 6000 and 7000 combat veterans after the war between 1982 and 1984 and found that 60–70% of them felt proud of their contribution while stationed in Vietnam.[11]

As the buildup of American advisors and eventually military personnel continued during the mid to late 1960s, many Americans who watched the television coverage of the war began to question and be critical of our involvement. But this generally did not affect most American soldiers, particularly before the Tet Offensive of 1968, who were very involved in their individual and collective missions. One of our patients spent 5 years in Vietnam, taking pride in being leader of a Ranger Team whose job it was to protect a number of South Vietnamese villages. He took his job seriously and believed that the villagers respected him and his work. Near the end of his stay in Vietnam, he met and married a Vietnamese woman, spent considerable time with her family, and took personal pride in being able to protect them during times when many other villagers were being killed.

Experiences like his were opportunities for individual Americans to learn about the customs and cultural differences of the Vietnamese people firsthand and to help individual Vietnamese in some personal way. If that would have been the primary American mission in Vietnam, it would most certainly have curtailed the increasing way in which American soldiers dehumanized the Vietnamese and eventually thought of them as subhumans, and curtailed atrocities that eventually became commonplace—by both sides—as the war escalated.

Although most American policymakers had the best intentions of protecting the South Vietnamese—and the world—from Communist invasion without the use of military troops, the rapidly spiraling war in Vietnam may be attributed, in large part, to the naiveté of our leaders in Washington, particularly President Johnson and his cabinet. They lacked firsthand involvement or understanding of the Vietnamese people and made major commitments of U.S. troops to escalate the war without any comprehension of the religious, social, and cultural factors of the country. They failed to understand that most Vietnamese perceived the American presence as just another case of domination, merely replacing the presence of the French colonialists who had been there for years. This perception, voiced openly by the NLF, many of whom were not Communists, was acted on silently by large numbers of villagers in both the South and the North. They were prepared to continue a struggle for independence and unification of their country for as long as necessary.[4]

President Johnson acted as if our actions in Vietnam required no preliminary understanding in any depth, of the Vietnamese language, culture, and religion; nor did he comprehend the need for a broad base of American understanding and support if this country were to undertake its "protective" military intervention. Yet, former Defense Department official Leslie Gelb along with coauthor Richard Betts have proposed that Johnson's failure was not based on limited knowledge since he was, in fact, thoroughly briefed. In fact, he was no different from his predecessors or his successor, Richard Nixon. They all failed to do anything more than what was minimally necessary at the time to stave off a Communist takeover, because it wasn't politically expedient.[12] Both Johnson and Nixon, however, were handicapped by decisions made by their predecessors, all the way back to President Truman, who reversed F.D.R's support of Vietnamese independence from the French in 1945. No new president chose to contravene Truman's action and thus none was able to begin with a fresh view or fresh solution and each failed to either prevent further escalation of the war, bring it to a halt, or attempt to achieve a military victory. And in order to minimize cognitive dissonance, the White House seemed to only want to receive information that substantiated the bias it had established—that the existing knowledge of the situation was both accurate and adequate.[12]

The bias they chose to follow was that the South Vietnamese, non-Communist regime was the most popular of two factions fighting a "civil war"; that American-backed South Vietnamese leaders could gather the support of the Vietnamese people; that our men placed in the background as merely "advisors," "guests," and "consultants" would not be perceived as part of just another self-serving foreign power; that the unlimited American financial support given to South Vietnamese leaders would not be misappropriated. In actuality, the willingness of the United States indiscriminately to bankroll any South Vietnamese plan to fight the "Communist North Vietnamese" made the United States the butt of many local jokes. In effect, tens of millions of dollars and American goods were openly squandered as a result of the dealings of corrupt South Vietnamese, as well as American, officials.[10]

What did our leaders fail to learn? They had a profound ignorance of the history of Southeast Asia, which extends back over 2000 years. And this ignorance ultimately cost the United States dearly. We knew little about such things as the Vietnamese people's long-standing resistance to change and their loyalty to traditional Chinese culture and religions. There was an ignorance of the reverence for family life and the land that bound people together in small villages. There was also ignorance and insensitivity to the emotional pain South Vietnamese villagers felt when displaced from their homes to concrete hamlets. Moreover, the United States was ignorant of the long-standing history of repeated and distressful internal struggles between warlords, especially between those in the North and the South, leaving the people with a strong sense of the division between these two parts of their country. Finally, the United States was insensitive to the Vietnamese people's willingness to endure pain and withstand suffering for years in order to gain their independence, having withstood a long history of subservience, the most recent being to French colonialism. They failed to understand the depth of the Vietnamese people's desire to be free of foreign domination, dating back to the first war against China in 1010 A.D.; to Ho Chi Minh and his Vietminh troops' battles with the French during and after World War II until victory was achieved in 1954; to the early 1960s with their intense desire to oust the Americans who replaced the French.[13]*

Perhaps America failed during its first encounters with those revolutionaries who later became its enemies. In relatively recent history, beginning with the modern Vietnamese "revolution" in 1941, the individual who was the moving force behind this movement was none other than Ho Chi Minh, who earlier had joined with American Intelligence Services (O.S.S.) to oppose Japanese occupation during World War II.

---

* Ironically, the Vietnamese now want to oust their Russian benefactors who financed the North Vietnamese military efforts and call the Russians "Americans without dollars"; hating them even more than they hated the Americans[4]

At that time, in 1941, 51-year-old Ho Chi Minh (later, ironically, to become the leader of North Vietnamese Communists who fought against the Americans) organized the Vietminh. This dedicated group of men fighting for independence worked in close collaboration with American forces who sent ammunition, advisors, and instructors to fight the Japanese.[1]

Ho Chi Minh appeared to have looked to the United States government as a benevolent big brother ever since he was a young man of 25 and traveled between Europe and the United States as a cabin boy on various ships. Then, as far back as World War I, he hoped for American support of Vietnamese freedom from French colonial rule and unofficially attended the Versailles Conference in Paris following the war hoping to get that support. Perhaps it was his feeling of familiarity with the United States and its revolutionary beginnings that led him to send a memo to the United States Secretary of State, asking for support of his movement for independence. But he left Paris empty-handed, without either a statement of support or official recognition of his request.[14]

Many have thought we should have recognized and even supported Ho Chi Minh and his ideas about independence for his country. In fact, he reportedly shared those ideas with the American O.S.S. personnel with whom he lived and worked closely together with for several months during the mutual fight against the Japanese during World War II. In fact, it was the American influence on Ho Chi Minh that influenced him to write the Vietminh's declaration of independence and began it with the familiar "All men are created equal. They are endowed by their Creator with certain unalienable rights, among these are Life, Liberty and the pursuit of Happiness."[10] Yet, there are others, realizing that he had Communist ties dating back into the 1920s, who believe that he ultimately hoped to conquer South Vietnam rather than liberate it.[4]

Partly because of American aid provided to Ho's Vietminh forces, they rapidly grew to 100,000 men by March 1945. Soon with the assistance of American-supplied radio communication, the Vietminh units began ambushing the Japanese, killing French informers for the Japanese, and raiding Japanese military-supply depots all over the country. The Japanese, who had expected the French to control the Vietnamese, angrily disarmed the French army and took over the country on March 11, 1945 several months before they surrendered to Allied forces. The Japanese proclaimed a Vietnamese leader, Bao Dai, as emperor, thereby voiding all French–Vietnamese treaties. They went on to announce, in spite of their ultimate intention of colonizing Southeast Asia, that Vietnam was now an independent country, although the announcement was unrecognized by Allied forces.[10]

Nevertheless, through this Japanese action, Vietnam considered itself an independent nation. Unification of North and South Vietnam was quickly accomplished by August 8, 1945 and continued after the Japanese surrendered to the Allies. Ho Chi Minh deposed Bao Dai and offered him a lesser position as chief advisor while Ho assumed the status of head of state. There appeared to be a groundswell of popular support for him as he quickly formed a Democratic Republican regime. Then he marred his achievement by permitting his Vietminh troops to execute 500 opposition leaders.[10]

On September 2, 1945, the Vietminh enthusiastically issued their own Declaration of Independence of the Republic of Vietnam with the unofficial recognition of President Roosevelt, but his later untimely death negated the presence of any substantive American support. Just shortly before the Japanese surrender, the Big Four powers—France, Great Britain, the Soviet Union, and the United States—met at Potsdam and decided to divide the responsibility of supervising the disarmament of Japanese troops in Vietnam. Great Britain was given the task of supervising Vietnam below the 16th parallel and Nationalist China was delegated supervision of North Vietnam, above the 16th parallel.[14] But on September 21, 1945, British troops, led by General Gracey who was sympathetic to French interests, proclaimed martial law, banned public meetings, and closed down only the Vietnamese newspapers. After releasing 1400 imprisoned French soldiers and legionnaires the following day, widespread violence erupted, first by the French and then by Vietnamese terrorists, quickly leading to a massive rearming of French troops.[10] The scene was similar in the North where 200,000 Chinese Nationalist troops plundered villages promiscuously. Ho Chi Minh soon found himself in the middle, trying to placate the Chinese in the North, hoping to accommodate the French and gain their support for national independence, and hoping to please the members of his own guerrilla forces who preferred a military solution.[1]

Ho Chi Minh, feeling trapped by demands on all sides, appealed to the United States. But the American government turned a deaf ear and was not receptive to the several formal letters that Vietnamese leaders sent to President Truman. Instead, in October 1945, the United States, by officially recognizing France's desire to resume control in South Vietnam and abandoning Ho Chi Minh and his nation's bid for independence, began to be perceived by the Vietnamese as an aggressor. This action even outraged General MacArthur: "If there is anything that makes my blood boil, it is to see our Allies in Indochina and Java deploying . . . troops to reconquer the little people we promised to liberate. It is the most ignoble kind of betrayal."[14]

Although the history of Ho Chi Minh's attempt to secure America's support for Vietnamese independence was generally not known by American soldiers during the early stages of the war in Vietnam, it had a major impact on them when they did find out about it. For example, one of our Vietnam veteran patients, a reconnaissance officer in Vietnam, read copies of Ho Chi Minh's letters during his second tour of duty. As a result, he grew angry and disillusioned, particularly after seeing the apathy of American commanders to respond to intelligence reports, an apathy that resulted in numbers of American squads being ambushed. He began to feel himself out of place, in a war that should not have come about in the first place, and was unable to continue his work.

The experience of betrayal and disillusionment became a pattern that repeated itself in a number of ways. Ho Chi Minh and his Vietminh forces, having become the victims of a betrayal by the British, French, and American governments, were faced with the return of the French aggressors. The trend of that war (which repeated itself 10 years later with the Americans) was marked by early expectations by the French that they would surely win. This was soon changed, partly because Russian and Chinese Communists sent armaments to the Vietminh in 1949 and 1950. This support by two Communist powers evoked fear in some Americans that not only would the French become victims, but also the free world.[1]

Falling back on its self-designated role as "protector of world freedom," the United States became actively involved in fighting the potential effects of Communist domination by supporting a non-Communist Saigon-based South Vietnamese government headed by Bao Dai, previously deposed by Ho Chi Minh, in February 1950. The lack of commitment in this anti-Communist effort by the South Vietnamese was marked by a continuously changing South Vietnamese leadership; given the nature of this leadership, corruption bred like flies and contributed to the degeneration of Bao Dai and each successive regime. After a series of changes in leadership, the United States covertly became the aggressors by assassinating Ngo Dinh Diem and his brother in January 1964 because of tiring of his failure to gain the trust of the people. Within 3 months, Diem was replaced by General Nguyen Khan, only to begin another unending cycle of instability.

Enormous amounts of American funds had been spent since before 1950 to support the French presence in Vietnam with the hope that this would stave off a Communist takeover. American money flowing to support French military endeavors between 1950 and 1954 amounted to $2.6 billion, 88% of the total cost of the French military effort.[14] President Eisenhower even considered providing troops to support the French in 1954, but Congress wisely balked. However, Secretary of State Dulles, a believer in the "domino theory," attempted to get congressional support for military involvement and was advised that Congress would support military intervention if three conditions were met, as Chester Cooper, advisor to American policymakers, reported: "1) U.S. intervention must be part of a coalition to include the other free nations of Southeast Asia, the Philippines, and the British Commonwealth. 2) The French must agree to accelerate their independence program . . . so there could be no interpretation that United States assistance meant support of French colonialism. 3) The French must agree not to pull their forces out of the war if we put our forces in."[14]

In spite of the United States' desire to remain in the background, increasing concern about the likelihood of a Communist victory over French forces prompted Vice President Nixon to say in an April 17, 1954 speech that the United States, as leader of the free world, must take an aggressively protective position by not retreating and by considering to send American troops there.[1]

At the battle of Dien Bien Phu in 1954, the French lost although they had urgently appealed to the Americans to rescue them. In the wake of what had happened in Korea, U.S. carriers and ships armed with atomic weapons were waiting in the Gulf of Tonkin if the Chinese Communists intervened. Since they did not, the United States remained militarily uninvolved.

With Ho Chi Minh's victory over the French, American leadership believed him and his Vietminh (Communist) forces to be a threat to the free world and not without good reason. Mass terror was inflicted on the rural Vietnamese population by the Vietnamese Communist Party. Modeled on a campaign that Mao Tse-tung had unleashed against the Chinese peasantry a few years earlier, the Communists committed the single greatest atrocity in Vietnamese history, executing 50,000 people and starving to death hundred of thousands.[15]

With the victory of Ho Chi Minh's forces in 1954, the United Nations-sponsored negotiations in Geneva led to a division between the North and South at the 17th parallel.* The American delegation, surprisingly, took a somewhat aggressive position, opposing direct negotiations between France and Ho Chi Minh even though the French government had preferred them, and refused to sign the final agreement which called for free reunification elections in 1956. Vietminh forces were supposed to return to the North, pending the results of those elections, but the American-supported Diem government, as well as China, North Vietnam, and the USSR, blocked the elections.

In response to a systematic repression of all groups that had been a part of the Vietminh, in May 1959, the North Vietnamese called for ·the overthrow of the Diem regime and expulsion of the United States. Widespread fighting broke out and the NLF was formed in 1960.

In a recent publication, *The Vietnam Experience,* authors Terrence Maitland and Stephen Weiss described the initial NLF as having strong idealistic and nationalistic motivations and not originally a Communist organization: "It would be a mistake . . . to see the early NLF (National Liberation Front) as nothing more than a Communist front, wholly directed by the North for its own interests. Its leadership was southern, its program reflected southern concerns, and these would not soon disappear. It is also true, however, that the Communists very quickly came to dominate the NLF."[9] However, in a 1980 publication, North Vietnamese Communists reported that they had been active in the South as early as 1957 at which time 37 armed companies were formed and remained in the South.[16]

Unfortunately, out of the idealistic beginnings of this independence movement came eventual terroristic activity. At first the NLF staged rallies

---

* Although this was unfortunate, it was a situation the country had been used to for hundred of years; inclusive of the building of two 18-foot-high dividing walls in the middle of the country in 1613 in order to keep two dissimilar groups of Vietnamese people apart.[11]

and attempted to instill within the people the wish for a mass uprising against the South Vietnamese government. But peaceful protest soon changed to violence. It was estimated that in 1959 one government official or government supporter was killed every other day and in 1962 there were 9000 kidnappings and 1700 assassinations. The NLF "victims" of oppression had become the aggressors.[9]

In 1960, the Kennedy administration was faced with decisions about American policy in Vietnam. Kennedy had inherited from Eisenhower an idealistic "save the world from Communism" attitude toward Indochina. He also benefited from 5 years of intelligence gathering about the Vietminh. His men, including General Maxwell Taylor and Secretary of Defense Robert McNamara, made numerous trips to the country in order to keep tabs of the effectiveness of the South Vietnamese leadership in spite of frequent changes which took place from day to day. They came away with an overly idealistic view of the situation, primarily through the interpretations of South Vietnamese leaders, who did not want, at any cost, to disturb their benefactors.

With the change of American leadership after Kennedy's death, American policymakers were prone to view this complex situation in overly simplistic terms—as a potential battleground between Communists and non-Communists. Furthermore, Secretary of Defense McNamara and President Johnson responded to all hints of escalating war from the NLF with step-by-step responses of increasing military strength. For example, on August 2 and August 4, 1964, Johnson was faced with making a response to the Gulf of Tonkin "attack" by torpedo-laden PT boats on two U.S. destroyers on August 2 and allegedly again on August 4, 1964. In spite of the fact that the second of these two incidents was not properly validated and may not have even occurred, the emotionally aroused President reacted, perhaps in part out of wounded pride, saying: "I not only want retaliation, I want to go all the way into the shore establishment that supports these PT boats and bomb them out of existence. . . . We can tuck our tails and run but if we do, these countries will feel that all they have to do to scare us is to shoot the American Flag."[17]

The American response was to bomb four North Vietnamese patrol-boat bases and a supporting oil complex in reprisal. The ensuing military conflict escalated rapidly month by month until by the end of 1964, there were 23,000 American personnel in Vietnam. By mid-1965, the United

States had brought 125,000 ground troops to Vietnam and by the time we officially abandoned hopes of military victory in 1973, we had sent nearly 2.8 million soldiers to that country.[1] In spite of the congressional backing for President Johnson's "emergency" response to the Gulf of Tonkin incident, there was no formal congressional "declaration of war" and Johnson's leadership in the Vietnam "war" remained both ambivalent and less than wholly honest with the American people. Political science professor Larry Berman has described Johnson's course of action as follows: "He chose a middle course, to fight the war at the lowest possible cost, on the cheap . . . and he lied about what he was doing. He staged a debate to create a war climate, so that when he announced the number of troops was only going up from 75,000 to 125,000, he looked like a moderate. But he knew there would be 300,000 troops in Vietnam in 1966."[18]

There was a continuing belief in Washington during the 1960s that the U.S.–South Vietnamese joint effort would result in a military victory. Officials continued to hold to the notion that South Vietnam would eventually assume full responsibility for driving out their Communist invaders. Washington maintained its expectation of success in the "Vietnamization" program and was prone to pattern the "truth" about the war's progress in order to sustain their optimism. Members of the Nixon administration were frightened to withdraw from Vietnam, continuing to hope that South Vietnamese leadership could sustain the protector role. And in spite of the growing widespread clamor by the American public and members of Congress to withdraw American troops, members of the Nixon administration feared the consequences if they gave in to such demands, as Stanley Karnow writes: "The specter of an ignominious finale in Vietnam haunted Kissinger. A humiliating collapse would shatter America's global credibility, he believed, and, as he put it, 'leave deep scars on our society, fueling impulses for recrimination.' Constantly on his mind was the tragedy of the Weimar Republic, a member of his staff later recalled, the democracy that had eventually been ripped asunder by the tensions that divided Germany after its defeat in World War I."[1]

Nixon's strategy, similar to that of his predecessor, emerged on an improvised basis.[19] Not wanting to withdraw dishonorably, he believed that he could withdraw American troops slowly, while the "Vietnamization" plan developed.[18] So beginning in 1969, troop strengths were reduced. All active ground combat ceased in 1972, leading to a final pullout of all U.S. combat forces by March 29, 1973. The withdrawal was met by considerable resistance on the part of the South Vietnamese government. Some observers have believed that Nixon's wish to speed up the withdrawal in 1972 because of elections resulted in his "bribe" to secure South Vietnamese President Thieu's cooperation. Nixon authorized the emergency shipment of $2 billion of American weapons and other materials to South Vietnam and the secret transfer of American installations to South Vietnamese ownership in October 1972. And when Kissinger's talks to gain "peace with honor" with the North Vietnamese bogged down, Nixon acted on his frustrations and retaliated. On December 14, 1972, he sent an ultimatum to North Vietnam to begin serious talks within 72 hours, and then ordered massive air attacks to demonstrate his seriousness, as Karnow reports: "He . . . ordered Admiral Thomas Moorer, chairman of the joint chiefs of staff, to prepare massive air attacks . . . [saying] "I don't want any more of this crap about the fact that we couldn't hit this target or that one. This is your chance to use military power to win this war, and if you don't, I'll hold you responsible." Thus, on December 18, he began 12 days of bombing. Twenty-six U.S. aircraft and ninety-three crew members were lost. Forty thousand tons of bombs were dropped at specific strategic targets, although over 1600 civilians were killed in Hanoi and Haiphong by the bombings.[1]

After an agreement had been signed with the North Vietnamese in Paris on January 27, 1973, wherein the United States capitulated at the conference table, Nixon kept up the illusion of success by publically announcing, "we have finally achieved peace with honor," while privately admitting the possibility of defeat in the future. That defeat soon became manifest after the flow of American cash into Thieu's government was reduced to a mere fraction of what it had been in 1969. For in 1974, the crumbling economy eroded army morale and corruption among South Vietnamese officials was of immense proportions. President Thieu, his wife, and cronies failed to change their ways in spite of the gradual demoralization of the South Vietnamese army. They reaped great personal fortunes in real estate and other deals, leading U.S. officials to reduce economic aid and direct the CIA to withdraw support for the South Vietnamese government. On April 21, 1975, Thieu resigned and fled to Taiwan where he described himself as having been victimized and abandoned by the United States, "an inhumane act by an inhuman ally."[1]

On April 29, after many battles won and lost between the North and the South, the Communists rocketed the Saigon airport and prompted the largest helicopter evacuation on record. Within an 18-hour span of time, 70 Marine helicopters lifted over 1000 Americans and almost 6000 Vietnamese out of Saigon. During that night, North Vietnamese forces moved into "liberated" Saigon. As the ranking officer assumed power in Saigon the next day from the hands of the South Vietnamese government, he was quoted as saying: "You have nothing to fear. Between Vietnamese, there are no victors and no vanquished. Only the Americans have been beaten. If you are patriots, consider this a moment of joy. The war for our country is over."[1] Unfortunately, as former NLF official Truong Nhu Tang has described, this turned out to be a massive deception: "On that day [when the North and South were pronounced as unified] the years of communist promises and assurances revealed themselves for the propaganda they were. Victory Day celebrated no victory for the NLF or for the South."[4]

Did American leaders learn from their mistakes? Some say that they did. On the one hand, they became more responsive to the American public which was disillusioned by the negative outcome of Washington's worldwide commitments of military forces, particularly to weak and corruptible governments. But, on the other hand, there has been a counterreaction to the U.S. experience of having become a victim in Vietnam. The present administration has sent military forces to Lebanon and Grenada and military "advisors" to Central America. Some onlookers fear the risk that this protective action will become a reenactment of the scenario that led Washington through the vicious cycle of protector, then aggressor, and finally victim, as it did in Vietnam. But it is not within the confines of this book to make a judgment here. Let us look instead at the men and women who have sacrificed themselves in fighting this complex, misconceived war.

Chapter 2 / BEING THERE: EXPERIENCING VIETNAM'S CLIMATE OF WAR

The experience of fighting in Vietnam's guerrilla war was different for each soldier, depending on his personality and values. Many aspects of the Vietnam experience, however, were shared in common by most soldiers in this gruesome theater of war.

The Americans who fought in Vietnam were the youngest soldiers in our history, the average age being 19.2 years, compared to 26 years for those in World War II. This relative youthfulness of our troops in Vietnam made them more susceptible to the stresses inherent in war. These stresses can obviously adversely affect most people regardless of age. However, we believe that the American soldier in Vietnam, with his relative psychological immaturity, was less mentally prepared for the carnage and terror that marked the Vietnam experience.

Erik Erikson observed the complexities of psychological development, particularly psychological *identity,** of returning World War II veterans. He was especially struck by the inner disorganization and loss of a sense of sameness and continuity in these men, and believed this to be related to the inability of the "inner agency" of the mind (or the ego) to control the disorganizing effects of traumatic war experiences. The mind's inability to oversee its own organization, he believed, meant that the soldier had lost his sense of ego-identity.[1] We would therefore suggest that if such psychological disorganization could be found in World War II veterans, it is reasonable to expect the relatively younger Vietnam veteran to have even more severe forms of identity disruption and confusion.

Thus, many soldiers in Vietnam struggled with serious fundamental questions as to *who* they were, *where* they were going, *how* they came to be involved in such a war, *what* they were fighting for, as well as *why* such "insanity" was necessary. These issues reflect concerns over identity. These questions were as significant and pressing to them as knowing how many days were left on their calendars before going home.

During the ordinary course of life, adolescents further their development as human beings by being exposed to increasingly diverse experiences with people, places, and things. This very important period in life was undercut in our troops in Vietnam by overwhelming anxieties, persistent threats of annihilation, terror, despair, and chronic frustrations in the war, far beyond in intensity and duration what any adolescent should be subjected to.

For many, there was the perpetual sense of having been uprooted, transplanted, and dislocated to a strange planet, where Western ways of life were replaced by a new reality. Vietnam was experienced as a place of strange customs, peoples, ideas, and expectations. Some soldiers found Vietnamese difficult to understand, and in addition felt they were misunderstood by the Vietnamese. Many of our troops had never before been away from home. Most of these late adolescents were forced to "grow up overnight" because of the overdemanding nature of combat. Some soldiers,

---

* "Identity" refers to the persisting temporal sense of one's sameness from moment to moment in space and through time, and the inner sense of security in one's historical and present continuity. Good identity development facilitates the feeling of being anchored psychologically, and thereby capable of orienting one's self to the world of people, of love, and work.

for example, had to assume responsibility for others' lives, and others for millions of dollars of military equipment. For many, such occupational stress, in conjunction with the psychological effects of being culturally uprooted, was sufficient to cause some adjustment problems.

In our clinical, community, and social work with Vietnam veterans over the years, it has been obvious that the soldiers in Vietnam were not a homogeneous group. Each soldier was different; each had his or her unique method of coping, style of perceiving, and capacities for tolerating cumulative stresses in the war. Vietnam itself was not a unidimensional or monolithic event, but comprised of a series of events—jigsaw pieces of events that made each soldier's inner mental puzzle a different configuration that the soldier was called upon to solve for himself. Each soldier, as an individual, with a consciousness of his own, sought his own path to find meaning, and to establish unique coping strategies to help survive Vietnam.

The soldiers' individual *coping strategy system* (CSS) became operative upon arriving in Vietnam (the "initial phase"), through the day-to-day experience of the war after assignment (the "mid phase"), to the period just prior to leaving Vietnam (the "end phase"). The soldier's CSS was toughened and seasoned as time progressed. It worked so well and became so automatic that some men still use those survival coping approaches to life today. Naturally, the development of an individual CSS was dependent upon a number of factors: the individual soldier's personality, age, combat experience, ethnocultural identity, religious beliefs, official military status, personal attitudes, and personal convictions.

During the initial phase of the Vietnam experience, soldiers typically entered the war alone. This is in stark contrast to previous American wars, in which soldiers entered the war in groups having trained for combat. In fact, in previous wars, group members would remain together for the duration of the military mission. Military planners in the past seemed to know the value of group cohesion to the fighting forces. However, for Vietnam, soldiers not only arrived there alone, they often left alone as well.

Typically, the soldier would arrive in Vietnam by airplane or ship. Just minutes before landing, the pilot would usually give the troop-passengers a "reading" of the enemy activity on the ground below, alerting everyone to the immediate dangers on the ground, especially when landing in Bien Hoa, Da Nang, and other areas where enemy hostilities were frequent and intense. The pilot would make such announcements as: "In two minutes we'll be on the ground. When we land, run as fast as you can, keeping low. Keep low!" One Vietnam veteran recalled having thought to himself at the time: "Oh man, this is the real thing. But I don't even have a weapon to defend myself with." Some of his fellow passengers often laughed it off, downplaying the imminent danger that awaited them.

Cam Ranh Bay was regarded as a relatively safe entry point from the States. Upon entering, the new GI would often hear loud and heavy shell bombardments. Feeling shaken up, he would later learn, as in Cam Ranh, that the noise came from American weapons in an antienemy military exercise called H & I (Harassment and Interdiction). H & I operations were basically to scare the enemy and discourage any advancements on their part. At the reception center, the GI would meet many other soldiers— young and scared just like himself—waiting hours or days to be transported to their assigned units. At these centers, soldiers would congregate in clusters, wondering aloud what Vietnam was going to be like for them. They wondered about their commanding officers, their noncommissioned officers (NCOs), their fellow grunts.* They also wondered whether they would leave Vietnam alive.

Nervously, they would tell jokes or "hairy" war stories they had heard from a brother, cousin, or friend who had written them from Vietnam. After a day or two of swapping stories, anxiety levels began to rise, particularly as the moment of their departure to their units became more imminent. Many of these young men, who had never before left home, now found themselves in a war. "Vietnam" was becoming less of an abstraction by the minute. Thus, even before leaving the reception center the abstract concept of Vietnam was already giving way to a harsh reality— that of a guerrilla war.

Some new soldiers were literally hit by reality en route to their unit. As Tim, an infantryman, was being driven by truck from Bien Hoa to Long Binh, the truck was attacked by a two-man VC sapper† team on a kamikaze-type mission to kill Americans at any cost. Tim's fellow soldiers

---

* Front-line foot soldier.

† Soldier trained in demolition and who attacks or infiltrates camps to destroy lives and property.

retaliated with their mounted M-60 machine gun, killing the VC. So much for the initial reception.

Arriving at their assigned combat units, the new soldiers were often greeted with a cool, suspicious, "wait and see" attitude from the "older," more seasoned troops. Met at times with outright hostility and expressed distrust, the new soldier knew that he had to prove himself at the first opportunity. But he would; he'd show these "seasoned turkeys" that he "had what it takes" to survive in 'Nam. Of course, underlying this self-"psyching up" were anxieties and fears over the uncertainty of survival, compounded by self-doubts and lowered self-esteem.

Called "green horn," "green troop," or just "FNG" ("fucking new guy"), the new entrant's value to the fighting force was at best dubious to the other unit troops. Some unit troops saw the new arrival as a source of worry; others saw him as a source of eagerly awaited news and gossip, especially if the newcomer was from their state or town. The FNG was especially avoided by the "short-timer"—a soldier with 2 or less months before returning to the United States. "Short-timers" became synonymous with "Careful and Cautious."

In terms of geographic origins, soldiers came from all over the United States: From the Northeast—New York, Connecticut, Masachusetts, New Hampshire, Vermont, and Maine; others from the rural deep South; some from the densely populated urban cities of the West. There were soldiers from Puerto Rico, from both urban and rural areas, as well as from the United States Virgin Islands (St. Thomas, St. Croix, and St. John).

Women served as nurses, physicians, secretaries, clerks, and as volunteers as in the Red Cross "Doughnut Dollies," which offered cheer, reassurance, and caring to the American GIs, as well as a hot cup of coffee and doughnuts. The largest number of women in Vietnam served as nurses, in a variety of military and civilian medical and nonmedical facilities. Men served as infantrymen, medics, clerks, RTOs (radiotelephone operators), gunners, a-gunners (assistant gunners), and nurses.

Mark remembers his first "firefight," and encountering the VC for the first time. He lost all bladder and bowel control—in a matter of a few minutes. In his own words, "I was scared and literally shitless; I pissed all over myself, and shit all over myself, too. Man, all hell broke loose. I tell you, I was so scared, I thought I would never make it out alive. I was convinced of that. Charlie had us pinned down and hitting the shit out of us for hours. We had to call in the napalm and the bombing."⸤During this first fight, Mark, an infantryman, experienced gruesome sights and strange sounds in battle. He witnessed headless bodies. "One guy said to me, 'Hey, Mark, new greenhorn *boy,* you saw that head go flying off that gook's shoulder. Isn't that something?' " Within 2 weeks Mark saw the head of a running comrade blown off his shoulders, the headless body moving for a few feet before falling to the ground. Mark, nauseous and vomiting for a long time, couldn't see himself surviving much longer: "I couldn't get that sight out of my head; it just kept on coming back to me in my dreams, nightmares. Like clockwork, I'd see R's head flying, and his headless body falling to the ground. One part goes up, the other part falls down to the ground. I knew the guy. He was very good to me when I first got to the unit. Nobody else seemed to give a damn about me; he broke me in. It's like I would see his head and body, you know, man, wow!" Mark often found himself crying during his first weeks of combat. "I wanted to go home. I was so lonely, helpless, and really scared. But I knew I could not go home until my year was up. After 3 weeks, though, I became numbed-out, really numbed-out; I was a zombie. I couldn't feel anything."⸥

Ted was a grunt with the 101st Airborne Division on his first firefight with Charlie (VC). His fighting Division, the "Screaming Eagles," had a tremendous reputation as a driven fighting force engaged in some of the most heated battles with the enemy. Though highly respected for their "airborne-trained" men, "nonairborne" soldiers were assigned to the Division, one of whom was Dan, a newcomer. Dan felt great pressure to prove himself worthy of being among "the greatest," good enough to be called a "Screaming Eagle." It took only one heavy engagement with the enemy to bring about an almost incredible transformation in him; the neophyte had become a respected "seasoned" soldier almost overnight. This lightning-fast change occurred in the majority of men after one or two engagements in heavy combat.

After the first battle, many a soldier feels the pain of killing another human being, and issues of morality arise within him. He must resolve this issue for himself, as best he can. No one else can do this for him. Most numb themselves psychologically, while others numb themselves through drugs and alcohol. Still others use diversionary thinking maneuvers that *deny* the psychotic reality of the war. Those soldiers who use denial of the war's reality and its impact on them, soon realize that denial is insufficient. Only psychic numbing seems for many to offer the kind of relief the soldier needs in order "to carry on." And as effective as psychic numbing might be for many soldiers, it is often not sufficient for the rest. This last group then has to resort to drugs and alcohol to help them cope, or to *deeper, second-stage numbing.*

Frank recollects his "first kill" in Vietnam: "I was guilty as all hell; and I did a number on myself—I tried to beat myself to death in atonement. I really felt bad, like no one would ever forgive me for what I had done. It was amazing; it was so easy to kill. Nothing to it. But later, I felt it a lot; but I also got over the guilt and self-flagellation." For Frank the new reality, the new order of things, had overthrown the old reality, the old order of things. Dr. Chaim Shatan, a New York City psychiatrist renowned for his astute observations of Vietnam veterans, has said of this transformation that "military reality eclipses civilian reality."[2] He goes on to state that the "acquisition of this new perceptual and experiential frame of reference completes the *transfiguration* of the personality."[2]

After this profound transformation of personality, the soldier is now ready to do what he came to Vietnam to do; that is, to kill and avoid being killed. This "warping of the self" phenomenon produces a "psychic realignment" to the reality of unimaginable butchery, terror, atrocity upon atrocity, and massive annihilation, destruction, and collapse—of human and physical worlds. JC felt himself becoming "like the walking dead," and "with a frayed, emotionless inner self." Though the transformation from being a "decent, red-blooded American boy" to becoming a "wanton, gruesome killer-machine" had probably begun in Basic Training, JC, after the "first kill," like most soldiers, felt "something inside had died with the first victim." But he also felt something within him spawned as well—the killer within him, and the need to kill, the desire to kill, the will to remain alive through it all.

The mental transformation in battle involves, then, both the processes of "self-death" as well as "self-resurrection," for as the "old self" dies after the first kill, the "new survivor-self" is born to carry on "the action" of killing and avoiding being killed. After this personal change had occurred, JC recollects, "Then I knew I had become an animal. But to be put in a cage, not let loose in the jungle!" JC's first encounter with the enemy was bloody. He lost two buddies who had "nurtured me along and psyched me into fighting and giving me confidence in myself to survive." Witnessing "all those mangled bodies, torn to bits by bullets, grenades, and heavy artillery" affected him profoundly. He would never fully forget that day as long as he lived. Within him waves of grief, sorrow, pain, fear, and anger converged into a deep sea that drowned the life within him: "The next time I went back into the field, I was now ready; I mean ready for anything, man, anybody, especially Charlie, that motherfucker. I mean I became a crazy motherfucker, just like Charlie. No one could touch me now. I was ready. During my second and third fights I was fucking excited, man; I mean erotically turned on, really fucking excited, wow, man." By the third fight, JC felt "old": "I felt like an old garment, torn and overworn; I was seasoned now. I had graduated from FNG status almost as fast as the blinking of your eye to 'hard-core,' battle-tested, and true. My buddies had told me that I would age fast after my first fight, but especially after my first kill. They were right."

Three or four weeks of being in Vietnam brought JC the realization that the war—in terms of success—centered on the *body count,* rather than on the traditional yardstick of the "spoils of war"—that is, land, weapons, and prisoners. In naive amazement, he exclaimed: "I couldn't fucking believe it! We fight like hell to take a hill or some land; we lose men, sometimes many men; lots of bloodshed and dying, for what? For what, I asked myself. It didn't make sense at all."

During a major battle in the northern provinces of Vietnam, JC's unit had fought very hard for several days, at times engaging the VC and the NVA (North Vietnam Army) for hours. This battle, JC's 12th in less than 3 months, had cost the lives of 18 men in his Company. After the battle, most of the soldiers were embittered by what they perceived to be poor leadership by their CO and platoon leader, an FNG lieutenant from the Midwest. This young officer had made a tactical error, misjudging the strength of a VC stronghold that he had been commissioned to find and destroy.

JC and his buddies in the unit were exceedingly angry, and wanted to vent their grievances to the lieutenant. Prior to the battle, "We tried to tell the asshole lieutenant that he was not to go in that direction, not at that angle, because we were bound to get the shit kicked out of us. He took the troops there anyway. And now all those guys got killed, They didn't even have a chance. He took us into this fantastic ambush. We were pissed off. We remember when he first came to the unit about a little over three weeks before. We all knew this guy was trouble." Officers entering combat units were observed with great suspicion and distrust, just like the EM (enlisted men) FNG grunt. Some men in the company had taken it upon themselves to closely watch the naive "greenhorn" lieutenant before the battle, "to see just how together" he was. "We thought we had to prevent him from foolishly trying to win the war singlehandedly, being a hero and making decisions that would kill our guys. But this is what happened, anyway." Too often the young lieutenant didn't protect his men and was viewed as a "dangerous man, not to be trusted; he could get you killed."

Men in the unit had been in a substantial number of firefights and ambushes and had survived. "That's why we don't want nobody putting our lives in jeopardy. Believe me, we would kill a motherfucker for not being trustworthy, and who won't listen to us when we try to tell him something." Seasoned troops had been on search-and-destroy patrols; they had been point men (special soldiers ahead of the squad to draw enemy fire and identify the enemy's position); Lurps (long-range reconnaissance patrolmen); and rangers. "We just did everything. A real good group of fighting guys." These hard-core troops had learned a great deal about the VC and the NVA—their rhythm and stealthy movements and tactical insurgency behaviors, their persistence, shrewdness, their general psychology of evoking terror, and also some of their vulnerabilities based on folklore and religious beliefs. These soldiers knew they could fight Charlie on his own turf, and they were proud of their accomplishments so far in the war. They had survived where others had not.

The troops were thus unwilling or disinclined to allow new officers (the "uninitiated") who were essentially "non-combat-effective" to risk their lives in what front-echelon troops believed to be a capricious manner of managing the war effort. Generally, soldiers believed that were their leaders more "jungle-adept" or more receptive, fewer of their buddies would have been killed, their own wounds would not have been as severe or would not even have occurred. Rational or not, these sentiments were real for the men who were there. And for those with prolonged frustration and disappointment over what they perceived as poor leadership, their "warring stamina" diminished, and demoralization and impotent anger set in.

Impotent rage in the jungle is always dangerous, because sooner or later it seeks expression in violence. Whether impotent rage is a consequence of the "senseless deaths of close buddies" or a reaction to the perception of poor leadership, "which gets guys killed," the results are the same—violence. Violence against Vietnamese civilians occurred from time to time, as a reaction to buddies being "wasted" by the VC or NVA. Torturing and atrocities committed against the VC or suspected VC or VC sympathizers were not uncommon in this environment of terror and counterterror. Extreme reactive violence is exemplified by the My Lai Massacre. When one highly respected leader had been killed by the Communists, the sorrow, grief, and rage of the men in his unit were activated in extraordinary violence, even for Vietnam. Several "mini My Lai's" also took place in Vietnam.

Violent acts in Vietnam also took the form of "American-against-American" violence. A number of soldiers committed violent acts against other Americans, especially during and after the Tet Offensive of 1968. The most frequent form of violence was the "fragging" of officers and NCOs by their troops, comprised mostly of enlisted men. "Fragging" is an assault on a superior by use of fragmenting grenades. Carl, an officer in one of Vietnam's most active combat units in the I Corps area (the northernmost military region in South Vietnam), had narrowly escaped death in a fragging attempt meant for the Company Commander, a close friend from West Point he was visiting that day. Apparently, frustrations had grown following a heated battle with VC and NVA forces in a northern province. Many men had been killed and dozens wounded. The enlisted men felt helpless, angry, and tense, believing they had lost buddies because of senseless military maneuvers ordered by superiors. Most blamed their CO, with whom they had wanted to talk for some time. However, he had again refused the men's entreaties to discuss military operations and review mistakes made in the last battle. The soldiers became even more infuriated. Some made subtle threats to the CO that he was going to be fragged. (These warnings were usually intended to cause fear and the desired change in orders.) Failing to have any effect, the threat was carried out; although Carl was wounded, the CO was unharmed.

Fragging was usually used only as a last resort. Once a threat was made, however, it was carried out within 24 hours.[2] Fragging was not inconsistent with the pervasive terrorist activities of this guerrilla war, and created yet another dimension of terror.

In World War I, World War II, and Korea, the number of court-martials for violent assaults on officers was low; in Vietnam, however, these incidents were of epidemic proportion. Between 1969 and 1972, almost 800 such incidents were reported, not including nonfragging assaults on officers, such as use of guns, knives, etc.[3] Rear-echelon troops even "shot it out" among themselves—"wasting each other like crazy," due to interpersonal conflicts that some believed could only be settled through violence. Both intraracial and interracial tensions, animosities, and mis-understandings, if unresolved, could result in violence. Having been taught to respond by reflex, the soldier in Vietnam was often quick to take "the shortcut" through violence.

Some officers thus had second thoughts about carrying out unpopular mandates in the field. Stu, for instance, made a conscious effort to listen to his men, and often felt "caught between a rock and a hard place," as he put it, in dealing with his superiors and the men in his Company. For one thing, "I needed their input, because I realized that they were the jungle experts; they had the battle-tested experience that many of us did not have as officers. Sure, we had the book knowledge, and even had some advanced training in guerrilla warfare and all that, but you've got to remember that it was those men out there on a daily basis that knew what the hell was going on. Most of them could smell Charlie miles away. Sure, as an officer I was scared sometimes, but it was also important to pay attention to the men from the military tactical planning perspective. There were some young officers, though, who would get real gung ho with the guys' lives. The grunts would resent this, because the men knew that the new officer just wanted to achieve quick promotions and rank on their blood. He would take unnecessary and dangerous risks."

From an overall point of view, the field officers' experience in Vietnam was similar in many respects to that of the grunt. Male and female officers, on average, were older and more educated than the teenaged foot soldiers. Officers were generally divided into two groups: those who were West Point (WP) graduates, and those who were Officer Candidate School (OCS) graduates. WP officers were considered by OCS and enlisted men as being "snooty, as if their shit don't stink; they were high-browed and looked

down on OCS officers and on enlisted men. They felt they knew it all."
Graduates of the same class at WP usually came to Vietnam together.
Regardless of whether or not the new officer was a WP or OCS graduate,
seasoned jungle troops were uneasy and distrustful, because most young
officers had no experience in leading men in combat. They were thus called
"asshole green officers."

All soldiers, officer and grunt alike, were exposed to terror and counterterror. Conventional weapons in some respects were virtually useless.
Strategies of terror became, for many, the preferred manner of defeating
the enemy. In this psychotic theater of war, American troops as well as
the VC devised methods of terror and counterterror. Soldiers would capture
enemy soldiers and castrate them, cut off their ears, scalp them, and commit
other heinous acts (before killing them). Americans often engaged in this
kind of barbarism to let the VC and NVA know that no prisoners would
be allowed to live. As a former medic in Vietnam said, reflecting on his
experience: "We had no intentions of capturing any of these people; we
just wanted to get home, and to get home, we would do anything."

Terrorism on the part of the VC often took the form of torturing a
prisoner followed by a painful and very slow death. As the soldier was
dying, his genitals were brutally chopped off, placed in his mouth, and
his lips sewn together. Another well-known atrocity of the VC was de-
capitation of American prisoners and placement of the heads on stakes.
These would then be displayed along paths American troops would likely
travel. This was a war of the macabre, the grisly.

The VC also forced captured GIs to watch as their friends were being
decapitated or castrated or were dying slowly of some other torture. Disem-
bowelment was another well-known atrocity of the VC. This was performed
on GIs, village officials who would not pay taxes, as well as young Vietnamese who resisted their Communist orientation. The stomach would
be cut open and the innards pulled out while the victim was conscious.
Other "imaginable" atrocities were meted out as well.

The VC expanded the horrifying aspects of the war by constructing
numerous ingenious booby traps, placed strategically and in abundance.
Among these were *punji sticks,* sharp bamboo sticks tempered in human
feces, which when "tripped" became fatal or near-fatal projectiles striking
the midsection. Signs with derogatory statements or epithets against Americans were posted on trees and walls, If removed, a grenade was detonated,

killing the unsuspecting soldier. There were also snake pits, into which the unwary soldier in pursuit would fall, after being "seduced" into a chase by the VC. At other times such a pursuit would occur after GIs located a sniper.

Highly sophisticated and intricate underground labyrinth networks were also part of the VC's strategy of terror. These networks were, for the most part, located in the jungle and covered with thick grass. The VC would emerge during the day or night, but especially at night, to terrorize, maim, and kill, disappearing without a trace. As Slim recounts: "It seemed that I was always frightened out there. I didn't know when it was coming. I looked at and under my feet where I walked; I watched ahead, behind; I watched the trees, and left and right. In town I watched the children, the women, the old men, the young men, not knowing when or where or by whom the bullet, poisoned arrow, grenade, or shell would come from. This paranoid 'hyper' quality sapped my energies out, kept me tired, drained and just wiped out, just about all the time."

This pervasive terror touched every soldier in Vietnam regardless of rank or location. It didn't matter whether he was on foot or in a "Huey" (utility helicopter), whether a "front man" (or point man) or in the "rear" (areas of *relative* safety), or whether on the compound or in the "boonies" (jungle). It didn't matter whether the soldier was a nurse in the field or in an evacuation hospital area or a medic attending the wounded in a firefight. The soldier was *always* in danger, though the degree of peril varied from one area to another, and from one particular time to another. Some places that were safe became "hot" hostile areas in a matter of weeks. In Vietnam, then, the "war zone" concept was virtually nonexistent, since terrorist activities were ubiquitous.

Danger was everywhere because this was a guerrilla war: all the people of the country were at war—men, women, boys, girls, the very young, the aged, and the infirmed. And all were caught between the two fighting forces, both competing for the people's "hearts and minds." As in most guerrilla wars, no one could be trusted, *no one*. At restaurants in town, soldiers had to be very careful about what they ate and who had prepared it. At a bar, either they made their drinks themselves or watched as they were being mixed and poured. On the compound, some Vietnamese hired by U.S. forces to help in the kitchen, laundry, and in other support capacities, were later found to be VC, VC suspects, or VC sympathizers.

As Luke put it, "We were really trying to help some of these people. We treated them well on the compound. And, to top it all off, we were supposedly here for them in the first place. These are South Vietnamese we were fighting for; you couldn't even trust them!"

Many American soldiers, after becoming drunk in town, were beaten severely with sticks and bats by groups of three or four Vietnamese nationals. Visiting a local brothel was fraught with danger: the prostitute could be a VC, or could "set up" the GI to be killed by a VC. Driving through towns or in rural villages was also hazardous, since VC and children were known to throw grenades into the vehicle. Some GIs placed meshed wire on the windows of their vehicles to keep explosives out. This pervasive web of terror made everywhere the soldier went a potential trap. Because no one could be trusted, the soldier had to develop profound hypervigilance—out of a deep sense of vulnerability and uncertainty. Survival became dependent on sharpening one's senses. Danger confronted American soldiers in "harmless" guises. GIs had to contend with the nightmare of whether an approaching Vietnamese child was booby-trapped, and whether to avoid or kill the child. South Vietnamese women intimate with GIs might become their executioners. Buildings were booby-trapped. Roads once known to be safe might later be mined. Since the South Vietnamese resembled the VC and NVA, it was extremely difficult, if not impossible, to differentiate among them. American soldiers were often dismayed, frustrated, and murderously incensed to discover that South Vietnamese Army soldiers could not be trusted to fight for their own country. South Vietnamese troops (of the ARVN—Army of the Republic of Vietnam) were known to abandon their posts in the heat of battle, leaving their Vietnamese and American comrades vulnerable and in danger. Needless to say, many Americans became anxious when ordered to fight alongside ARVN troops.

American soldiers were also beset by such mistakes or accidents as American pilots inadvertently dropping napalm on American troops. In an eyewitness account of napalm falling short of its target and landing on an American, Joe stated, "In less than no time he was nothing but charcoal. I still have memories of the terrible sight, smell and horrible odor that I will never get over."

Aside from their booby traps, the VC were seemingly invincible as snipers. In this "game of death" they were persistent and highly effective, picking off GIs and ARVN troops seemingly at will, whether perched in trees or remaining hidden from sight. Of such exploits in the jungle, Terry, an American infantryman, comments: "One thing I can say about Charlie [VC] is that he knew what he was doing. He knew his business—frustrating, terrorizing, and killing GIs. It seems strange of me saying this, because Charlie hurt me twice in the 'Nam. He was a bad motherfucker. He did his action right. Just fucked everybody up; just like that. He was some scary sucker, too. Yeah, he kept me humping in the bush. He was very scary and he was everywhere. We were so much aware of that dude's presence around us in the bush that no soldier ever saluted an officer, not in the bush. You could feel Charlie's presence—you knew he was watching you, you just didn't know from where, but he *was* there. Oh, yeah, man, shit, Charlie had a thing for those officers and NCOs. He would go after them with all he's got. Also, at one time Charlie had a thing for medics, too. He knew that nothing was more demoralizing to a group of fighting men than not to have leaders and medics. The men just wouldn't want to fight. Yeah, Charlie was a scary bastard. I used to just dream about the bastard all the time—for months in Vietnam. He scared the shit out of me and made me piss in my pants many times, no lie, no lie."

Ambushes were another terrorist tactic. Quite often, the VC planned attacks and ambushes on weekends and holidays, especially on sentimental holidays, such as Christmas, Thanksgiving, and the Fourth of July. The basic VC objective was to terrorize and harass, not necessarily to maim or kill. Yet these surprise attacks resulted in heavy casualties anyway. A special drill routine conducted by the "Aussies" (Australian combat soldiers) proved an effective counterambush tactic, which gained great respect in Vietnam.[4] This military maneuver was based on rapid movement through the center of the ambush, and enveloping the ambushing forces from the rear.

Land mines, some dating back to the French involvement in Vietnam, were another source of danger. Ted was a point man for his squad. An important part of his job was detecting antipersonnel mines, booby traps, and antitank bombs. Though well trained, he always felt anxious when engaged in road-clearing operations. Very dedicated to the men in his squad, he took great care that he did not miss a single mine, booby trap, or bomb. Another point man, Seth, with a different fighting unit in the Central Highlands, recalled a frightening episode in which 12 of his men were killed by a Russian Claymore mine. Seth still suffers tremendous guilt and remorse over the incident, blaming himself for not detecting the mine. As typical mine-planting practice, the VC would choose the center or near-center of a trail; at other times, however, mines would be planted at the edge of the path.

In Vietnam, terror was also fostered by special psychological operations and propaganda campaigns, on both sides; this is generally referred to as "psychological warfare" ("psywar") or "psychological operations" ("psyops"). For psywar, the North Vietnamese used Radio Hanoi to erode the confidence and morale of American troops. For example, messages addressed to black American soldiers told them that they were fighting, not to free Vietnam as they had been misled to believe, but rather a white man's war of imperialist colonialism, and that they, as black soldiers, should have no part in fighting and killing a Third World people (the Vietnamese). Communist propaganda also advised black troops to defect and save themselves from a moral dilemma and certain destruction. The American counterpart to Radio Hanoi was its "Chieu Hoi" (Open Arms) tactical propaganda campaign, incorporating an in-depth knowledge and understanding of the Vietnamese culture, values, and beliefs, particularly their superstitions. Vietnamese superstitions were exploited by American psyops propaganda operations. Bill, specifically trained in this area, admitted: "It is unbelievable the things we'd say and do to psyche out the VC and NVA forces." For example, the "Big Red One" (First Infantry Division) launched a harassment daytime program involving loudspeakers and broadcasts intended to keep the VC awake during the day in order to make them ineffective in their nighttime terrorist operations. Their resistance lowered by lack of sleep, the VC were then subjected to strange, eerie, and deathly sounds. These sounds represented the "wandering souls" of the VC dead for whom a resting place had not yet been found.[4] Bill also served as an interrogation officer in a military intelligence group, and was assigned to the Phoenix Program. This program involved interrogating key officials within the VC organization (which, unlike prevailing beliefs, was a highly sophisticated system), learning the identities of other VC, and then assassinating them. In addition to the Phoenix Program, such programs as the Census Grievance and Rural Development (RD) Cadre aimed to "rout out" VC institutions one at a time.[5] The American military had come to terms with the reality that it could not win militarily in the face of the powerfully entrenched ideals of the VC and NVA, and that it was far better to win the people over by understanding and showing respect for their way of life by protecting the Vietnamese people from the cruelty, torture, and illegal tax collection by the VC.

The Census Grievance Program, based on its census of the Vietnamese people, sought to win them over by identifying problems they experienced with the VC in their villages, and by attempting to correct these problems; for example, the need for sanitation, bridges, the rebuilding of a village after destruction by the VC or by the Americans.

The Phoenix Program would then follow: any VC collecting taxes or levies were taken into custody, and uncooperative village chiefs and villagers were harassed or tortured. Using interrogation to learn the whereabouts of other VC, Phoenix would then set out to assassinate each of them. The overall objective of the Phoenix Program was to undermine the infrastructure of VC village operations.

Two of the most valued and feared groups of American soldiers in Vietnam (aside from the 101st Airborne "Screaming Eagles" and some Marine Corps fighting groups) were the "Lurps" and the U.S. SEALS. As long-range recon patrollers, the Lurps stalked the enemy by stealthily creeping up on VC camps or NVA troops during the night. In Vietnam, the VC were said to own the night, the Americans the day. The Lurps and SEALS were exceptions to this. These groups were the night ambushers, the American counterparts to the VC insurgency fighters and infiltrators. Lurps were strange people, for the most part, even frightening to regular Division troops seasoned in search-and-destroy missions and frequent firefights. Non-Lurp troops stayed out of their way, and in some Divisions, Lurps had living quarters separate from the other soldiers. Whereas the point man went ahead of the platoon to draw enemy fire, detect trip-wired booby traps and land mines, the Lurps attacked the enemy, on his own turf, using the same "tried-and-true" insurgency and counterinsurgency tactics of the VC that Americans had learned so well in the bush.

Most Lurps were peculiar people, manifesting strange behavior characteristic of the deranged. They would withdraw from other troops, wear peculiar headbands, neckbands, and clothing, and, at times, wear around their necks a band of VC ears, which had been cut off during infiltration or ambushes. These men practiced the art of terrorism. They looked terrifying to others and, at times, even to themselves. They psyched themselves into believing in their insurgency activities, that they were fierce and frightening automatons devoid of feeling, who killed on reflex.

Not everyone could become a Lurp. One had to look mean, *be* mean, determined, heartless, with a strong hate for the VC. Some men, intent on revenge, became Lurps after having survived a near-total "wipeout" of their unit by the VC or NVA. For many of these men, becoming a Lurp was their way of dealing with their grief and loss, of releasing pent-up feelings. This intent on revenge was the primary motivating force for many men in volunteering to become Lurps.

The SEAL insurgency and counterinsurgency teams were begun by President Kennedy, who believed that a new type of soldier was needed to provide insurgency capability to the military. SEAL ("Sea, Air, and Land") featured personnel trained to survive and fight on sea, air, or land, often in support of military land activities such as those of the Phoenix Program. Like the Lurps (mostly Army troops), the SEALS were Navy insurgents, perhaps even more determined and ruthless than the Lurps. These men would infiltrate the most perilous VC strongholds at night and leave with their target VC. After completing their mission—that is, after kidnapping or assassinating the target VC official(s) they had been sent to kill or capture for interrogation—they would "sign" their work—the body was painted green and dismembered. As Michael Beamon, a Scout with the SEALS in Vietnam, put it,". . . the PRUs [Provincial Reconnaissance Unit insurgents] would . . . cut the liver out and take a bite out of it, and that would symbolize that the person would not go into Buddha heaven intact . . . . Finding a loved one with a green face and stabbed—in the middle of the road—was incredible terror."[5]

Another fighting force was the CRIP (Combined Recon and Intelligence Platoon). This platoon was organized to integrate reconnaissance and intelligence to provide better cooperative activities between our forces and the ARVN for the purpose of undermining the VC's village infrastructures.[5] By associating with Vietnamese villagers—talking with them, eating at their restaurants, visiting their laundries—CRIP learned important information, as well as discovered "a honeycomb of tunnels . . . [northwest of Go Dau Ha] from a couple of operations [where] people would disappear . . . underground."[5]

The Small Independent Action Forces (SIAFs) were tactical units made up of conventional soldiers who engaged in insurgency military operations. SIAFs usually set up impregnable camps in VC-held territories to subvert VC and NVA influences in South Vietnam. Other important fighting forces in Vietnam included, but were not limited to: the First Infantry Division, the Ninth Infantry Division, the Twenty-fifth Infantry Division, U.S. Navy Beachmasters; the Marine Divisions; First Cavalry Division; River Patrol Groups; the 101st Airborne Division; the 173rd Airborne Division; Americal Division; U.S. Navy Light Attack Squadron; U.S. Marine Combined Action Platoon (CAP) [Marines and Navy soldiers (usually a medic)]; Central Intelligence Agency (CIA) operations; the 717th Air Cavalry; various aircraft carriers, such as the *America, Midday,* and others.

At some point during their tour of duty in Vietnam, soldiers were encouraged to go on R & R (rest and recuperation) to Japan, Bangkok (Thailand), Kuala Lumpur (Malaysia), and other places either within Vietnam itself or not. R & R served to give the soldier a respite from the stresses of war, recuperating his spirit, his physical and mental energies. R & R was always experienced as a "grand taste" of the *world* and would make each more determined to survive and return home to the United States.

Some men did rather unsoldierly things to get out of the fighting. They would shoot themselves in the foot, or shoot off a finger, or engage in some assignment of calculated risk to receive injuries of sufficient severity to be sent to the "rear." Others did whatever was necessary to be put in jail. Tiger T., a Marine, had fought for almost 6 months in the jungle. After several close calls, he decided that he wanted to go home rather than continuing as a "superhero," humping the bush and being killed. He "became rambunctious, wild, assaultive, and a real bastard. No one could believe I was the same person. I was sent to the LBJ [the Long Binh Jail] near Saigon where I did time." Another soldier, "Bullseye" Mack, had volunteered for the most dangerous assignments anywhere in Vietnam or in Southeast Asia "where the action was." Highly valued by his Division, Company, and platoon, he had served as point man, as a Lurp, and did TDY (temporary duty) with Phoenix, Special Forces, and other special tactical forces. After 8 months of hard fighting and risking his life, "something snapped in my head—I don't know what happened." He was tired and wanted to go home alive, "not in some body-bag." Bullseye Mack changed when, about 10 minutes into a battle, he saw Mitch, his best buddy with whom he had grown up in the Midwest, "catch his lunch" (get killed) by a barrage of enemy fire. "Man, this was freaky. I really freaked out for the first time in 'Nam. What happened was that the fucking bullets kept my buddy doing sommersaults. He was dead, but the steady precision and rhythm of the bullets kept his body moving. That was weird; I considered myself to be *hard*, real *hard*. I have proven myself as such. But that day I cried and cried and couldn't stop—a very dangerous thing to do in the field. I was later depressed. I just wanted out. I just said, 'Fuck it, what am I doing all this crazy shit in this man's Army for, anyway? Is it for myself, for my family, for my buddy, for America, for the Vietnamese? Who gives a ranking fuck anyway? Who gives a goddam? Who cares? I am going to the LBJ.' I want to be a jailbird; it's safer and it makes sense to me now."

Increased stresses of the war during and after the Tet Offensive of 1968 intensified the already mounting sense of unrest, frustration, and anger among American troops in the field. Many men felt that lack of superior leadership lay at the heart of the confusion and seeming lack of confidence of American troops. "Men were dying everywhere, like flies. It made no sense at all. All these young dudes. We just were a bunch of kids killing other kids." These are the words of Mike, an RTO in an infantry unit. He went on to say that during the Offensive he and many others in his unit believed that they "were getting wasted because officers were too inexperienced in Vietnam's jungle situation." They felt that a leader must be as tough, battle-tested, and sharp as the *punji sticks* lurking in the jungle. They believed that the military's theoretical strategists were inferior to leaders with an experiential grasp of the war—an insurgency and counterinsurgency tactician, leading his men from victory to victory, with the least number of deaths and casualties. Because the soldiers were so relatively young, they often depended on protective and dependable leadership for their very survival, especially during the time of eroding support for the war at home. Many soldiers believed that good leadership would have given them a "beacon of orientation" that would offer some modicum of stability and meaning to their involvement in the war. Since, for the most part, COs and platoon leaders were themselves unsure of the mission in Vietnam, they were unable to give the soldier a framework within which he could understand and make sense of his suffering, misery, pain, disappointments, the futility of the war effort, not to mention the American rejection of the war and its warriors at home.

It was during this period of the Vietnam experience that assaults on officers peaked. John, an infantryman, expressed the idea that no one in his unit seemed "to know what the fuck was going on; only guys and more guys getting fucked up—dead and mangled bodies, that's all! . . . All we were being told was, 'Go here, go there, no, stop, go the other way, and so on. I meant over there, not here,' etc. That's the way it felt. Everybody was confused and going crazy."

Being an officer in Vietnam, especially during these times was certainly not easy. It was a job that was very demanding, frustrating, and filled with uncertainty. Officers did not always know the right action to be taken, and their own superiors were often not very helpful in mapping out effective strategic options. Many officers still retain scars related to decisions made in Vietnam that resulted in the death of soldiers under their command.

In addition, officers discovered they were not permitted to implement strategic and tactical ideas they felt would work in a given situation, and thus felt their hands were tied by their superiors. In the "boonies," it seemed that control was as unstable as vapor on a hot day. Things were fluid, one thing passing into another, and on and on. Boredom, fatigue, and frustration—important "enemies" of survival[4]—were the order of the day, with terror at night. Terror also moved by day, but intensified manifold by night. During Tet and after, the psychotic reality of constant slaughter, mutilations, and atrocities moved onward with no end in sight. Pete, a grunt, recalled: "Those days of fighting Charlie and the NVA I will never forget. Khe Sanh, the city of Hue, the DMZ, Kontum, Hoi An, Da Nang, Gan Me Thuot, Pleiku, Qui Nhon, Bien Hoa—all these areas were involved in the Tet Offensive, and many more, believe me. I thought I would never get out alive, though I did lose a leg and an arm. They were hitting us from every which way—in all directions, all over the place, from below and from above—grenading, mortaring, bombing, machine gunning, you name it, man, they claimed it. Guys were falling like flies!"

Increasing racial tensions also contributed to Vietnam's experience of terror and uncertainty. During 1968, the assassination of Dr. Martin Luther King, Jr. affected race relations in a detrimental way, especially in the "rear." Blacks were angry; they viewed the assassination as a direct blow to black values and the determination of some black people to struggle for racial equality in a peaceful way. Moreover, they felt betrayed and harmed by a racist society they were now "protecting" by fighting and risking their lives in Vietnam. Consequently, blacks began to segregate themselves from whites. Many blacks in Vietnam frequented Saigon's "Soul Kitchen" and joined black militancy groups such as the Ju Ju's and the Mau Mau's.[6]

One group of investigators found that "race consciousness" caused emotional conflicts in non-white American soldiers during the "bad war" (late '60s and early '70s) in Vietnam[7] and on various military bases (Air Force, Navy, Marines, and Army). They reported hearing epithets such as "reindeer," "Jig," "spook," "Brownie," "coon," "warrior," "spade," and "nigger."[8] During this time, many black soldiers felt they should have been home defending their own freedom as Americans—on American soil, not Vietnamese. They felt, further, that their families, homes, and communities were unprotected from the American "VCs"—brutal police and antiblack rallyists. Especially during the 1970s, white officers feared that blacks would turn their weapons on them in Vietnam.[6] Despite this underlying racial tension—on both sides—a general feeling of comradeship prevailed which was essential for survival.

The overwhelming tensions of war within each soldier—particularly the dreaded fear of being "blown away"—called for some effective method of quelling the anticipated catastrophe. For many soldiers in Vietnam, drugs and alcohol were used as effective agents in helping the soldier to sleep; in dulling his senses and shutting out disturbing memories; making it possible to anesthetize himself to moral anxieties that derive from killing, atrocities, and from surviving. We prefer the term "self-medication" in discussions of drug use or misuse in the war zone, because these substances were used instrumentally. In contrast to popular images portraying the Vietnam veteran as a "drug-crazed and wanton killer" who indulged in Vietnam's bountiful supplies of mind- and mood-altering drugs, most soldiers in Vietnam who used drugs, took these substances instrumentally—that is, to survive mentally. These men and women were committed to surviving and going home.

There were others who used these substances as a way of life—as an inflexible life-style, "stuck in glue." Soldiers who drank too much or took large amounts of drugs, increased their chances of losing control over thought, action, and judgment in combat encounters. These men were shunned and distrusted, for obvious reasons. In addition, commissioned and noncommissioned officers were reported to have been unable to lead their men into battle due to their own use of drugs and alcohol. Doctors and nurses were no exception, many of them succumbing to the extraordinary stresses inherent in their work.

Overuse of these substances invariably undermined unit morale for those who found other more adaptive ways of coping with the stresses of combat. This situation eroded confidence, and shattered the illusion of having a protector and wise counsel in battle, when combat leaders became virtually "inoperative and dysfunctional in the bush." Heavy use of drugs, however, was restricted to the "rear."

In addition to the treacherousness of Vietnam's guerrilla warfare, the soldier was confronted with yet another pernicious dimension of reality there: an abundance of diseases. There was, for example. bubonic plague, cholera, fevers of unknown origins, melioidosis, internal parasites, rabies, tropical sprue, tuberculosis, leprosy, various strains of venereal diseases, and Japanese encephalitis (found mostly in Da Nang), in addition to malaria, the communicable disease that affected the largest number of American troops and accounted for a large proportion of man-hours lost on the battlefield. Another danger was being bitten by monkeys, who were always suspected of having rabies.

When a soldier had 2 months or less remaining before returning to the United States, he assumed the status of "short-timer." As we mentioned earlier, the short-timer became more cautious and suspicious than ever. He had survived thus far, and wanted to "make it back home, in one piece." Company Commanders would often allow these soldiers to leave the field and take a "safer" job until their departure. Paul, having only 6 days left in Vietnam before the "great day," relates: "I now walk very carefully. All of a sudden that I am now a short-timer, time has stood still; the sun stands still; the moon stands still; everything stands still. I can't believe it. I just can't take no chances now; I am coming home, baby!" Some soldiers leaving Vietnam nonetheless felt they were betraying their buddies left behind. For this and other reasons, they returned to the jungles of Vietnam for another tour of duty after having gone home to the United States.

Paul's last days and hours were reminiscent of his early days a year earlier as a "greenhorn," filled with apprehension and the dread of uncertainty. And because he had seen so much heavy combat and had surprised himself with his capacity for killing, even to the extent of becoming excited over the combat "action," Paul was not certain he would be able to turn off the "killer within" upon arriving home. There was doubt whether he could maintain his "cool" if confronted with negative conceptions of him and the war by family or friends. But foremost in his mind was whether he would leave Vietnam alive or "in one of those plastic body bags. Will I finally, really make it home after all I have been through, after all I have done?"

Like most other short-timers, Paul became superstitious, particularly after hearing tales such as the last 21 days being the time of greatest danger of getting killed in Vietnam. His superstition abated only when he had boarded the plane, his "freedom bird." Even up in the air, he had more than a fleeting thought, "What if we're hit from below? What if the plane crashes?" He got up and sat in the place he felt was safest—just in case. After an hour or so, Paul was able to relax, and fell into a deep sleep. When he awoke, he "felt relaxed, but *not too* relaxed."

Chapter 3 / BEING BACK: THE TREACHEROUS TERRAIN BACK HOME

For officers and enlisted men of all military rank in Vietnam, crossing each day off the calendar was an important daily ritual. Indeed, the most envied situation was that of the "short-timer." Though most soldiers had looked forward from the first day to the time they would be returning to the United States, going home, for many, was not as easy as they had believed. For many, going home meant breaking up close, meaningful relationships with fellow soldiers; it meant leaving a part of one's youth and life behind. And it meant leaving one's innocence behind, because a killer is no longer innocent, his hands now tainted with blood that no washing can ever clean. Moreover, for some, going home meant relinquishing a sense of omnipotence—that they could do anything, without punishment or guilt. For many, going home also meant giving up excitement, intense excitement—to return, as one GI put it, "to an unknown quantity" back home in the United States. After the thrill of Vietnam, going home for some meant being thrust into an unintriguing, humdrum existence.

Moreover, for some, going home meant "copping out" and "abandoning" their comrades. Large numbers of soldiers felt guilty about leaving without their friends. And, back home, they would often wonder about the fate of those they left behind. Many had to wait from 7 to as many as 17 years to find out whether certain friends had survived Vietnam. They went to "The Wall"* in 1982 in Washington, D.C., to search feverishly through over 59,000 names inscribed on the Memorial to see if their friends had died in Vietnam.

The actuality of leaving Vietnam after completing a year of duty—to be united finally with one's family and friends—was the event the soldier had lived for. Most soldiers had fantasized that once they were home all their troubles would be over. Everything would certainly be at least as good as it had been prior to going to Vietnam. The soldiers, in anticipating the repatriation experience, neglected to consider the possibility of anything going awry.

Upon returning home, however, the returnee found that "people, buildings, cars, dogs, everything looked like clever imitations of the real world."[1] For the *real world* had now become Vietnam, not the United States. "The World [U.S.A.] that they had talked about and dreamed of every day in Nam was gone, replaced with a flat, lifeless *forgery of reality*"[1] [italics added]. This forgery of reality was experienced by the veteran as going "from a free-fire zone to the twilight zone"[1]—from Vietnam's reality to the unreality of repatriation. Thus, the two worlds of the veteran—the Vietnam-acquired *real* world of action and what seemed to be the *unreal* world of inaction—were in sharp conflict. When he had first entered Vietnam, the soldier had been faced with the "culture shock" of that country. Now, back home as a veteran, he was faced with the challenge of "reconciling" the two clashing worlds in his mind.

In *Strangers at Home,* a book that examines the stresses, crises, and readjustment problems of Vietnam veterans, Alfred Schuetz's account of the post-World War II readjustment difficulties of veterans parallels to some extent the problems we observe in today's Vietnam veterans. His

---

* "The Wall" is a term given to the National Memorial of Vietnam Veterans in Washington, D.C. The monument was dedicated in November, 1982.

insightful analysis of Odysseus's historic return to Ithaca reveals a similarity to that of the Vietnam veteran. He writes[2]:

> The Phaecian sailors deposited the sleeping Odysseus on the shore of Ithaca, his homeland, to reach which he had struggled for 20 years of unspeakable suffering. He stirred and woke from sleep in the land of his fathers, but he knew not his whereabouts. Ithaca showed to him an unaccustomed face; he did not recognize the pathways stretching far into the distance, the quiet bays, the crags and precipices. He rose to his feet and stood staring at what was his own land, crying mournfully: "Alas! and now where on earth am I? What do I here myself?" That he had been absent for so long was not the whole reason why he did not recognize his own country; in part it was because goddess Pallas Athene had thickened the air about him to keep him unknown "while she made him wise to things." Thus Homer tells the story of the most famous homecoming in the literature of the world.

Returning home after war is bewildering even under the best of circumstances, that is, when the war—fully sanctioned—has been won. No returnee is spared the feelings of disorientation, self-strangeness, and varying degrees of anger and alienation, albeit short-lived. In our observations, a parallel can also be drawn between Odysseus having fought in Troy and the veteran having fought in Vietnam. Though Odysseus returned to his home in Ithaca after 20 years, and the Vietnam veteran after only 1 year, that 1 year, for many veterans, seemed endless. Lucas, a combat marine who had fought a bloody battle defending the northern city of Hue during the Tet Offensive, felt he had aged "30 years during my 13 months in Vietnam." He explained: "When I got home everybody seemed to believe that I was strange. They looked at me as if I had been away for a long many years. My parents were home when I got in from 'Nam, and they said, 'Hi, nice to see you again; we're going out to supper. See you when we get back.' Out they went, and down I went into depression."

Once home, the Vietnam veteran felt very strange within himself, and some felt others were strange. He had, after all, changed in some very important ways. Now less tolerant of trivial matters, he was concerned only about "the bottom line"—the heart of the matter. He felt he had special knowledge about life and death that most people around him did not have. Though not always apparent to others, and in fact sometimes not even to the veteran himself, he felt great pride over having survived in Vietnam—a feat nearly impossible to communicate to others, even one's own family. Having been habitually conditioned to respond in battle by reflex to reality (Vietnam), he was now jittery, nervous, a mild fluttering in his stomach, a continuous feeling of disorientation. As Lucas said: "I had no way of knowing in what way I was different. The feeling was there, though. Even my block looked different; the steps felt a little lower, the size of the house looked smaller. My girlfriend looked sexier and prettier than I remembered her to be." Such perceptual and cognitive alterations and distortions usually accompany the veteran's reorientation to home—an aspect of a normal process of returning home not only physically but psychologically as well. Picking up where they had left off in intimate relationships is often extremely difficult. Issues of closeness, sex, and fidelity emerge early. As Lucas recollects:

> After a short while, my girlfriend told me she didn't know how to relate to me; or how she really felt about me now. I had expected things to be the way they were; but they weren't. She said she thought I had been killed in the war, because I stopped writing to her. Honestly, I didn't know how to relate to her now either. I dreaded going to bed with her; I just didn't know how I'd do. She also said that I wasn't the loving guy she used to know and love, that something horrible must have happened to me over there to change me so completely. I told her I didn't know what she was talking about. She said that the look in my eyes was the look of a deeply terrorized person, with a long-distance stare, looking off into the beyond—not into the present with her at this time. She also mentioned that my frightened look and pallid complexion, my uptight way of sitting, talking, walking, you name it, my aloofness, and all that, made her too uncomfortable for us to continue our relationship. She said that besides, she had found somebody else anyway. That really hurt me; it burned me up inside to hear this.

> When it came to my family, my mother told me that I wasn't as considerate and sweet as I used to be. My dad felt I wasn't diligent and committed as he remembered me to be prior to Vietnam. I didn't know what any of these people were saying. I knew I was getting pissed off more and more by hearing all of this bullshit, I know that.

My Aunt Tilda and Uncle Josey felt the same as the others. Finally, as time went on, I realized that so many people couldn't all be wrong about me. The change in me began to seem deep to me— deeper than I would ever have imagined to be the case. I myself was not fully aware of just how profound my transformation had been. I guess killing and hurting human beings have a way of catching up with you; just seeing so many guys die, some died in my arms; seeing guys die of snake bites; getting sick from malaria; feeling so tired and emotionally drained for so long, feeling so intensely angry and used; being terrorized myself so many times, so many close calls. I got hit three times with bullets. I guess that can change somebody, maybe most people.

Like Odysseus who awoke in his homeland and yet didn't know his whereabouts, so Lucas had experienced his house, neighborhood, community, and self as Odysseus had experienced Ithaca—as having "an unaccustomed face." Again, like Odysseus, who asked "Alas! and now where on earth am I? What do I here myself?", Vietnam veterans reflected on their altered sense of time, space, and relationship with other human beings. Odysseus's lamentation and query, "What do I here myself?", has a special significance for Vietnam veterans. Indeed, they also felt isolated and alone, psychologically and culturally dislocated. These important and fundamental questions, then, bear on the veteran's basic alteration in the concepts of self and reality, as well as express a profound sense of alienation and loneliness.

Now, in great contrast to Odysseus's homecoming, Vietnam veterans were not given the opportunity to be "made . . . wise to things" through a transitional period between war and repatriation. From Homer: "Pallas Athene had thickened the air about him to keep him unknown," thus offering Odysseus a chance to gain his bearings and gradually become a member of society once again. Pallas Athene, unlike the American people and the military, knew of the importance of this transitional period. What of the Vietnam veteran's transitional period? Thirty-six hours! In that time, men left the jungles of Vietnam, were driven to a departure post, boarded on an American plane and processed at a Reception Center in Oakland (California) or Seattle. Within 18 hours or less at the Reception Center, the returnee was officially discharged to civilian life, or reassigned to a new military unit in the United States if the soldier had additional service in the military.

Service in the military, after Vietnam, had its own brand of "culture shock" for the returnee. Thus, for some, going home meant returning not only to civilian communities in the United States, but also to a strict, highly disciplined and regimented military system they had grown unaccustomed to in Vietnam. Difficulties in readjusting to military life after Vietnam were experienced by many. Considered a "seasoned" soldier who had seen a lot of action in Vietnam, the returnee was both respected and derided. And he was feared because of the impression that he could become easily "unglued," and go off on rampages of violence if bothered. Officers and NCOs were often seen by the returnee as insensitive to his sacrifices and combat experience in Vietnam, creating an adversarial relationship between them. "Back-home" military life seemed boring to many returnees, who opted to return to serve in Vietnam.

As Schuetz[2] notes, the veteran expects little change when he returns home, but finds substantial; those to whom he returns expect little change, but find much. Schuetz goes on to stress the need for both veteran and community to be adequately prepared for the veteran's return home. In the case of Vietnam, the veteran was not prepared to become a civilian; neither was the community prepared for his homecoming. Thus, the very vital transitional phase for an "inhuman killer" to become "rehumanized" (or "recivilianized") was neglected by the military and society. Moreover, such transition is a process; and process takes time. If Homer's Pallas Athene knew this during ancient times, what can be said of modern-day military planners, military psychologists, and society, who failed to devise and implement a useful transitional plan for Vietnam veterans?

The Vietnam veteran was not only deprived the vital transitionary period, but was treated with intense scorn, disgust, and hatred by a nation that refused to look at itself honestly. Thus, anger and hostility over the war were displaced onto the veteran, and blaming the veteran became the American *modus operandi*. Because of the unwillingness of the government and the people to take responsibility for the war, the soldier became the victim of the war. And this was after all the sacrifices he had made in Vietnam. Thus, he was twice sacrificed; this time on the altar of shame and guilt in order to appease the national "conscience." This *double sacrifice* of the Vietnam veteran is intimately connected to what psychologist

William Ryan calls "blaming the victim."[3] Victimizing the Vietnam veteran occurred subtly, systematically, and completely. First, the veteran was told by nearly everyone that he had been foolish to fight in an immoral war where American soldiers must have been depraved for killing women and children in Vietnam. Worse, veterans of other wars told him that he fought in the only war that America lost. This he heard constantly. Even worse, he was told by some that he didn't even have the honor of having fought in a *war*, since this had been a "police action" or a "conflict." Then his sense of self was attacked most directly and painfully, for the media portrayed him as depraved, immoral, drug-crazed, and psychopathic. Moreover, he was accused both directly and indirectly by family and peers of killing wantonly because he enjoyed it, and that he was and will hopelessly remain an "animal."

The experience of being a stranger at home is a profound one; it is a painful one, with critical psychological implication for the veteran's readjustment and ultimate well-being. We present the repatriation or homecoming stories of three Vietnam veterans, in their own words:

> I got back about 6:00 in the morning. Everybody was asleep. They got up, welcomed me back. I got a few hugs and kisses. The whole scene lasted 15 minutes or thereabouts. They went to bed. Next morning my sisters went to school as usual, while my brother went to college. Everything seemed the same to them, real routine, you know. I didn't feel "routine," I felt out of it. I felt nervous, tense, jittery, even shaky. I wasn't able to fall asleep, so I got up at 10:00 A.M. I was home alone. So I walked down to the package store and bought me some liquor to help me out—you know, with the nervousness, *and* my anger about everything.
>
> I had started drinking heavily in Vietnam after a battle at Khe Sanh. Alcohol usually worked for me. As I walked down the street, I was trying to avoid drawing attention to myself. I saw a good friend but I tried to hurry by so he wouldn't see me. I knew he might be glad to see me, but I didn't want him to see me, so I hurried by, hoping he or anyone else wouldn't see me pass by. I just wanted to get my bottle and make it back to my parents' crib [house] so I could get myself together quick.
>
> In spite of all my efforts to avoid having anyone see me, a long-time friend saw me and really welcomed me home. It was really nice. Then, like out of nowhere, six guys showed up on the scene; I knew

most of them. They wanted to know about the "good dope" in Vietnam. They didn't seem interested in me as a person. They had heard of the Thai red, the opium, and all that stuff. They asked me about the Vietnamese whores; and how many times I caught the clap [gonorrhea].

They also wanted to know what it was like having sex with Vietnamese women. One of them yelled out, "How many babies you've burned, man? How many young children don't have their fathers because of guys like you. Yeah, you killers, man; you heard me." Before I knew what had happened the cops were there. I had beaten four guys up severely; three had to be taken to the hospital. I seemed to have lost my head totally. I didn't want to hurt anybody. I had done a lot of killing in the 'Nam; I just wanted to be left alone, now. But I was really mad; I felt I had to defend myself against and kill the new "gooks"—the American gooks.

I was disappointed, so hurt, and bitter at myself for "going off" and losing control of myself. I was told later that I was attacked first; I don't remember. I came back to my room, and began really drinking. I just kept thinking to myself that the streets of Cholon, Saigon, Nha Trang, and other cities and villages in Vietnam were probably safer for me than back in the United States.

My mother came in from the market and asked me how I was feeling. She told me she was aware of what I had just done, "to shame the family name." She was referring to the fight I just had on the street. She later told me she was going to make my favorite dish for supper, and a special welcome home cake. She was awfully quiet. This was not like her at all. She didn't seem too enthusiastic to see me; it seemed that way to me. It really hurt, because we used to be very close. Actually, she barely looked me in the eyes; almost never looked my way. I was getting real angry. Actually, she barely seemed to notice I was around. I shouted, "Mom, you can't even look at me; what's the matter, mom, talk to me."

I felt like a total stranger in my own home. I told her I was her son; that I was just back from fighting for my country—an important family value she and pop had instilled in me. I thought she had read all those letters I wrote to her, my dad, and brother from Vietnam telling them how happy I was going to be when I came home. I was not happy at all. "Tell me, mom, what's going on?" "Well, I'll tell you," she began. Now, I wasn't sure I wanted to hear it. I'd been "traumatized" already since I was back home, I didn't need any more. She went on, "I want to feel proud of you, but I don't. I just keep hearing those awful things on TV about what you guys are doing over there—just killing innocent people. " She said that was why she was so distant from me, but told me that she still loved me; and that her problem was what she kept on hearing from the media about the soldiers in Vietnam.

Another Vietnam veteran tells of his return home after the war, in 1971:

> The first few days were nice. My family came to the airport for me and drove me to a local banquet hall. The family had planned a party for me; I was excited. I felt special, just like my father, grandfather, and greatgrandfather when they returned from war. I was alive; I made it back through some of the most intense fighting in Vietnam. I wondered whether anyone felt as proud of me as I was of myself at the moment. I was looking forward to a big chat with my father about my experiences in Vietnam. I wanted him to be proud of me. One whole week went by before we could sit down and talk. I soon became aware of his true feelings about me and my war involvement. He started to give me a "song and dance" about how different the wars had been, that World War I was different than World War II and that Vietnam was different than all the other wars. I felt he was putting me on, bullshitting me, and I felt myself getting "hot under the collar." I was very upset, and getting more and more angry. He told me we shouldn't have been in Vietnam in the first place. I told him "we" weren't in Vietnam, "I" was; and that he was embarrassed of me. I told him that he had raised me to believe in our country and that service in the military was a noble thing to do. He said that had he been in my shoes, he would have gone to Canada or Europe, but not to Vietnam, never! I was confused, and my anger was mounting to a dangerous point inside me. He downplayed the war, and put me down—right down with it. I was really sick. I wanted him to feel proud of me. But he wasn't.
>
> What he said to me since that time was that my war wasn't really a war—not like World War II. He said that Congress had declared that the war in Southeast Asia was a "conflict," not a war per se. I said to myself, "I don't fucking believe it; I put my life on the line for Americans, and even my family does not seem to care."
>
> It was one thing that America was cruel to its men and women sent to fight in Vietnam, but I never thought my own family would treat me in the same shabby manner as everyone else. My disap-

pointment, isolation, bitterness, depression, and hopelessness got real deep from this point on. I just didn't care anymore. Later I looked up shrinks to help me with my nightmares. But all three shrinks didn't know anything about Vietnam and combat. I didn't feel they understood me at all. The would say things like: "What you need is to grow up, James; that'll do it." Or, "It's all over, James, give up the war or it'll kill you. Just tell yourself, 'Vietnam never happened.' If you do this, all those fears, nightmares, headaches, and problems in your head will just evaporate into thin air.' " I couldn't believe the shit these so-called professionals were telling me.

My shrinks never asked me about Vietnam, so I stopped talking about Vietnam. They said it was my "resistance" which kept me talking about Vietnam so much. They believed it was more therapeutic if I didn't bring Vietnam up in the therapy, if you can call it that. They were unable to reach me; I was unable to reach them too. Now that I am talking about this, I also remember that even my pastor could not help me. I went to see him after three months of not going to church, at my family's insistence—*they* wanted me to go. I grew up very religious. I took my religion to Vietnam, and either lost it or left it there. In either case, I don't have any now. I asked him questions such as, "Where was God?" "Why all the killing, why all the loss? Doesn't He see all this, doesn't He care?" "Why did all this have to happen?" I haven't been back to church in the 12 years after Vietnam. I think it's because I lost my faith over there, but especially back over here in the United States.

Now that those Vietnam veterans Outreach Centers are in existence they have made a difference in my life. I have visited six of them over parts of the country in my travels. I have been impressed with just how excellent the service is. They really understand me when I talk about Khe Sanh, An Khe, Da Nang, Quantri Province, Hue, the Mekong Delta, the DMZ, the Iron Triangle, and other places in the 'Nam. I am finally being helped.

Joe, a Marine who served three tours in Vietnam and saw some of the most brutal combat during Tet, tells this story:

When I got back, I was a young kid about 20 years old; I had done three tours to the 'Nam and I saw some pretty heavy stuff over there, a lot of action. I was home now. I wanted to forget the killing, the fears, the terrors inside me. I just wanted to forget, period. I didn't think that was asking too much. Being home meant that I would have people around me who cared—who respected me for what I had done in 'Nam, for putting my life on the line. I wanted pay-back, I guess; I thought I deserved at least something—a job or something. I didn't know for sure. It was just this feeling I had.

My best friend and I grew up in Brooklyn—this really pisses me off when I think of it—my best friend stole my girl when I was away in 'Nam and now works in a top-notch law firm making "boo-coo"* bucks. You ought to see his pad; it's the greatest place. I remember we used to like the same things, the same kind of girls, foods. We went to church together, dated together, and all that. We were like brothers, you know. You name it, we did it—together. But our similarities and friendship ended when I went to 'Nam; he didn't go. Lucky dog. He went to Canada and parts of Europe—he really wanted to get lost from the draft. See, I went to 'Nam, he didn't. It burns me up inside; it tears at my guts when I think of this. I came back with nothing; he came back with a profession. He had had sense and gone to school; me, I had no sense and I ended up in 'Nam. Yeah, we have changed; we are different now in every respect. He is now a lawyer; I am a bum. He has so much more, but it's the American dream he got. I lost out on it. I hate to admit it, but I hate him, I envy him and all that he's got. I just keep on getting those feelings that I want revenge. I feel ripped off.

I am so angry, it eats me up inside. I am mad because we used to be so close; I miss that. Now, we are so distant. We are very different people now. He married my girlfriend; he was my "Jody"† while I was in the war. I hate him for it. He took everything from me. The same people who knew us growing up together, now look at him and then at me, and say, "What happened to you?" They seem to despise me a lot. After hearing this for a while, I had to ask my own question, "What do you mean by that?" They claimed to be responsible, patriotic Americans, and all that. They ain't shit; if they can treat American soldiers this way, I can't say much for them. They claimed to be responding to my pallid skin color, my looking anemic all the time, and my "shiftlessness"—you know, not wanting to do very much of anything. They told me I looked scared, and that I must have seen a lot of terrible things in the war. I told them I had, but that I was still an American—their native son, and that they were not to ever forget it.

* Vietnamized version of the French *beau coup*, meaning plenty, very much, or a lot.
† Name given to a male who "steals" a GI's girlfriend when he is away in military service.

Though they didn't say it directly, they saw me as a sore loser—as just one of those fucked-up 'Nam vets—yes, those "super-crazies," "super-losers," motherfuckers. I know what the fuck they are thinking. My friend is a community star—an idol, if you will; I am the community bum, the fuck-up. He is happy as all hell; I have nothing, no money, no friends, but a lot of PTSD troubles all the time. I had no one to love, no one to care about. I can't even get myself together. I've gotten no government help. No one from the government helped me to get over 'Nam before throwing me into "this den of civilian lions," that always seems to be eating me up—inside and outside. I don't know; I don't know what I am even saying right now. But I am feeling a lot of pain; I am afraid to turn this pain onto somebody else, or turn it more on me. I just ache all over—mentally, socially, spiritually. I am trapped. I need someone to teach me how to give up the past, how to overcome my reflexive killing instincts, how to become a human being again. I was placed in a boot camp to learn to be a killer. I succeeded—they succeeded—at that. A responsible government would also help retrain me to become a person suitable to live with people again. I just don't feel like being around people. I feel they are looking at me and saying, "Wow! Look at that nut, doesn't he look awful?" "Let's get him out of society; he's a misfit." I just kept on having those thoughts. I had no family support. My father and uncle who fought in World War II all abandoned me. They are ashamed of me. They refuse to help me find work. Employers seem to "see me coming," so to speak, so they are ready with all the lies and fantastic stories as to why the job is no longer available even though I knew the job was not taken an hour and a half ago.

I was a wreck for over three years. Then, bingo! I found a job; but I was unable to hold the job. But just because somebody trusted that once, I decided to get some help for my mental and social problems. It was hard for me to take orders from anybody, especially bosses who were much younger than myself, because I figure that I should be their boss because I have been to war and know a lot about leading people, making decisions, and carrying out directives. This burned me up too. These young bosses didn't go to Vietnam; I did. Because I went I am "light-years" behind these guys. I am also behind them mentally, too. They don't have my headaches, flashbacks, anxieties, these weird sensations, funny thoughts going through my head. They can be normal; they can be crazy. At least they have a choice in this matter. I don't seem able to do so. Like I said, I sought treatment and was lucky to find someone who wanted to work with me in the Veterans Administration. This shrink had been in Vietnam; and he was sympathetic to me. He was there, so I felt he understood me and wanted to help me. He was "for real"; not a phony. He seemed to like me. This was the first time in many years that somebody really liked me and respected me for myself as a person—just for me.

Many Vietnam veterans' fathers who had served in earlier wars often refused to discuss Vietnam with them. Or, if Vietnam was discussed, the war and its soldiers were spoken of as losers and in a disparaging way. Many fathers compared *their* war of World War II—the "war to end all wars"—with their sons' "police action." Moreover, the battles the fathers had fought were *real* battles, not the little skirmishes and tame firefights of Vietnam. According to some veteran-fathers, the only real dangers in Vietnam were those created by the soldiers themselves by their overuse or overabuse of drugs and alcohol.

Much the same was said, whether aloud or in subtle but unmistakable ways, by the Vietnam veteran's uncle who had fought in World War II: The Vietnam veteran was an inferior soldier, inferior veteran, and inferior human being. And it hadn't taken a man to do a boy's job in fighting the VC, who was nothing more than a "Commie," in a paltry "nation of peasants," a low-grade Third World agrarian country somewhere in Southeast Asia. The Vietnam veteran had fought a "forgery of a war." His wounds were not real wounds; he didn't know what real pain or real wounds were.

Most mothers of Vietnam veterans tried very hard to understand, but in many instances were unable to comprehend the changes seen in their sons. Though mothers still cared for them, they found their sons caring very little about anyone, not even themselves or their families. It was very difficult to accept that their sons were no longer the caring and gentle human beings they had been before going to Vietnam. Comparing their husbands' return from World War II with their sons' return from Vietnam, the mothers often concluded that their veteran-sons had fought in a depraved war and thus had themselves become depraved. Most mothers did continue loving their sons but often found themselves having to choose sides between their World War II husbands and their Vietnam War sons.

Many Vietnam veterans found it hard to communicate their feelings to their wives or girlfriends. Some seemed to demand total empathy and understanding without first making their feelings and needs known. It was difficult for her to comprehend his moodiness and his preference for solitude. She often blamed herself for not being able to meet all of his needs, and to make him happy. She believed that if she were good enough, he would have behaved differently with her, been more loving and more attentive to their relationship.

Many veterans needed to be alone—away from *everyone*. In Vietnam, they had been exposed daily to a multitude of noises—helicopters, mortar rounds, rockets, tanks, machine guns, rifles, the screams and groans of wounded, dying children, of soldiers covered with napalm, and on and on. In what appears to have been a *somatopsychic programming,* the Vietnam veteran returned "neurologically wired" to respond to even the most low-intensity mental, social, and environmental stimuli with hyperalertness, irritability, physiological and emotional arousal. In this state, many interpersonal encounters from a spouse, lover, or child could cause a veteran to withdraw, become irritable, or even violent.

Many veterans found that they needed to withdraw from people in order to reflect upon and make sense of their Vietnam experience. Withdrawing from loved ones, moreover, helped the veteran to regain an equilibrium in his civilian life. Other veterans found that solitude helped them work out their conflict, while still others chose isolation to avoid "going off on somebody violently." Since many veterans experienced their new environment as fraught with temptations to violent outbursts, and because they were tired of "hurting and killing people,"* some sought an opportunity to "get themselves together," but on their own terms and "on their own turf" (a temporary self-imposed solitude).

Although there also existed within the veteran the desire to be close to others, especially to family and friends, there was a basic generalized "aversion" toward people, most of whom the veteran believed sold him down the river of despair and personal anguish. For a number of veterans, the feeling of having been disowned by their country was the greatest and most profound insult, causing "deep wound[s] . . . [in] the self-as-a-whole."[4]

---

* Many veterans are hypersensitive to what we refer to as *emotional equivalents of destruction and killing* in human relationships. Thus, these veterans equate interpersonally or socially directed anger, and mental and physical violence with destroying and killing.

Most felt they had given up their innocence, their physical, mental, and spiritual wholeness, for no meaningful reason. And to have to defend themselves for responding to America's call to protect its democratic values and ideals, compounded the hurt. Few can comprehend and cope psychologically with such rejection and violence to their pride and humanity. It is thus not very difficult to understand why it has been extraordinarily taxing for these men and women to regain their psychological and social equilibrium.

The war may have been over for them, but another war was just beginning—the war at home. Some veterans found it easier to dodge the enemy's bullets and punji sticks, circumvent the mines, snipers, grenades hidden in streams and other booby traps, and adjust to the cruel terrain and climate of the jungle than to encounter and confront American disfavor and outright hatred. As pointed out in an article, entitled "The Vietnam Vet: The Inner Battle Rages On," these men and women "are America's 'boat people' abandoned on the waters of uncertainty and on the unchartered seas of despair, anguish, and personal pain."[5] Because of this widespread animosity, one of us has applied the term "dysreception" to the prevailing response the Vietnam veteran received from his countrymen.

Just as family members had found the repatriated veteran, his friends had difficulty comprehending his behavior and the changes in his personality. He was less responsive, less like them, and less able to engage them in conversation on any subject, especially on the subject of Vietnam. He seemed off by himself in an intrapsychic or intrapersonal dialogue with himself, "in his own world—inside his head." As had his family, friends asked questions regarding his combat experiences, questions that were demeaning and cruel. They asked: "How many children did you kill?" "How many women and children did you burn?" "What was it like to kill somebody, a human being?" These and other such questions are not ones a veteran is willing or able to talk about. For one thing, he often felt ashamed of having killed; he often felt "different." Responding to such questions only made him "stand out" in a nonoutstanding manner—far more than he felt able to tolerate. Though some family members and friends asked these questions in sincerity, the veteran knew that most of the time these questions were asked out of condemnation and hostility. To the veteran, they were intrusive, insensitive, condescending, and degrading.

Typically, when the veteran's friends asked, "What's wrong?", his response was, "Nothing." These exchanges seemed direct enough, except that no one, including the veteran, believed the response to be genuine. The natural tendency of friends was to "push for the truth," which further alienated and angered the veteran. He was angry because he felt "put down" and distrusted. Such intrusiveness was experienced as disrespectful and insulting. Some veterans withdrew from social activities because they were tired "of having to explain and defend [themselves] all the time." "Besides," as another veteran put it, "They wouldn't understand anyway, so why bother."

This *non-self-disclosing* attitude had replaced in many Vietnam veterans a relative openness to others during the first several days or even weeks after repatriation. Non-self-disclosure was the consequence of numerous interpersonal interactions, most of which were upsetting to the veteran. Upon first coming home, many veterans had felt comfortable telling people—family, friends, or anyone else—about what had happened to them and others in Vietnam, as well as about their pride in having done a good job in their military positions. They would often recount specific battles and military operations. In fact, most Vietnam veterans, at first, felt very proud of their performance in Vietnam. It was only later that they realized that as they spoke of their war experiences, those to whom they were talking seemed bored, scared, repulsed, anxious, or even angry. After observing this reaction a few times, most Vietnam veterans "shut off" and adopted a personal policy of silence about Vietnam. With this, it became difficult for anyone, including therapists, to get them to talk about Vietnam.

The three veterans' stories are typical of those of a large number of Vietnam veterans who struggle daily to regain psychological equilibrium, inner balance, and control. The reader is asked to keep in mind that though the situations and issues are typical, certain generalizations have had to be made in many instances throughout this chapter in order to convey very complex issues affecting many Vietnam veterans, their families, friends, and society.

There are certain recurrent themes in these veterans' stories that should be emphasized. Many Vietnam veterans are bitter because they have been misunderstood, disliked, unfairly treated, and institutionally neglected. Many have become embittered over not being able to hold a job because of their irritability, anxiety, and difficulties in interpersonal and social situations—emotional problems stemming from combat experiences. For some, bitterness is the only tolerable emotional response. It replaces grief, intractable guilt, and enormous sadness because they have disappointed families, friends, and government institutions. Other veterans have become bitter because they feel themselves immersed in perpetual helplessness and hopelessness, without the prospect of a better tomorrow. They have grown tired of remembering and do not want to relive the war every night for the rest of their lives. They want relief and because many have not found it, they are bitter.

An equal source of bitterness in many cases is the loss of pride due to failed traditional masculine achievements—taking responsibility for working and providing for their families. Soldiers in Vietnam, had been given responsibility for military equipment and weapons costing up to millions of dollars. Doing those jobs well left them with a sense of achievement. Consequently, most Vietnam veterans look back on their Vietnam experience with great joy and pride, despite society's ill-regard of it.[6] Their Vietnam experience holds "deep personal joys" for most returnees, but these feelings are soon suppressed. Many have become angry because they cannot reconcile the conflicting images of themselves: *competent warrior* vs. *incompetent civilian*. In the face of chronic unemployment, difficulty paying the bills, and the inability to give their children those things they believe they deserve, a severe blow is struck to the veterans' sense of manhood. Because many veterans have been unable to reconcile these images, psychological conflicts have resulted.

In American society, *maleness* is imbued with great respectability. Culture requires that a man be resourceful and productive to provide adequately for his family, and make important contributions to society. Of those veterans who have been unable to readjust and live competently and productively in society, most are very aware of their shortcomings in these areas. This awareness is a source of great personal pain and lowered self-esteem. Chronic self-hate over perceived failures fosters an ever escalating sense of bitterness that many Vietnam veterans continue to struggle with.

Intense bitterness upon returning home from war is not new. In fact, it has been felt by warriors returning from *all* wars. Whereas this bitterness is modulated in so-called primitive cultures through rites of purification and culturally appropriate rituals, it is left to warriors of modern societies to deal with in the best way they can.

World War I returnees expressed bitterness and hate toward those who seemed to reap the harvest of their wartime sacrifices, and toward those Americans who seemed indifferent to them and their experiences in the war. Like Vietnam veterans, they felt ignored and taken for granted by their government and by society. There are widespread accounts in 1919 of the bitterness of World War I veterans.[7] As sociologist Willard Waller notes, these older veterans were bitter toward those who did not serve, toward those employers who were indifferent, and those in government who didn't seem to care. Moreover, they were angry because they had given all they had, and had received very little, if anything, in return. They were embittered toward those "happy speech makers" who did not serve, but used the occasion of the war to build their own personal gain and platforms of power. The angry veteran would have found it rather difficult to fight for their country again: "They said, 'The next war, if they want me, they'll have to burn the woods and sift the ashes.' "[7]

The repatriated veteran's success in readjusting depends on whether he fought a "good" war or a "bad" war. The labels "good" and "bad" are, of course, value-laden judgments originating within a given social context. Good wars are those in which the mission and objectives are clear to those within the hierarchy of the government, within the echelons of the military, and in which the soldiers are given a chance to fight and win. Such wars are predominantly free of "no-win" situations, and military planning is geared to defeat the enemy. Moreover, the vast majority of the citizens of that country sanction the war, conferring on it and its warriors respectability, and supporting them without reservation. Furthermore, the demarcation between "hawks" and "doves" is less clearly drawn, because the country is not in great conflict over the war. Finally, success can be measured along more traditional lines such as land taken, prisoners of war, intelligence gained, equipment and weapons seized, etc.

Bad wars are "undeclared" wars; they are wars no one wants to take responsibility for. These are wars that such institutions as the Congress of the United States choose not to sanction fully. It should be noted that the Grenada Invasion of 1983 and the peace-making presence of United States Marines in Lebanon during 1983 and 1984 are exceptions here, though they featured some characteristics of "bad" wars (for example, there was little or no public or congressional support for either). Small-scale military operations such as these do not fit the "good war–bad war" schema, since they are on such a minute scale. In good wars the soldier feels that his is a legitimate mission: what he does in the war is shared symbolically with the entire country. However, in bad wars, what the soldier does in the war falls squarely on his shoulders. He alone bears the burden for killing, for it is unshared, unshareable. Furthermore, in bad wars, what the soldier experiences must also be borne alone.

In a bad war, the soldier moves through the war experience adrift, without moorings, and hence without a useful personal perspective that would aid him in formulating and weaving his own "tapestry of meaning."[8] Some civilians have asked, "Were the fighting soldiers unaware of what those at home thought about the war?" The answer is certainly "no." Soldiers in Vietnam knew the sentiments of their fellow Americans through the various channels of communication that were available in Vietnam. They received newspapers from home. Relatives of soldiers sent newspaper clippings of specific events in America. Moreover, shortwave radios broadcasted American opinions and controversies about the war from a number of countries.

Every soldier who fights needs to acquire some meaning for his actions in war. In bad wars, however, meaning is either never acquired or is soon lost as disillusionment sets in and frustrations rise to overwhelming levels. Meaning follows nationwide and even worldwide acceptance, which confers legitimacy to a war and recognition for the mission as a worthwhile cause.

All good wars do not necessarily produce contented veterans, however, as exemplified by the World War I returnees. Though this war, according to our analysis, was a good war insofar as there was widespread support, its veterans were very bitter and discontented, as mentioned earlier. Perhaps the relative satisfaction of World War II veterans is an example of a good war *and* postwar support. We contend that a very critical factor that distinguishes the World War I/Vietnam War veteran from the World War II veteran is the nature of the social, political, community, and governmental support. The kind of support World War II soldiers received helped their later readjustment by instilling meaning and hope to their mission—important positive psychological after effects of most good wars.

The Vietnam War was a bad war, especially after the 1968 Tet Offensive.[9] The war not only lacked sanction from the world community, but also lacked the endorsement of the American people. Having fought in a bad war, many Vietnam veterans felt doubly wounded and crushed to discover that family members and relatives who were World War II veterans lost respect for them because they had fought in this country's "infamous" unsanctioned, undeclared war. As a "bad" war, the Vietnam War produced "villains" rather than "heroes."

But what makes the Vietnam War so different from the other wars, aside from the aforementioned characteristics of good and bad wars? Much of the answer emerges from the sociopolitical ethos of the 1960s, and the turmoil generated during this era. In stark contrast to the "silent generation" of the 1950s, which had essentially acquiesced to the status quo, the youth of the 1960s were contumaciously opposed to the status quo.

Young people in the 1960s were stirred by the Civil Rights struggles of black people, which focused attention on our nation's social and political ills and injustices. To this generation, if the system was to work for a privileged few, it had to work for the unprivileged masses as well—for everyone. An active examination of old, "static" values was under way. And a call for new initiatives on behalf of the poor, the minorities, and the helpless was generated. This new generation wanted to make life better for all—Americans and mankind as a whole. Not resigned to existing values nor bound to obsolete creeds and precepts, they wanted to bring about changes in perceptions, attitudes, and values.

The Vietnam War became the concrete and symbolic embodiment of America's moral ills and distorted value system. As the number of soldiers increased, and the controversies multiplied around the nation and around the world, the intensity of the 1960s grew ever greater. Dissidents pointed to the need for a new age of values—a transvaluation—an examination of our values and belief systems. In actuality, during the 1960s it is unlikely that any war, for any reason, would have escaped the scathing scrutiny and severe criticism that was directed toward the Vietnam War. This is partly because every facet of American life was under intense scrutiny, especially the weaknesses in our social, political, and moral fabric. Social critics pointed to the Vietnam War as "evidence" of America's moral depravity, injustice, and short-sightedness. The increased media attention to the war and the daily reports of killings and atrocities by American troops added fuel to already heated controversies, debate, and protests.

Though killing has always been repugnant to civilized people through-out history, the subject of killing in Vietnam took on new dimensions during this epoch. The soldiers in Vietnam and those returning home were held as responsible for the war as were public officials and the President. The increasing number of American casualties also fueled the social and political controversies. Americans came from all walks of life—including some Vietnam veterans—to join in protesting the war. The America that called the war immoral came to regard its warriors as immoral too.

It was abundantly clear to the returnee that he had been condemned by the American people, but he did not know why. He could not understand why they had turned on him, why they did not try to understand him, why they lacked empathy for him and his readjustment needs. The returnee was baffled over how the American people could view him as a villain— as a criminal—and themselves as blameless. Even psychotherapists, whose profession prohibits moralizing, judged their Vietnam veteran patients in moral terms and seemed unable, for the most part, to leave personal moralizing and political values and biases outside the treatment relationship. By not providing a supportive home environment, more turmoil began. Furthermore, when veterans sought psychotherapy and help in rehabilitation centers, physicians were unable to comprehend the emotional components of their patients' physical problems. They, moreover, chose to interpret the veterans' psychological symptoms and interpersonal and social problems—stemming from the war—as evidence of their disrespect for civilized modes of personal conduct. Under such circumstances, it is no wonder more trouble was on the way.

Chapter 4 / FROM SHELL SHOCK TO "PTSD"

There can be no overstatement of how frightening the experience of war is. At times there are sporadic moments of terror. At other times the shelling doesn't let up for hours or even days. In the words of one veteran: "You're lying face down in the dirt, trying to keep from getting your head blown off while machine gun fire is strafing the ground next to you and over your head . . . the noise from rockets and artillery is so damn loud that you can't hear a person yelling next to you. You're scared that you are gonna die but it's so unbearable that you'd like to die to get it over with . . . and you're scared of that too. When a buddy is killed, the grief is overwhelming but you learn not to break down and cry or even admit to anyone you might be afraid for fear of being considered less than a man."

Under such conditions without benefit of emotional release, it is no wonder that war has produced so many psychological casualties. Those who have broken down in battle have historically been labeled by the military as cowards. Tragically, the untried soldier experiences war as a violation of his mind and body, goes on to become a hardened veteran, and leaves military service only to suffer the later effects of deep emotional scars.

Combatants during World War I fought a war very different from that of Vietnam. Nevertheless, many World War I veterans as well as their successors were plagued with postwar disorders. Protracted artillery barrages and exploding shells deadened the sense of hearing and caused a variety of posttraumatic symptoms thought to result from physiological damage. During World War I, it became apparent that a number of symptoms were present in the acutely disturbed soldier; the term "shell shock" seemed to fit the disorder well.[1]

Physicians at that time noted that the sudden onset of the overwhelming noise of combat was accompanied by pain, upset stomach, headache, perspiration, rapid heart rate, breathlessness, tightness in the chest, and sometimes loss of all bladder and bowel control. These symptoms reflected a repeated attempt by the autonomic nervous system to prepare the body, now sensitized, to defend against attack.

Fear alone has triggered any number of physical responses and even a good soldier has sometimes done little more than shake, tremble, or run like hell, instead of what he was trained to do. The unexpected appearance of charging enemy troops might paralyze a soldier in the way fear elicits the survival instinct in certain primitive forms of life, only to be followed later by delayed shaking and tremulousness. After 4 months or more of this, a soldier is likely to develop a persistent muscle tremor.

The physical and psychological exhaustion overwhelming soldiers who have been continually exposed to the stress of war was given the label "battle exhaustion" during World War II. But it had already been observed in World War I, as this description by news correspondent Ernie Pyle will attest[2]:

> A narrow path comes like a ribbon over a hill miles away . . . along [which] there is now a thin line of men. For four days and nights they have fought hard, eaten little, washed once, and slept hardly at all. Their nights have been violent with attack . . . and their days sleepless and miserable with the crash of artillery. . . . Their walk is slow, for they are dead weary . . . every line and sag of their bodies speaks their inhuman exhaustion. On their shoulders and backs they

carry heavy [equipment]. Their feet seem to sink into the ground from the overload they are bearing. . . . It is the terrible deliberation of each step that spells out their appalling tiredness. Their faces are black and unshaven. They are young men, but the grime and whiskers and exhaustion make them look middle-aged . . . as though they had been here doing this forever, and nothing else.

While any untrained observer might correctly have ascertained the physical aftereffects of combat, he would likely not have been aware of the emotional aftereffects, which often remained a secret, perhaps due to the tradition that soldiers are expected to hide their feelings. Thus, it took a psychological revolution in the form of Sigmund Freud's psychoanalytic theory of "neuroses" to replace the "shell shock" theory. In 1919, Freud gave testimony to a German national commission that was investigating the treatment of German soldiers. He declared that postwar symptoms were a "war neurosis," an emotional disorder rather than an organic disturbance. Furthermore, in place of the impersonal, perhaps even frightening treatment of electric shock, he advocated recalling and talking about traumatic experiences, a therapy he called "psychoanalysis"—a therapy he had been using with patients with other problems.[3]

During World War II military psychiatrists took greater pains than physicians had in earlier times to recognize potential psychiatric problems in young enlistees and draftees. After administering psychological tests, they screened out all whom they believed could not handle the emotional stress of military service: by this, two out of every five were rejected. Interestingly enough, by 1944, over a million combatants had been relieved from service for psychological reasons. To understand this phenomenon, Dr. William Menninger, Neuropsychiatric Consultant to the Surgeon General, appointed a commission of five civilian psychiatrists to investigate in more detail the nature of the symptoms caused by war. They reported a number of emotions and reactions that soldiers had to the stress of battle, including fear, helplessness, distrust, loneliness, anger at feeling abandoned or betrayed, guilt over inadequate performance, horror and grief at the loss of buddies, and physical exhaustion from constant exposure to the stress of war. They used the term "combat exhaustion" to describe those symptoms that began with irritability, sleep disturbance, and unusual sensitivity; these worsened into withdrawal, depression, confusion, and then resulted in eventual complete mental and emotional disorganization.[4] Psychiatrist Harry Kormos described the conclusions of this commission: "It is noteworthy that the report of this high-level commission, written after an extensive tour of the European Theater of War, turned out to be quite tentative. The final conclusion concentrates on what battle fatigue was not: ' . . . this picture of psychological disorganization does not correspond, either in its moderate or its extreme form, to any recognized or established psychiatric syndrome . . . it certainly is not merely a state of exhaustion . . . it certainly is not a neurosis in the ordinary sense . . . it certainly cannot be adequately described as anxiety or fear . . . it comes closer to a situation psychosis than anything else but its subsequent clinical course is quite different'."[5]

Psychiatrists held a symposium in 1944 to discuss the cause of the high rate of psychological casualties in World War II combatants. They believed the contributing factors to be: the combatant's personality makeup; the extremely long time many soldiers had remained in a fighting zone; poor leadership, leading to low morale and defeat in battle; and lack of belief systems and will power.[6] Dr. William Menninger explained that the trauma of killing, the absence of morale-building support by leadership, and the death of comrades all worked together in psychologically unraveling the soldier: "The cumulative effect is a major factor, so that whenever the specific traumatic event does occur, it may in some cases appear trival. . . . The soldier may or may not be able to describe certain events which may have been the final straw—the death of a comrade, the hopelessness of a particular assignment, or a broken promise."[7]

Following the war, veterans' chronic symptoms, such as guilt-laden agitated and hostile behavior, were said to be manifestations of "personality disturbances" linked to prewar and childhood problems.[8] However, the more specific symptoms related to war such as anxiety, depression, dreams and nightmares were eventually referred to as "traumatic war neuroses."[9]

In contrast to the traditional labels psychiatrists generally used for posttraumatic symptoms, Robert Lifton's more vivid portrayal of the symptoms of Hiroshima's survivors paved the way for a broader and more descriptive terminology. For example, Lifton stressed a "death imprint" as well as a "numbing" defense against any emotional response to a devastating experience. This death imprint and numbing of emotion are apparent in the following description by a survivor of Hiroshima: "Their skin [was all] blackened by burns. They had no hair because the hair was burned.

At a glance, you couldn't tell whether you were looking at them in front or in back. They held their arms bent forward . . . and their skin, not only on their hands but on their faces and bodies too, hung down. Wherever I walked, I met these people. Many of them died along the road. I can still picture them in my mind, like walking ghosts. They didn't seem to look like people of this world. They had a special way of walking—very slowly; I myself was one of them."[10]

From Lifton's research, survivors of overwhelming catastrophes were found to have been changed. They experienced a bond to those who had died and a sense of being "contaminated" by guilt, which in turn damaged their relations with others.

Lifton not only noted the response by survivors to vividly imprint traumatic imagery, but their astonishing capacity to forget, deny, or remain emotionally numb. This is a capacity that affects entire societies and countries as well. When a disaster is profoundly disturbing to the people of a society, it can cause a massive "cultural denial" response, particularly when associated with guilt. Understandably, few attempts by writers and filmmakers were made to show audiences a candid picture of nuclear holocaust until the last few years. And why did so many Europeans and Americans appear to deny the reality of the deaths of millions in Nazi gas chambers until 20 years later? And why did the Vietnam War remain a taboo subject to most Americans, until a decade after it ended, when the media finally gave it their attention?

Because of cultural denial, there were relatively few scientific reports on the nature of postwar symptoms and treatment following both world wars, Korea, and Vietnam. Studies on military performance did, however, appear. Peter Watson reported in 1978 that soldiers during the Korean War were studied more thoroughly by the military than at any previous time in order to determine the qualities of combat behavior and improve the fighting forces. Good fighters were found to take risks by readily exposing themselves to enemy fire, taking aggressive action, being strong leaders, and remaining calm under stress. Poor fighters were depicted as withdrawing under fire, freezing, trembling, crying, or overreacting to fear.[11]

Clearly, this research distinguishes between "good" and "bad" soldiers without acknowledging the normal responses of fear and withdrawal to the threat of being killed. If anything, it portrays the expectations of career military personnel: that soldiers, in spite of having fear and anxiety, should be trained to deny these feelings so as to become pure fighting machines. The unfortunate outcome of such denial too frequently is a fixed posttraumatic symptom of emotional detachment and denial of feeling.

Military psychiatrists in Vietnam relied primarily on preventive measures to keep psychiatric casualties to a minimum. Foremost of these measures were limiting combat duty to 12 or 13 months and providing regular periods of rest and recuperation (R & R). They were trained to return combatants to battle as soon as possible, however. Doctors intervened by evacuating severely disturbed soldiers for brief psychiatric hospitalizations or transferring them from active combat to other duty. Military psychiatrists were often frustrated, however, by conflicting responsibilities—to their soldier patients and to their military superiors. While their official mandate was to return soldiers to battle as quickly as possible, their personal wishes often led them to take different approaches. As one ex-Army psychiatrist declared: "It was like Catch 22. An infantryman was having an acute grief reaction but wouldn't allow himself to cry after his closest buddy was killed. He was confused, depressed, and having some bad nightmares. I had no choice but to remove him from his duties until his symptoms cleared up, for if he went back out there in his present state of mind, he was at risk to blindly stumble over a mine or get himself killed in some other way. As a military psychiatrist, I was expected to get him back into action as soon as possible, but if he had been a civilian, I would have insisted he remove himself from any stress for awhile and also scheduled several psychotherapy sessions with him for a period of several weeks."

The enormous demands on a single military psychiatrist serving 16,000 men in a combat zone[11] made only the briefest psychiatric intervention possible for an emotionally distraught soldier. If the psychiatrist determined that the combatant's psychiatric disturbance was too severe for him to return quickly to battle, he would admit him to the base hospital, transfer him to a less stressful job, and in some instances, give him a medical discharge if his symptoms were so severe that they didn't respond to treatment.

Sometimes none of the available psychiatric interventions were adequate for a soldier's problems: "I was beginning to have trouble dealing with what was happening to me after several of my friends were killed. I couldn't sleep and had to do a lot of drinking to quiet my nerves. They thought I was taking too many chances, particularly when I would chase the gooks with a knife because I hated them so much after two of my closest buddies got killed. They put me in a hospital for about a week, then sent me back into the bush because I hated the hospital. I kept chasing gooks and they transferred me to other duty. But I didn't give a fuck after that. Then they sent me back to the states, but when I screwed up a few penny ante orders and got sent to the brig, they decided I wasn't worth it and let me out."

Military psychiatrists, representing military authority, could not grant their "patients" the privilege of confidentiality about matters pertaining to their military duties. For that reason, the few available chaplains, one for every 1400 men, were called upon to provide counseling services. They were particularly needed by soldiers who were grieving, guilt-ridden, or wanted to confess to atrocities.

To alleviate the constant and intense level of stress, every man was offered periodic R & R in safe areas, including the Philippines, Thailand, Australia, or Hawaii. In some instances, R & R was granted as a reward to a successful soldier, particularly if he had a high body count. These rest periods led to a frantic and all-too-temporary attempt to put the horrors of combat experience out of mind. As Mike, now a teacher, recalled with some guilt: "I had a good body count one week and the commander rewarded me with an R & R in Bangkok. I had a good time. I shacked up with a whore for the weekend and stayed smashed on liquor so I could forget what had happened to me out in the bush." But he did not talk about this R & R as a meaningful experience providing emotional strength for enduring future combat.

On the other hand, some soldiers recalled their R & R's with fondness and appreciation: "They sent me to Hawaii and flew my wife there too. It is the only positive memories I have from being in Vietnam."

The policy of limiting the tour of duty in Vietnam to 12 months, and 13 months for a Marine (unless the soldier himself volunteered for a second tour) was thought to reduce feelings of hopelessness about a never-ending war. This plan, called DEROS (Date of Expected Return from Overseas), was believed to have a major effect on reducing the psychiatric casualty rate compared to that of World War II combatants.

Impressively, the psychiatric casualty rate of Vietnam combatants—psychiatric problems requiring medical discharge from the service—was reduced to an all-time low of 1.5% compared to 23% during World War II. It appeared that the new military psychiatry was working very well.[12]

The low incidence of psychiatric casualties was hidden, ironically, in the excessive use by young soldiers of narcotics, alcohol, and marijuana. Those who investigated the reports of high rates of drug addiction, minimized the significance of these reports by saying that the problem was merely the result of easy access to very cheap drugs, overlooking the fact that the drugs were used as self-medication for serious traumatic aftereffects. And a study of the drug habits of Vietnam veterans shortly after their return to the United States reported that most had spontaneously discontinued using them. Yet, we have found that nearly all Vietnam veterans who request help for posttraumatic symptoms, report having medicated themselves against anxiety, depression, and sleeplessness with alcohol, marijuana, and narcotics soon after they arrived in Vietnam and have continued to do so for many years up until the time they get help.

Many of the veterans that we have treated for serious problems have also made the surprising claim that these drugs, particularly marijuana, did not seem to interfere with their ability to fight in battle. They often relate that marijuana was condoned to some extent, particularly during the early years of the war; and there may have been widespread, though unofficial, acceptance of alcohol. As one veteran reported, "They gave us plenty of booze when we wanted it and it was easy to smoke a reefer any time even though they told us we couldn't. And if we wanted the hard stuff, it was cheap and easy to get from the Vietnamese. It got so that I couldn't get along unless I was half stoned. But it calmed me down and never interfered with my ability to fight." Thus, many Vietnam veterans have said that if it had not been for the easy access of alcohol and marijuana, they would have had many more emotional breakdowns from the constant stress of the war.

In the Vietnam War, the new policy was begun of flying combatants home quickly; combatants often were back home with their families in the United States 36 hours from the time they were processed out of Vietnam. To civilians sitting at a desk in Washington, this idea seemed both efficient and altruistic. But for many of the young men, transformed by a year in Vietnam, it proved disastrous. Leaving in an abrupt manner a life of day-to-day survival, and leaving men who had become their closest friends, they were thrust too quickly into an environment that was frequently insensitive and even hostile. As one veteran said, "One day I was out in the bush, killing gooks, seeing buddies get killed, covered in mud, trying to sleep at night with the threat of ambush by the VC and two days later I was trying to talk to my family at the dinner table. I couldn't tell them what I had been through. They couldn't have understood it."

On this whirlwind schedule, soldiers were given little opportunity to talk through their traumatic experiences, unlike their predecessors of World War II, who had a more gradual reintegration into society. In the words of another veteran: "I thought I was going to be debriefed when I was sent back to the States. But it was like they wanted us to forget about everything. I never had any opportunity to talk about it again . . . even at the base where I went, they treated me like a new recruit. Giving me chicken shit things to do. I said 'Fuck you!' "

Ironically, a number of seriously wounded soldiers who had lengthy convalescent stays, had more opportunity to talk through their combat experiences and feel better integrated into society than their counterparts who weren't so severely wounded. Jeff, who has become a successful businessman, explained: "When I left Vietnam I was seriously wounded and spent 21 months in Walter Reed Hospital recovering. There were a lot of other guys from Vietnam in the hospital when I was there. The nursing staff didn't understand us, either ignored us or wanted us to stop talking about what we went through. So we would get together off in the corner and rap about what happened. After spending almost two years doing that, I got it all out of my system. I haven't had a need to talk about it since that time."

For Vietnam veterans who lost limbs or bodily functions, there is a very singular sense of vulnerability. Yet, those with emotional disabilities may suffer from at least as severe a sense of vulnerability as well as associated anxiety. For example, several men with posttraumatic emotional symptoms have told us: "We can't work. We can't get along with people, and our disability is just as severe as those who are physically disabled. But we sometimes look normal to people so they expect much more out of us than we can give. We'd rather have an arm or a leg missing."

However, there are those plagued with both posttraumatic emotional symptoms and physical disabilities. Dan, a veteran with double amputations after serving two tours of duty in Vietnam, found that both the emotional and the physical difficulties worked against each other, compounding his problem with his self-image: "I don't like my body. I think of myself as a physical cripple and different from other people. And even though a lot of people treat me like I'm normal and have both arms and legs, I resent that too. They completely overlook the fact that I am a Vietnam veteran and am disabled."

During the late 1960s and early 1970s, there were a handful of mental health professionals who seemed interested in providing psychological help for those whose emotional wounds were painful but not obvious to others. Psychiatrist Robert Lifton,[13] who sought the help of Chaim Shatan[14] and other colleagues, were instrumental in leading an ongoing "rap group" with Vietnam veterans. Out of this ongoing dialogue emerged a nucleus of veterans and mental health professionals to educate the broader psychiatric community about their problems. Most important, their efforts bore fruit and they went on to formulate a special diagnostic category for these veterans.

That a special diagnostic category would be necessary at all for Vietnam veterans was at first surprising, considering the fact that American war veterans have been diagnosed and treated by psychiatrists since World War I. Professionals had published reports about the psychiatric symptoms in soldiers following each major war, particularly between 1944 and 1947. The memory of the mental health professional community, however, seemed short-lived. The literature on the posttraumatic symptoms of veterans of both world wars has not been read by many during the last 25 or 30 years. Yet, in all fairness, it was not entirely applicable to Vietnam veterans. The diagnostic labels used in our previous wars have become outdated. No psychiatrist during the 1970s would diagnosis Vietnam veterans as suffering from "shell shock" or "battle exhaustion" and only a few believed that the World War II category of "traumatic war neurosis" now applied to Vietnam veterans.

Moreover, the meaning of the term "neurosis," coined by Freud and his colleagues over a century ago, had changed. First used to categorize a serious psychological disturbance caused by childhood traumatic events, neurosis 100 years later became defined as a relatively minor or circumscribed emotional problem—a depression of limited time, an episode of anxiety, or a phobia. And while Vietnam veterans certainly have suffered from anxieties, depressions, and phobias, their symptoms were often found to be more serious and varied. Many had developed personality problems, alcohol and drug addiction, and difficulties with the legal system, often without a history of prewar personality disturbances.

Though scores of veterans were seriously in need of counseling, it is sad to say that mental health professionals rarely involved themselves with veterans. The self-destructive nature of these veterans was so overwhelming that the morticians were too often summoned first. As early as 1971, the National Council of Churches had reported that 49,000 Vietnam veterans had died after returning to the United States. Moreover, rough estimates lead officials to believe that Vietnam veteran deaths have continued at a rate of 800 a year. Their deaths have often been of a violent nature: suicides, vehicular accidents, drug overdoses, police shootouts, and the like. The post-Vietnam syndrome seemed to have fatal results in a disproportionate percentage of cases; the number of Vietnam veterans who died prematurely was staggering.[15]

If these men survived the first 10 years, they were often to be found within the confines of police, prisons, probation officers, or parole counselors. The antisocial feature of their problems was an all too common form of self-destruction—although not always irreversible. According to a presidential review in 1979, over 400,000 Vietnam veterans were in some way caught up by the legal system: 29,000 in state or federal prisons, 37,500 on parole, 250,000 under probation supervision, and 87,000 awaiting trial, a tragic revelation.[16]

A typical history of criminal behavior is that of Doug, a helicopter pilot who had survived several near-fatal experiences while many of his friends had been killed. During the summer of 1978, he and his wife participated in a bank robbery that remained unsolved for 2 years until their separation. His wife reported the crime and turned state's evidence in exchange for leniency. At his trial, he admitted the crime but stated that it had been committed after years of depression and flashbacks of the war. He had not been able to keep a job as a pilot because every attempt at flying brought back feelings of panic. Feeling episodically enraged about his life in general, he believed he had been forsaken by his country and his wife. He admitted that at a particularly angry moment when under the influence of drugs, he had coerced his wife to assist him in the bank robbery. He described having been in an altered state of consciousness during the robbery; his mind depersonalized the experience, as if he were observing someone else doing it. Nevertheless, he was sentenced to 5 years in a state prison. During this period, he was a model prisoner, using the time profitably to educate himself about the law, and undergoing therapy for emotional problems with a psychiatrist, who fortunately took a special interest in him. After 3 years, he was granted parole on the condition that he continue psychiatric treatment. Upon his release, he was admitted to a VA Hospital, where he received specialized treatment to continue the recovery process. He was the exception.

Many others who sought help in VA hospitals during the 1970s were misdiagnosed. Psychiatrist M. Straker, for instance, reported in 1976 that 77% of Vietnam veterans admitted to VA hosptials received the wrong diagnosis of schizophrenia.[17] Their "flashbacks" or hallucinations of being in combat, were often so real that psychiatrists unfamiliar with the nature of postwar symptoms diagnosed the veterans as suffering from acute schizophrenic episodes. Hence, patients were primarily drugged with heavy doses of "antipsychotic" medications. Though these medications temporarily proved helpful in many cases, they were too often the only treatment provided. For those who had committed a violent act with a weapon—40% of the cases[18]—mental health professionals usually ended up labeling them as having Antisocial or Borderline Personalities. More often than not, this diagnostic approach led to the wrong kind of treatment or none at all.

Many other Vietnam veterans, estimated to have been as high as 60% of hospitalized patients, were found to be dependent on alcohol, marijuana, or other street drugs that they had used to suppress their anxieties, depression, sleep disturbances, and urges to pick fights. If they were treated without any attention to their specific posttraumatic symptoms through methods exclusively used for addicts, they soon reverted back to their old drug habits when their nightmares, bad dreams, and fear of losing control returned.

This serious problem of misdiagnosis demanded a remedy. During the late 1970s a few Vietnam veterans, who had received help from "rap groups," and a handful of mental health professionals got together to discuss this problem and sought the advice of nationally recognized experts. This group eventually convinced enough people that the symptoms of Vietnam veterans warranted a new diagnostic category. In 1980 the American Psychiatric Association's new *Diagnostic and Statistical Manual of Mental Disorders* (DSM-III) gave these symptoms the name "Posttraumatic Stress Disorder" (PTSD) and described it in detail[19]:

> The essential feature is the development of characteristic symptoms following a psychologically traumatic event that is generally outside the range of usual human experience.
>
> The characteristic symptoms involve reexperiencing the traumatic event; numbing of responsiveness to, or reduced involvement with, the external world; and a variety of autonomic dysphoric, or cognitive symptoms.
>
> The traumatic event can be reexperienced in a variety of ways. Commonly the individual has recurrent painful, intrusive recollections of the event or recurrent dreams or nightmares during which the event is reexperienced. In rare instances there are dissociative-like states, lasting from a few minutes to several hours or even days, during which components of the event are relived and the individual behaves as though experiencing the event at that moment. Diminished responsiveness to the external world, referred to as "psychic numbing" or "emotional anesthesia," usually begins soon after the traumatic occurrence. A person may complain of feeling detached or estranged from other people, that he or she has lost the ability to become interested in previously enjoyed significant activities, or that the ability to feel emotions of any type, especially those associated with intimacy, tenderness, and sexuality, is markedly decreased.
>
> After experiencing the stressor, many develop symptoms of excessive autonomic arousal, such as hyperalertness, exaggerated startle response, and difficulty falling asleep. Recurrent nightmares during which the traumatic event is relived and which are sometimes accompanied by sleep disturbance may be present. Some complain of impaired memory or difficulty in concentrating or completing tasks. In the case of a life-threatening trauma shared with others, survivors often describe painful guilt feelings about surviving when many did not, or about the things they had to do in order to survive. Activities or situations that may arouse recollections of the traumatic occurrence are often avoided. Symptoms characteristic of Post-traumatic Stress Disorder are often intensified when the individual is exposed to situations or activities that resemble or symbolize the original trauma.
>
> Associated features: Symptoms of depression and anxiety are

common. Increased irritability may be associated with sporadic and unpredictable explosions of aggressive behavior, with even minimal or no provocation. The latter symptom has been reported to be particularly characteristic of war veterans with this disorder.

Diagnostic criteria for Post-traumatic Stress Disorder:

A. Existence of a recognizable stressor that would evoke significant symptoms of distress in almost everyone.

B. Reexperiencing of the trauma as evidenced by at least one of the following:

1) recurrent and intrusive recollections of the event

2) recurrent dreams of the event

3) sudden acting or feeling as if the traumatic event were reoccurring, because of an association with an environmental or ideational stimulus

C. Numbing of responsiveness to or reduced involvement with the external world, beginning some time after the trauma, as shown by at least one of the following:

1) markedly diminished interest in one or more significant activities

2) feeling of detachment or estrangement from others

3) constricted affect [emotions]

D. At least two of the following symptoms that were not present before the trauma:

1) hyperalertness or exaggerated startle response

2) sleep disturbance

3) guilt about surviving when others have not, or about behavior required for survival

4) memory impairment or trouble concentrating

5) avoidance of activities that arouse recollection of the traumatic event

6) intensification of symptoms by exposure to events that symbolize or resemble the traumatic event

The new diagnosis of PTSD resolved many of the difficulties resulting from the inadequacies of the World War II diagnosis, Traumatic War Neurosis. The word "stress," an engineering term, came to replace the word "neurosis." Hans Selye is generally credited for borrowing the term for medical application when he described how an organism adapts to the impact of the stress of illness or injury, first with a large defensive reaction, then with a lesser reaction. Dr. Selye found that the initial shock response to a stressful event included releasing adrenalin and the adrenal cortical hormones into the system. The body would then indicate a slight adaptation response, seeming to show that it was learning to get used to an undesirable situation. Selye's pioneering work was soon broadened by other researchers to explain responses of the psyche as well; that following a response to stress, there can be psychological adaptation.[20]

With this new label, PTSD, it seemed permissible for mental health professionals to rediscover that traumatic experiences caused psychiatric disturbances, as had been first described over a century ago. They were able to abandon, however, misapplied stereotypical labels of neurosis, psychosis, or personality disorder. Furthermore, this diagnostic category was broad enough to encompass the survivors of any major stressful event, including those of natural catastrophes such as floods, tornadoes, and earthquakes; accidental disasters brought on by man such as car accidents, airplane crashes, and large fires; and disasters deliberately perpetrated by man such as rape, war, bombing, torture, and death camps.

Those who formulated this new diagnosis drew not only on the work of Selye but on findings of researchers who specialized in trauma, particularly Dr. Mardi Horowitz of the Center for the Study of the Neuroses in San Francisco. He determined that following all traumatic occurrences, survivors develop a pattern of symptoms characterized by the "intrusion vs. denial/numbing" phenomenon. In other words, a victim of a severe accident would likely experience immediate denial of the memory of the traumatic event as well as a "numbing" of the associated fear, emotional pain, and sometimes even physical pain. The victim would then be unexpectedly overwhelmed with fear and pain at a later time when reexperiencing the traumatic event in the form of intrusive memories, images, or nightmares.[21] Psychologist Victor DeFazio has described the frightening nature of the veteran's traumatic dream, found to occur in 75% of all Vietnam veterans: "In a typical dream, almost regardless of setting, the individual tends to be helpless in the face of attack. He may be stuck in one place, unable to run or hide. His weapon may not fire. He usually awakens in a cold sweat, terrified. Sometimes the dreamer cries out."[22]

While such symptoms are common in war veterans, they also occur in others who have been exposed to traumatic situations. Dr. Horowitz undertook an interesting experiment testing "normal people" watching disturbing movies, and found that they too, for a period after, were plagued by intrusive images and memories. This finding substantiated what many mothers fear, that children who watch violent television programs before bedtime will have nightmares. It also suggested the significant finding that observers of a traumatic event are likely to have nearly as intense an emotional involvement in the event as the victim.

A less extreme example of the intrusion phenomenon was described by a friend of ours who had a potentially life threatening experience as a teenager: "My sister and I were attending a sporting event where hundreds of people were seated in bleachers. My sister and I climbed down from our seats and walked under the bleachers when we were leaving. All of a sudden there was a cracking sound and when I looked up, people were screaming and falling. The bleachers just collapsed."

Fortunately a bystander pushed him out of the way of the bleachers as they were about to cave in on him. Though unhurt, he nonetheless had the frightening experience imprinted on his mind in the form of "intrusive imagery." Many years later he still periodically "hears" and "sees" the people as they are beginning to fall as if he were still there. Our friend's experience is not uncommon insofar as others have experienced sensory "imprinting"; its function is to provide protection for the future and prepare a previously unsuspecting victim to be on guard the next time.

In some cases, Vietnam veterans have suffered from an extreme form of this phenomenon—the "flashback." Psychoanalyst and researcher Herbert Hendin, along with colleagues, has reported that flashbacks occur in 20% of all Vietnam veterans, who "suddenly acted or felt as if traumatic events which they had experienced in Vietnam were recurring."[23]

Mark, a veteran from the Midwest, commented: "When I got home from 'Nam, I'd walk down to the river on our land and the water and the thick bushes made me think I was back in 'Nam. I had to take a gun with me 'cause I'd see the VC and start firing."

Greg, a veteran from a middle-class family near New York City, experienced a flashback while on a train: "I started feeling strange when these two guys in dark uniforms got on the train. They looked like 'gooks.' Then I saw some kids on the train that looked like 'gooks' too. Four hours later I was huddling in the corner of my friend's apartment in Manhattan . . . my skin was all blackened and I'd cut my shoes down to sandals, like I was identifying with the enemy. My friend told me that I'd climbed up the fire escape during the night. I guess I was back in 'Nam. It was pretty scary. My friend spent the next three hours calming me down."

On the other side of the same coin as flashbacks or periodic intrusions of traumatic images is the posttraumatic phenomenon of denial/numbing. An example of this was that of a friend who spilled scalding hot water over her body. She calmly instructed her husband to help her remove her clothing, along with a superficial layer of skin that had been burned, and then told him to drive her to the hospital. As she walked calmly down the hospital corridor, a nurse, who had been awaiting her arrival, said, "The burn victim is here." The moment she heard the words "burn victim," the denial/numbing phenomenon, which had allowed her to cope with the immediate emergency of the traumatic event, was suddenly replaced by overwhelming fear, trembling, and excruciating pain.

This phenomenon appears to be part of a physiological readiness that includes time distortion, panoramic memory, superhuman strength, clarity of thought, and automatic physical responses to cope with danger. A friend of ours, who is a sailor, recalled: "During one calm Sunday afternoon, a gust of wind came up and caught the sail in the back of our sail boat, which was attached to a rope lying on the deck. The rope suddenly wrapped itself around my leg and jerked me off my feet while pulling me rapidly toward the end of the boat and open water. My hands automatically grabbed the mast and held on for dear life. No one of my crew seemed to know what to do. But I suddenly had an enormous feeling of calm and strength come over me. I was able to think clearly as if time had slowed down. I began to give instructions to my crew members and within seconds they had freed my leg from the rope which was now strangling the circulation out of my leg. I would otherwise have most certainly drowned."

While the calmness and numbing sensation permitted him to cope with the danger, survivors of repeated traumatic events, such as veterans of war, have sometimes remained emotionally "numb" for long periods of time after the event to the point of feeling detached or estranged from other people. An extension of this is the loss of interest in activities previously enjoyed and, in some cases, an inability to feel any emotion, especially those associated with intimacy, tenderness, and sexuality. Sometimes this problem manifests itself in impaired memory, difficulty in concentration, inability to complete tasks, dulling of alertness, and even episodes of staring off into space. John, a Vietnam veteran from Missouri, explained: "I feel like something is missing in me. Sometimes I feel like I'm dead inside. I go through the motions of living and being with people but I can't think. I can't feel anything. My wife tells me that I can't show any affection. And she's right."

Vietnam veterans have often taken unusual risks as an unconscious means of breaking through the emotional detachment. In doing so, they ironically enjoy the thrill of the familiar "adrenalin rush" associated with danger. Bill, an unemployed veteran, experienced nothing but a sense of "deadness" unless taking chances while racing his motorcycle. At such times he felt the "adrenalin surge" go through his body. Even after having a severe accident when his cycle missed a curve at breakneck speed, he continued taking significant risks with his life.

Conversely, Vietnam veterans also become upset and startled when reminders of that danger are unexpectedly thrust upon them. Craig, a veteran from Oklahoma, said: "For the first two years after I returned from Vietnam, if I heard a helicopter overhead, I'd hit the ground and take cover immediately." This ever-present expectation of danger in these men may be associated with their past behavior in Vietnam, when they had to be constantly on guard, primed for immediate survival action. This excessive readiness on the home front often extends into the night so that a Vietnam veteran sleeps "with one eye open," creating difficulties. Donna, the wife of a veteran from Florida, related: "For the last five years, Jim has been getting out of bed several times during the night. He's only told his Vietnam friends, who understand, that he has to check for possible danger, as if we might be attacked. He's too embarrassed to tell me anything other than he just can't sleep well."

Many survivors suffer from hyperalertness and exaggerated startle reactions for years. Ralph, a 47-year-old career Army veteran, explained 15 years after his time in Vietnam: "I have to sit against the wall, even if it means sitting on the floor. I just can't sit in the open. I don't feel safe. I feel all tensed up, like I have to be on guard against someone coming up behind me. I can't even sleep at night. It's like I have one eye open and one closed. If someone comes into my room during the dark, I immediately wake up. I know it isn't logical but it's been that way ever since I was in the war."

He has never forgotten the 3 days of constant attack and subsequent terror he experienced in the war: "It happened so fast and none of us were ready that night when our base camp was overrun. First the Vietcong sneaked through and laid down explosives after cutting through four lines of constantina wire. And then all hell broke loose. They caught us off guard coming in hordes from all directions and they killed a lot of our men. I've never gotten over that."

Soldiers in Vietnam were conditioned to fight instinctively when the situation called for it. This conditioning phenomenon was first discovered by psychiatrist A. Kardiner as causing postwar symptoms in veterans of World War I.[9] Researcher and psychiatrist Lawrence Kolb has described the same phenomenon, calling it the "conditioned emotional response in Vietnam veterans."[24] The instinctive behavior is generated by the soldier's "regression" back to the primitive law of survival of the mammalian species.[25] Neuropsychiatrist P. D. MacLean describes this primitive survival behavior as directed by the brain's "limbic system."[26] This system is the part of the brain that operates as a primitive mammalian brain. The slightest stimulus may set off a message to the limbic system, as in a "short circuit," triggering an automatic survival response. The message will bypass all reflective thought and planning associated with the cerebral cortex. Rob, a Vietnam veteran, recounted: "The calm that I experienced when I started shooting at the enemy is a part of me waiting to come out. It happened so many times and I know that something changed inside me. I just don't react like normal people. I'm always waiting for something to happen and I'd like it to happen. If I got into a fight with someone, I'd probably feel better. That calm would come over me. But I know better because if I get into a fight, I can't stop. It's like I've been programmed to complete a task and something inside of me says 'don't stop until the task has been completed even if it means killing.' "

Chapter 5 / WAR: ITS EFFECTS ON IDENTITY

War can alter normal human experience in such a way as to cause profound changes in identity. Perhaps there was no other battleground where this transformation later became more apparent than that of Vietnam—a war that "sent more permanently disabled veterans back into civilian society than any previous war," according to authors Charles Figley and Seymour Leventman.[2] The changes that overwhelmed these soldiers are compounded by their relative youth (their average age being only 19).[3] According to research psychologist Dr. John Wilson, this made them more malleable to altering or consolidation of their self concepts.[4] These boys, having just graduated from high school, believed they were fighting to preserve the freedom of their country, as their fathers had done during World War II. While some of their friends were pledging fraternities and playing college football and others at universities were demonstrating against the war, they were fighting. When they returned to join their friends, they did so with profound changes in character. As one veteran said: "When I returned from my tour of duty in Vietnam, I tried to go to the university where all of my friends were. But I couldn't enjoy the ridiculous parties, games, and childish fun they were caught up in. I didn't understand their world and they didn't seem to understand mine. It was a depressing experience to know that I just didn't fit in—particularly since I had been looking forward to it when I was in Vietnam. There wasn't anything else I could do, so I volunteered to go back to Vietnam where I did fit in."

Psychologist John Wilson describes Vietnam veterans' perception of their own ages as paradoxically both excessively young and excessively old. On the one hand, they still feel like the teenagers they were when they first went to Vietnam. On the other hand, they feel as if they were prematurely aged by the experiences they endured.[3]

A group of small-town Midwestern veterans in their mid-30's, participating in a 4-week alcohol recovery program, described it well: "We feel like there isn't any more to experience in life. It's like we are 75 years old and have seen it all. We also feel 18. But it's impossible for us to start all over again now. We're caught in a time capsule and don't fit in anywhere. And people just don't understand that."

The identity transformation of a combat veteran begins with basic training, as recognized nearly 40 years ago by Dr. William Menninger, who wrote about the young World War II recruit: "When [a young] man became a soldier . . . he had to give up his individual identity [and make an identification] with that of the team. . . . [He learned to accept] severe privations in return for very restricted gratification."[5]

The green recruit entering military service in the 1960s painfully discovered when he first entered boot camp that he was stripped of all of the symbolic visible markings of his own identity. His clothes, hairstyle, address, property, education, and social status (unless he was an officer) vanished within a week. If he sought personal recognition, he found his only symbol of identity to be his rank and if he resisted an order, he could lose that. Thus, he was not only an impressionable 18-year-old soldier looking for a cause and a sense of identity but, bereft of any other identity, he was now receptive to the "indoctrination" process providing him with a new cause and a new identity. Consequently, the duly trained soldier left basic training for Vietnam fully "programmed" to kill the Vietcong and stop Communism under an illusion of certainty that he was part of a just cause.

That illusion of certainty in the justness of the Vietnam War was maintained until near its end, although doubts began to creep into the minds of some men after the major "Tet Offensive," which caught Americans by surprise in 1968. Until that time, young soldiers rarely doubted the validity of America's role in Vietnam. But during the late 1960s and early 1970s, some Vietnam veterans, particularly those who returned for a second tour of duty, became disillusioned with the war. Others, after returning to the United States, were influenced by the message of the many antiwar protests. Still others were skeptical of the validity of the war from the time they were drafted and could not share in the sense of purpose that others had as a result of the indoctrination of basic training. They entered the war without wholeheartedly embracing the cause. Paul, who came from a strongly religious background, had been refused change of combat duty in spite of his objection to the war and his request for conscientious objector status. After a year in Vietnam, during which time he was placed in a situation where he had to kill in order to survive, he believed that he had been forced to betray his own values and suffered a pervasive sense of shame after returning home.

Some remained certain of the war's rightness while surrounded by others who didn't, more out of a need to justify their own participation than for any other reason. One highly decorated Vietnam veteran, Harold, wore his combat fatigues to all of his counseling sessions, indicating that he was hanging on to his military identity 15 years after leaving the service: "I learned everything that there was to learn about survival, weapons, and fighting a war. For the first time in my life, I was really good at what I did. I believed that I was fighting for my country and I would do it again. In fact, I feel like my purpose will not be completed until I go back there and fight to win or die trying."

Even though many soldiers became confused about American participation in the war, they recalled good memories of basic training, learning how to survive, how to fight as a team, how to take orders, and how to accept responsibility. They not only felt like men, but even more, they felt as if they were a part of something bigger and more important than a single individual. Some who were part of an elite group, such as the Marine

Corps, particularly had a sense of pride that was often deepened as they survived combat together. A group of ex-Marines described their feelings this way: "It was not easy to become a Marine. They made us do things that were impossible, until we discovered we could do 'em. We developed a special pride about what we went through together. Being a Marine never changes—once a Marine, always a Marine."

Thus, the painful process of giving up the trappings of civilian status was made easier as each man developed a more intense sense of belonging to the military, that is, believing in a common ideology, learning loyalty to one another, and sharing a common purpose. In fact, being in close proximity without race or class distinctions often broke down social barriers. It created a feeling of exhilaration and liberation as close personal bonds emerged. This unique identification with comrades became fraught with new meaning. "I" became "we," the nucleus for an identity that was prepared to fight and die together, as one unit.

Buddies felt linked together as if they were different parts of a single organism. A highly dedicated former team leader, Sergeant White tried to relate this feeling of unity: "We relied on one another in my team so well that we could read each other's minds. My two best buddies were like my right and left hands. There was no other way that any of us could have survived."

Few civilians are capable of comprehending the intensity of the unity and common bond that each soldier felt with one another in combat. The loss of any one of them had a devastating effect on all the others of the group left behind. This was a phenomenon observed by Dr. Karl Menninger while a member of a commission appointed to study "combat exhaustion" in World War II combatants: "The resistance [of even the most hardened soldier] has been subjected . . . to . . . the experience of losing comrades. In the opinion of many observers, this is the most destructive influence bearing upon personality integrity in the battle situation. The maintenance of the psychic equilibrium, the defense against yielding to fear and chucking the whole business has its chief emotional anchorage in personal attachments and unit identification. The loss of a comrade, of a respected commanding officer, or of a member of the squad . . . may constitute a wound more painful than that of a bullet through the body."[6]

Menninger has described the psychotic nature of some soldiers' reactions to such a loss: "They are brought to the battalion aid station, strapped to a litter fighting, struggling, screaming, and yelling . . . still others demonstrate equal demoralization by standing mute, trembling, fumbling, staring into space and making no response."[6]

The loss of buddies was equally devastating for combatants in Vietnam: "Sarge," a Vietnam veteran from Kansas, entered a hospital for treatment of severe PTSD. He had nightmares and nearly took his life a month before seeking help. He described "playing" Russian roulette by loading a bullet into one of the five chambers of the barrel of his pistol, spinning the barrel, and pulling the trigger. When "fate" decided that he would not die, he decided to enter a treatment program. Within 3 months at the hospital, he finally unburdened himself of a very painful memory: "We were feared by the Vietcong as one of the best killer teams in Vietnam. The North Vietnamese finally placed a bounty on our heads and planned an almost perfect ambush. Normally one of us would've sensed something was wrong but we walked right into this one. The VC were hiding in tree trunks and buried in the ground. We were fired on from all directions at once. Jack got hit first and then Bill caught a round in the chest. He died in my arms. It was the worst pain I've ever had . . . it was like losing a part of me. I insisted on staying with them in the mortuary and spent three days and nights there talking to them. If anyone had tried to stop me from being there, I'd have blown them away. I was never the same after that."

With little or no way to grieve adequately for his closest comrades, this once proud and capable Army sergeant filled his inner emptiness with rage and covered it with a hardened shell. Now he is unable to express his affection or tell his wife he loves her. Though she yearns for closeness with him, he is afraid to respond affectionately to her. He says: "I've never had such close friends as I've had in Vietnam. They were like part of me and there's been nothing like that before or since. But every time one of them died, it was like part of me died. I don't want that to happen again so I guard against getting too close to people now."

Others, including noncommissioned officers fighting side by side with men who were killed, were never able to accept responsibility again. George, a career Marine gunnery sergeant in Vietnam, lost 24 loyal soldiers—half of his men—during a 25-day seige in the city of Hue. It shattered his self-esteem and his career: "I was never able to go back into combat after that. All I did was pick fights. And when the commander wouldn't listen to me tell about what happened, I went over a desk after him. They let me out of the service after I gave them 18 years of my life. Since then, those faces keep coming back in my mind. I've never wanted to have anyone ever depend on me again."

Others have had similar experiences of loss. Frequently, they not only avoid responsibility but find it nearly impossible to fill their inner emptiness with new people, spouses, or family members. When they have reproduced the sense of oneness they felt for their comrades, it is often expressed as an intense loyalty. This intense loyalty often translates into an aggressive need to protect the other person, as if the experience of being in the same unit in Vietnam was being reenacted. Veterans have often described, for example, the intent to kill anyone who might threaten members of their family. Those who have established close bonds, not only with members of their family but also with each other—particularly when in treatment programs together for several months—begin to feel as if their survival were based on maintaining this common bond.

While mental health professionals believe this behavior represents the need to reestablish an intense interpersonal bond to fill the loss of a prior relationship and enhance the sense of well-being, there is a special quality to this "bonding" in Vietnam veterans. They respond aggressively and protectively to their closest friends and family when it is perceived that they are being victimized, as if there were a "protective-self" within each of them.[7] This "protective-self" was evident in Pete as he reacted to what he believed was the victimization of a fellow veteran by the system: "I can tell Tom's about ready to lose it. He don't say nothin' about how he's doing but he don't have to. If he don't get some help right now, he's goin' kill somebody. If things don't change, I'll kill them motherfuckers myself!"

During the treatment of Vietnam veterans, therapists have come to comprehend their patients' need for close relationships, but also their concomitant fear of losing anyone close to them. It is important that veterans be encouraged to recognize the positive aspects of their "protective" wishes toward their families and even their therapists. In this way, they can feel pride about their inner "protective-selves" at a time when they have few other personal qualities for which they feel proud. And they can be encouraged to go a step further by "protectively" caring for one another even when there are no aggressors to attack.

Some veterans have experienced a sense of self-protection that enabled them to remain relatively free from the devastation of posttraumatic symptoms suffered by others. Research performed by Drs. Hendin and Pollinger-Haas found them to have inner resources protecting them from fear, guilt, and shame and enabling them to carry out their military endeavors.[8] Unfortunately, there were many others who became guilt-ridden and ashamed of their combat experiences.

Educator Peter Marin has described Vietnam veterans' guilt feelings resulting from two kinds of violence. The first was the planned slaughter of civilian village populations suspected of being VC sympathizers and the second was the "recreational" violence in which a GI might, for the fun of it, gun down a woman crossing a field or a child on the road.[9]

Related to committing such atrocities is the soldier's loss of conscience. With each step of involvement in the war, the soldier would lose more of his sense of conscience, although in some cases the conscience would suddenly turn off completely. Raoul, a veteran who suffered frequent "flashbacks" after his discharge, recalled his sudden loss of conscience: "They made a psychopath out of me in Vietnam after I killed for the first time. The lieutenant was with me and we saw a Montagnard native coming toward us with a machete. I saw that he wasn't armed well but the lieutenant kept saying to me, 'Kill that Montagnard! Kill him!' It was barbaric . . . but I opened fire. A part of his face just blew right off. . . .There was only one native and all he had was a machete. I coulda taken him out by hand. I didn't have to kill him. And after that I just didn't care any more. I became a trained robot that killed people in villages . . . women and children, and even babies."

Although this veteran's experience was sudden and dramatic, he was the product of a gradual process of "programming" that began in basic training whereby the dissolution of consience began to take place. Dr. William Menninger describes this occurrence in World War II trainees as an essential indoctrination process whereby prior ethical and moral principles are set aside so that soldiers are able to kill.[5]

Dr. John Russell Smith, director of The National Center for Stress Recovery, describes a process he calls "sanction and sealing over," which permits the individual soldier to suspend his conscience and give meaning to acts committed during war: "Like hot wax which can permeate each strand of a ball of loose ends of string, so too, in sealing over, sanction permeates the loose ends of experience, giving them meaning and bending them into a unit, immune from [previous ethical demands]."[10] The sanction by those who sent their warriors into battle, provided a group conscience that justified individual actions and neutralized individual guilt feelings that would ordinarily result from these acts.

During a "rap group" of Marine veterans, they described their basic training experiences wherein they began the indoctrination process that enabled them to kill: "They used to have us fire our weapons or run forward with our bayonets fixed while we yelled, 'Kill! Kill! Kill!' " When they did this maneuver in a state of highly charged emotion, trainees began to imprint an image of killing within their minds that became a "blueprint" for future combat situations.

Psychoanalyst Chaim Shatan has described yet a further step of indoctrination as occurring during basic combat training: " 'Harassing the troops' in basic combat training promotes obedience through maltreatment and humiliation. In line with the principle, 'If you can't beat 'em, join 'em,' the trainee learns to ape his persecutors, that is his officers."[11] Dr. Shatan has described the final transformation of Vietnam trainees: "When the 'induction phase' of counter guerrilla training succeeds . . . the trainee surrenders his personal identity to the corporate identity of his military legion . . . . The soldier patterns himself after his persecutors . . . [who humiliated him during basic combat training] and . . . his character is restructured into a combat personality. "[12]

The commonly used phrase "identification with the aggressor" has been given to describe how a frightened and helpless victim can become aggressive in order to suppress the pain of being abandoned or betrayed. This concept may be applied not only to combat trainees but also to American troops in Vietnam who felt abandoned and betrayed on a variety of levels. Out of profound disillusionment, many described their utter rage with the lack of support by their leaders. One NCO, who spent a full tour of duty in Vietnam and then returned to his California home, recounted: "I was willing to give my life if necessary and I took my men out on very dangerous missions. One time we were trapped in a mine field and couldn't get out without help. So I radioed my captain for help. He came out in a helicopter but when he saw where we were, he refused to land. I was so furious that I nearly shot him out of the sky and when I saw him after that, I wanted to kill him."

Men became demoralized by the sole measurement of victory—the body count. And they could not understand why they were repeatedly ordered to evacuate territory that had been paid for with the lives of their buddies. Frank, an NCO, described: "They told us to take the fucking hill two times before and every time told us to retreat. Finally the motherfuckers told us to take it again. So we did. But my best buddy was killed during that last time. I didn't give a goddam after that and started killing civilians and anyone that looked like a gook!"

Many of the officers, except for those few who actively fought side by side with their men, were unwilling to risk their own lives and abandoned their positions as both active and symbolic leaders, as well-known author John Del Vecchio, himself a Vietnam veteran, has portrayed with apt cynicism:

> For heroism and gallantry in ground combat in the Republic of Vietnam, 13 to 25 August 1970, Lieutenant Colonel Dinky Dau GreenMan distinguished himself while serving as commanding officer of a bunch of dumb-ass troops during operations near firebase Barnett. During the entire operation the GreenMan repeatedly supervised ground and air forces which got fucked up looking for a meaningless bunker complex. The GreenMan directed artillery and tactical air support against enemy hills, trees and grass. He listened on the radio repeatedly as his units were ambushed and attacked. After the enemy forces were routed, he, without regard for his personal safety, tabulated the reported dead. . . . During the operation the GreenMan also managed to take twelve hot showers in the rear, eat thirty hot meals and read twenty-seven Fantastic Four comic books. The GreenMan's personal bravery and devotion to duty are in keeping with the highest traditions of the military service and reflect great credit upon himself, his unit, and the United States Army."[13]

The rage of the enlisted men, resulting from the belief that their leaders had betrayed their trust, was often much more direct. Some American soldiers began to distrust any new officer joining their unit; thus began fragging (wounding or killing) officers, as described by a former squad leader, Todd: "It had gotten so bad that we began to lose more men from the mistakes made by 90-day wonders [second lieutenants graduating from officer training school] than from the enemy. I was elected to be the chairman of a secret committee in our unit to decide which one we would keep. We fragged six of 'em while I was there—wounded them all so they got shipped back to the States." If officers discovered their lives were in jeopardy, they frequently requested transfer to other units, or took special precautions to protect themselves, since it was nearly impossible to prove that an "errant" bullet or grenade was not a result of enemy attack.

Incompetent leadership contributed to a feeling of futility, a feeling that was compounded by the degrading and dehumanizing way that the success of the war came to be measured—the body count. As a Vietnam veteran recalled, "They told us that the only thing that mattered was body counts. So we would get them any way we could, even if it meant bringing in dead civilians or even parts of bodies we found on the road."

Soldiers in Vietnam who felt their leaders were inept or even destructive, could not identify with them as respected role models. Refusing to accept leadership from men they distrusted, they took on the task of "taking care of themselves" and depending on none but their closest buddies. With their feelings of disrespect for men in power, they began to assume that any power other than their own was not to be trusted. One man recalled: "We learned to turn off our feelings and never admit to any weakness or need for someone else to tell us what to do. We didn't trust most of the officers and certainly didn't want to be like them."

Thus, soldiers who angrily closed themselves off to being "led" by officers, were more likely to become aggressive, frequently displacing that rage toward the enemy. And given an environment that rewarded killing and devalued the expression of human feelings of fear and helplessness, it was easy for a soldier to readily assume the identity of "killer." It was not unusual for his transformation to take yet another step, to the point where killing became more than just a necessary evil. It, in some cases, eventually became a source of pleasure. In fact, for the soldier who believed he had godlike powers to determine life and death, killing became an addiction. Only later—once home—might such a veteran be able to realize that he had become a completely different person. And then, confused about his identity, he might withdraw from relationships with other people and become emotionally detached. Or he might succumb to the other side of the coin, embarking on relationships in which he could become violent or even kill again.

This process of transformation has been recalled by veterans who described killing as a source of emotional pleasure. They associated zeroing in on a target with a feeling of calmness and tranquility, and the completion of the kill with an exhilarating "adrenalin rush." A veteran who still has urges to harm people said: "I got to be kill crazy in 'Nam. It was like going duck hunting. The more I killed the more I liked it. It's the best high I ever had. The wish to kill is still there but I don't tell anyone about it. Most of the time I don't feel anything until somebody makes me mad and then I feel the rush come up through me. I like that feeling but I've also got to control it. I still would like to kill someone if the situation was right. But I know I can't."

In some Vietnam veterans there remains a residual of the "killer-self" ready to make an appearance with the slightest provocation. Even talking about events related to Vietnam can trigger such a response. For example, an infantryman who attended church regularly when he was a boy, had a major personality change in Vietnam following the death of a number of his friends in battle. Robert proceeded to become cruel and sadistic in his treatment of VC prisoners. After his return from the war, two of his war buddies visited him at his home. They noted that he acted strangely: "We were talking about Vietnam and Robert seemed to really be getting excited as he talked about killing VC prisoners. He started to change in front of our eyes. His face took on a pale, waxy deathlike appearance, his mouth became frothy, and his eyes glassy and crazy looking. It was like another person took over who went into the house and came back out with an M-16. He was scary looking. I tried to talk him into putting that gun back. But Robert seemed to be in his own world and didn't pay any attention to me. He pointed the M-16 into the swimming pool. First he fired a short burst and another burst. With the third burst, he yelled like he was killing a gook which released the pressure in him for he turned and looked at me and said, 'I just had to do that,' as if he knew what he had been doing. But I don't think Robert really was aware of the seriousness of what had happened because he acted surprised when we told him what he had just done. It seemed like he is a Jekyll and Hyde because he is usually one of the nicest guys in the world."

Soldiers in Vietnam were conditioned to idealize killing and devalue normal expressions of fear, helplessness, guilt, and grief, which resulted in a dehumanization of themselves and others. Scott, who had led many search-and-destroy missions, described it this way: "It was easy killing them gooks. They wasn't even people, they was lower down than animals." The dehumanization process worsened when close buddies were killed in grotesque ways. "My best friend walked into a mine field and all that was left of him was a head. I can still see it in my mind. It freaked me out and after that, killing gooks was easy. I even killed civilians and it got so that I loved to torture prisoners. I used to see bodies all mutilated and it never bothered me," recalled Scott.

After continuous exposure to death in its most grotesque forms, many soldiers came to identify themselves with death and killing. Dr. Chaim Shatan believes that this results from the need to remain sane within an insane environment: "Surrounded by death coming from everywhere and nowhere . . . the soldier must embrace it as the only reality. Only then can inner and outer reality feel at one again."[11]

Another contributing factor to a veteran's strong identification with death is for the soldier to survive while friends next to him are killed. In such situations he may be subject to "survival guilt," one of the manifestations of PTSD. The surviving soldier with this symptom believes that his survival was paid for by another's death, that if he had not survived, some other(s), more deserving, might have lived in his place. As Mike, who became an alcoholic, declared: "I almost died. I shoulda died. If I am alive, it is not right that I should be. I really feel more dead than alive anyway. I'd give anything if I could change places with those guys who died in Vietnam."

Another veteran who identified strongly with those who had died, said: "Sometimes I have a strange feeling that comes over me and it happened a month ago when I was drawn out of the house and to the cemetery. I didn't really feel like I had any control over myself. I stayed out there for four hours. I don't know why. I can't even remember all of the details of what happened. It was almost like being taken over by another force. Maybe I felt like I should be there with them."

Vietnam veterans who have killed others, particularly enemy soldiers, frequently suffer from a persistent identification with those who have been killed, which we, as counselors, refer to as the "victim-self." Its presence, not apparent on the surface, results from the absence of a boundary between aggression and victimization, which Dr. Karl Menninger described in suicide victims.[14] Vietnam veterans harbor various manifestations of this internalized "victim-self," including a variety of self-destructive symptoms among which are dreams of victimization. For example, a veteran receiving hospital treatment for severe symptoms of PTSD, suffered intrusive images and dreams of a VC soldier whose hand he had cut off before killing him:

"At least twice a week I keep having this dream of a gook's hand that comes up onto my face. I try to pull it off and I can't get it off. Then, sometimes I have a dream where I see a gook's face and as I look, it changes into my face."

Fred, another soldier who had been in many battles and ambushes where friends and enemy were killed, recounted a recurrent dream of walking through the "bush" in Vietnam. He would suddenly discover that he looked like a VC soldier and be ambushed by the Americans. At this point he would suddenly wake up in a cold sweat. Another veteran in a hospital treatment program, who had had many close calls during which his buddies were killed, described this recurrent dream: "This dream I keep havin'—I'm hit by a rocket in the chest and this fucking blood comes outa my chest. It's so damn real I can reach down and feel the warm blood in my hands. They think I'm dead but there's kinda a wall between me and them. I yell out that I'm still alive but they don't hear me."

"Victim-self"-related symptoms may be less specific in other Vietnam veterans and may surface as vague anxiety, unpleasant memories, nightmares, headaches, dizzy spells, and muscle pain. In our own sessions with veterans, we have come to recognize the presence of such a new or persistent symptom as the external manifestation of a persistent hidden guilt and grief associated with death, killing, or friends dying. This symptom is often precipitated by a current event that triggers feelings of helplessness. For instance, one hospitalized former squad leader developed weakness and dizzy spells when he thought he might be prematurely discharged from the hospital. He kept dreaming of seeing himself gunned down in a violent shootout. During his treatment, he was helped to see the relationship between these events; he was also assured that he would not be discharged from the hospital, and encouraged to recall violent memories from Vietnam. He then vividly remembered his two best friends being killed in an ambush to which he responded by singlehandedly wiping out most of the enemy.

The vivid recollection and reexperiencing of a traumatic event with all associated emotions is an important part of treating symptoms related to the "victim-self." Historically, the most common treatment technique is hypnosis. One outstanding soldier, who had been receiving outpatient therapy for over a year, underwent hypnosis after he developed a new symptom of pain and tingling in the right side of his face. During the trance, Anthony described vividly that while in Vietnam, he was nearly killed by a bullet striking that side of his face. During the same hypnotic trance, Anthony reexperienced fear of dying and grief at the thought of not surviving to return home. Reliving the experience with the associated emotions relieved the physical symptom, which disappeared after the treatment session.

Because of the absence of a boundary between aggression and victimization, there is a close affiliation between the "victim-self" and the "killer-self." Consequently, Vietnam veterans cannot express aggressive outbursts without suffering subsequently from "victim-self" symptoms. Josh, for instance, described his wishes to kill his VA doctor who had failed to provide him with the medication he wanted; and his dreams of killing several hospital staff personnel in which he was then killed during a shootout. When he finally revealed these dreams, it was helpful for Josh to admit openly his rage toward his doctor. This revelation lessened his fear of his own violence, purged him of some guilt and anxiety, and relieved him of his violent killer–victim dreams.

The perception of having embraced evil in Vietnam is another expression of victim identification, described previously by psychiatrist and psychohistorian Robert Lifton.[15] Some veterans have the feeling of being possessed or contaminated by evil. One veteran "confessed" of this inner sense of contamination: "ever since I came back from 'Nam, I have felt as if I was possessed and lost my soul."

The concept of being vitiated by an evil presence is so encompassing that most Vietnam veterans fear that they can infect other people. Such a belief was voiced by a former helicopter pilot who had been divorced twice, lost a close friend by suicide, and saw his wife and child killed in a car accident: "I started to believe that I had caused the deaths of everyone who was ever close to me. I had to get away from people in order to keep from hurting them." It was not until after he entered a treatment program for Vietnam veterans that he began to discover for the first time in years that his presence with people and his descriptions of violent battles would not hurt other people, in particular his therapist.

Some have admitted during private counseling sessions that they feel possessed by spirits of dead Vietnamese. This was described by a former Army NCO who thought his physical and emotional pain emanated from having the spirit of a dead gook within him: "One time a VC prisoner cursed me just before I killed him and said he would never let me forget him . . . and he hasn't. I wish I could get my hands on that VC. I'd kill 'im for good 'cause I've killed that sucker a million times in the last 10 years, but the motherfucker keeps coming at me in more shapes and ways than you can shake a stick at."

This veteran's recovery process was very lengthy and complicated, since he had the strong conviction that it was impossible for him to be forgiven: "I don't believe in a God and if there is a God or a heaven or hell, I'm sure I won't be going to no heaven."

Peter Marin interviewed a number of psychologists and psychiatrists, all of whom found it difficult to help Vietnam veterans resolve pervasive guilt about having committed atrocities. One group therapist said that whenever a group member talked about an atrocity, the other group members remained silent as the leaders struggled to be helpful.[9] The therapists' own feelings may sometimes get in the way of helping the veterans with theirs, as reported by other group therapists: "The tales of such atrocities stimulated . . . feelings of anxiety and disgust . . . so much so that one of us had nightmares about Vietnam. We also experienced a kind of primitive admiration, awe, and even envy about the depth and intensity of their experiences with life and death, and at times found ourselves getting caught up in the excitement of their sadism."[16]

Sarah Haley, an experienced social worker and therapist for Vietnam veterans, has described how important it was for her to empathically listen to a Vietnam veteran talk about atrocities and experiences with death.[17] She and her patients' identities appeared to merge during their regular therapy sessions when she listened to her patients' reports of violent and guilt-ridden experiences. She considered that she too, even though unlikely, could also have been an aggressor and committed the same violent acts if placed in the same environment. And her patient discovered, after recounting reports of atrocities, that she did not become the victim he feared she might become or cease being the protector he hoped she would continue to be.

Some veterans who are burdened with enormous guilt find relief through religious expiation. One veteran reported to us that he had a religious conversion that purged his sense of evil contamination after his minister and members of his congregation prayed for him. More commonly, Vietnam veterans with such serious problems have told us that they avoid priests and ministers. Perhaps this is a reaction to those clergy who don't understand the problems associated with war or tend to oversimplify their approach without recognizing all of the hidden complexities of each individual. One Vietnam veteran in a hospital treatment program recalled that he had felt a sense of evil contamination after his discharge from the service and went to confession, talking to a priest in his hometown. He consequently said that he will never return to church again because the priest refused to believe that he had killed women and children, and added, moreover, that he was in danger of eternal condemnation if it were true.

Robert Lifton has given us perhaps more insights about the complexities of the self-experience of contamination by death and evil than anyone else. From his research while meeting with Vietnam veterans in the early 1970s, he found that they sensed themselves as having transgressed boundaries related to witnessing and inflicting death, and suffered from guilt and indelible changes in their identities. He explained, first, the survivor experiences guilt about being alive while others died. Second, the survivor experiences anxiety about being alive because of its association with being "invulnerable." Third, the survivor senses a linkage with those who died and is deeply imprinted with a "death taint" that he believes will rub off on others, thus causing him to remain alienated. Fourth, there is a profound numbing of his emotional life, causing him to be apathetic and uninvolved. Fifth, he suffers from a loss of purpose and inability to find significance in his life experiences.[15] In therapy sessions, we have frequently provided Vietnam veterans with Lifton's concepts and they have felt some comfort in knowing that many other survivors have experienced such feelings.

For many veterans, there remains a continuing identification with death, as if they are unable to establish a normal boundary between living and dying. It seems even more profound than the temporary loss of boundary between life and death described by World War I veterans who felt penetrated by smells of death and decomposed victims in the trenches.[1] For a large number of Vietnam veterans, their attempts to protect themselves from the enormous pain of guilt and depression cause emptiness, numbing, and fragmentation of their sense of who they are.[18,19] It is not unusual for them to describe themselves as if already dead. Thus, they remain in a continual struggle to hang onto the sensation of being alive, even if it means feeling physical pain to signal life instead of death. A former soldier with 5 years of violent experiences in Vietnam, spent ten years in his hometown in the South without being troubled by memories or symptoms. However, a severe injury from a fall that nearly killed him produced within him a sense of momentary loss of boundary between life and death: "When I hit the ground, it knocked me out and then I came to. At that moment I felt absolutely nothing. I thought I musta died and gone to hell. Then all of a sudden, my back started hurting terribly and I knew I was alive. It still hasn't stopped hurting."

This veteran, as well as others who have been plagued with various manifestations of PTSD, struggled to understand why he survived this accident as well as his stint in Vietnam. When he came to believe that his survival had a purpose—taking care of his wife and children—his treatment progressed. Others too have found a purpose for surviving: some in actively participating in helping other Vietnam veterans. Thus, in therapy sessions, we always ask veterans to describe close calls with death and to render their opinions about why they survived. Many have listed 10 or 20 such close calls and say: "There's no reason why I survived Vietnam unless it's to be punished. That's the only reason I can think of."

Those who cannot find a purpose in their survival, often come to fear their own omnipotence. They have learned to distrust power, particularly their own. Yet, during the treatment process, we persist in asking the questions, "Why do you think you survived? And do you think you have a purpose in life?" When they continue to say no, we respond, "Your task is to discover that purpose and I do not believe it is to suffer or to punish yourself any more."

As difficult as it has been for Vietnam veterans to resolve such a crucial question, their lives can become purposeful after they cease being victims in a world without meaning.

The most tragic outcome of a persistent identification with death is suicide. An example of such an outcome was reported concerning a Vietnam veteran who sought treatment after surviving a shootout with police but vowed that he would never go to prison. Unfortunately, during the course of recovery when he had begun to recall some of his most guilt-ridden Vietnam experiences, he was arrested for disturbing the peace and put in a jail cell. Four hours later he was found dead by hanging.

Although this was a tragic death, many of his friends, who had been patients in the treatment program with him, were helped, through him, to grieve in a therapeutic way. As one of his friends said, "While I was standing at the cemetery during the service, I began to see images of my friends in Vietnam who had died. I couldn't hold the tears back anymore. They finally came and I cried for all of them." Grieving his friend's death, with the support of the group who attended the funeral with him, and shedding tears for the first time since leaving Vietnam helped to break down the emotional detachment that had interfered with his life for the past 12 years. For him, at least, hope for recovery became a reality.

Chapter 6 / FAMILY LIFE AFTER VIETNAM

Vietnam has had a devastating effect on family life. Tens of thousands of family members have experienced severe losses and disruptions to their lives because of the war. By the end of 1970, 5 years before the final departure of American troops from Vietnam, 18,000 women had become widows, 12,000 children became orphans and 250,000 Americans had been bereaved by death of an immediate family member. Of the enlisted men alone, 40% were married and 20% were fathers.[1]

Psychologists Charles Figley, M. Robertson, and G. Lester did a noteworthy review of studies on the families of repatriated Vietnam prisoners of war (POWs) and found significant problems. Wives could not relax from their previous dominant positions and children had more psychological problems, presumably because their ex-POW fathers remained emotionally distant from them.[2]

In spite of the family problems of POWs and an estimated 20% of Vietnam veterans' families, research evidence indicates that not only have most Vietnam veterans adjusted well, but some men are now better adjusted than before going to Vietnam.[3] But for those husbands and fathers who remain victims of "the terror and horrors of war . . . inside their minds and hearts,"[4] family difficulties painfully linger on and on.

Many of the thought patterns learned in Vietnam were deeply ingrained in the impressionable young serving there. The veteran may carry within him a "museum of mind," filled with old dead objects that are kept alive in the present through memory only. These painful recollections of the past interfere with the veteran's present: they intrude and disrupt his functioning in the work setting, in recreation, and in human relationships, particularly those of his family. The veteran's basic "trained inability to feel"[5] and his "countertender tendency" (that is, a basic discomfort with tender feelings)[6] in relating to others adversely have affected his desire to be close to anyone. Most veterans, each profoundly affected by the war, do have a desire to love and to accept love in return, but may be unable to do so.

For many veterans, this difficulty began in Vietnam where it was necessary to keep one's feeling under control at all times. Losing control over feelings could mean instant annihilation for the soldier and his unit. In conjunction with numbing of feelings in the war zone, was the hypervigilance associated with staying alive. Not knowing when a sniper would strike, or where underfoot a booby trap or land mine was, made a continuous hypervigilant state necessary for survival. Hypervigilance, though adaptive in Vietnam, has proved destructive to relationships out of the war zone. It plagues the family relationship with suspicion, blame, and anger. Often very unsure of himself, the veteran is distrusting of his family's motives, and tends to accuse them of actions that have not occurred. These accusations lead to arguments, then to withdrawal, and finally, more anger on all sides. Pervasive suspiciousness, which one of us has called the "pansuspicious attitude," is a mental defense against fear. For to be suspicious is also to be forewarned for "expected" and "anticipated" attacks on one's well-being. Moreover, suspicious attitudes derive from the veteran's intense feelings of guilt he is unable to overcome. Because he is unable to forgive himself, he expects others to do him harm. Such expectations destroy the familial atmosphere and obstruct the growth of the family members.

The veteran's hypervigilance often becomes pervasive in most aspects of his life. The term "pansuspicious attitude"[7] describes the furtive, constricted, and pervasively suspicious veteran. This concept about self and the world attacks the most basic prerequisite to familial tranquility: trust. Family members feel misunderstood, unloved, fearful, and angry; and believe that nothing they might say or do matters—his mind is already closed. Whereas the soldier in Vietnam had to be hypervigilant to survive the jungles, the veteran back home with his family uses hypervigilance to survive his inner "jungle-world" of threatening emotions. Why is this the veteran's way of surviving back home? The answer is complex. For the severly disordered veteran, his pansuspiciousness is a response to the threat of danger. However, the danger he now fears has been internalized into the self, creating a new battle on a new terrain. This new terrain is within, which he cannot escape, and the dangers have moved from the physical domain to the emotional domain. These survival tactics are played out in the interpersonal arena among people he deeply cares about and who care about him.

The veteran's low self-esteem and depressions are related to his feelings of guilt and loss. His anger is often directed toward himself for being foolish in having heeded his country's call to fight and toward other Americans for not supporting his efforts. The veteran's basic inability to mourn and grieve is also a source of deep emotional problems. Veterans who lost close buddies now find it difficult to get close to others; they fear another precious loss. In the families of some veterans, the pansuspicious attitude serves to regulate interpersonal distance, thus avoiding yet another lost relationship.

Vietnam, indeed, is a legacy of loss. And the issues of loss and distance-regulation are central to the veteran's psychological outlook. He struggles with an intense dilemma. The fear of loss tends to keep him dependent on and close to his family, while at the same time he is fearful of intimacy. In some of these families, members are too close; in others, too distant. More often than not, this paradox of a "too close–too distant" family revolves primarily around the spouses.

From a "family systems" perspective, these vacillations in the family's functioning require a stabilizing force. Usually it is a child who steps in to protect the parents from being too close or too distant, thus bringing some temporary stability to the family system. This child is usually very fearful of losing his parents, while at the same time anxious and envious of his parents' closeness. Soon the worn-out child develops symptoms from the stress of regulating his parents' *too close–too distant* emotional life.

Interestingly enough, this pattern is found specifically in families where the veteran is doing well in most spheres of his life, except in that involving intimacy with his wife. Distrustful, but not abusive to his wife or children, he is an excellent provider and a successful person with a respectable position in the community. Typically, he had been directly involved in killing the enemy, but did not take part in atrocities. Thus, despite his apparent success in life, the veteran remains dull, deeply uncertain about his life, and very fearful of intimacy.

In most families of veterans seeking help, the veteran is the "identified problem" or "identified patient," "the sick one." In these family situations, the spouse clings to the children for emotional sustenance, and devotes most of her time to ensuring that "they are all right." On the conscious level, the wife perceives herself as the children's protector while on the unconscious level she is her husband's "savior." The wife who is caught in this dynamic situation is in need of relief, for the stress inherent in this situation is extraordinary. Family systems theory helps to illuminate her role and points to possible avenues for relief for her and her family.

Systems theory is an approach to understanding how the family functions, how it enters into conflict, and how it gains and maintains equilibrium. The concept of *systems*[8] helps to explain the complex interactions among family members, the community, and society at large. The essential tenet of systems theory is that the family tends naturally toward psychological equilibrium, and that as long as this "family homeostasis"[8] is achieved and maintained, family members will experience well-being and emotional security. Conversely, when the equilibrium is lost, the system attempts to regain its stability by accommodating the disruptive element. When the latter cannot be overcome, familial well-being gives way to a breakdown of the family system. In the case of Jim, a veteran, and Mary, his wife, the disruptive force was the birth of their son. Under these conditions of imbalance, we speak of a *dysutile* family system; that is, a system that is

dysfunctional and thereby incapable of providing its members with emotional and spiritual support. Prior to their child's birth, Jim and Mary had been approaching marital equilibrium. His unresolved psychological symptoms, related to Vietnam, were reactivated by the birth of the baby. Though the system attempted to regain its balance, it was unable to do so.

In such instances of *system breakdown,* the family's *accommodation mechanisms* may take the form of symptoms. Around the elements of everyday life, a family ethos develops that represents the family's governing "constitution" of predictable attitudes. Systems theory, then, addresses the well-known "group feel–think" phenomenon; in other words, individual behavior cannot be understood isolated from the family system in which the behavior originated. As opposed to some other proponents of systems theory, we believe that, though family organization is stable for the most part, it is also in a steady state of movement and transformation. That is, family systems are not static, but "process-intensive"—the family system is movement-oriented and dynamic. Ilya Prigogine's concept of "order through fluctuation" lends itself readily to our conviction that family systems undergo continuous change. We thus believe that transformational aspects need to be taken into consideration when therapists work with Vietnam veterans and their families.

The Vietnam veteran's family system, like any other family system, struggles to fulfill three basic functions of the family: (1) the developmental well-being of the children, (2) the enculturation of the children, and (3) fulfillment for the parents. For a family system to fulfill these functions well, there needs to be a positive and loving family climate in which parents, honest and sharing, are reasonably happy with each other. There needs to be humor and mutual congeniality between parents, between children, and between parents and children. Children in such an environment feel secure, loved, and inspired to grow emotionally and achieve within society.

These family functions are basically inoperative under the adverse impact of PTSD on the wife, lover, or children. The well-being of the children in these families appears to always be in jeopardy. For example, Ronald and Jeannie have two daughters, ages 11 and 13. These girls have been subjected to an atmosphere of constant hostility and fear at home since they were very young. Their dreams, verbal accounts, and "family" drawings reflect that the family climate has had a profound influence on their current behavior and outlook on life. Their drawings of human and inanimate objects display a peculiar sense of pessimism, anxiety, insecurity, low self-esteem, and vulnerability. Despondent, unprotected, resentful, and bitter, they have strong feelings of having been "ripped off" and deprived of nurturing parents. Their preoccupation with themes of violence, revenge, and anger has taken its toll in their poor performance at school.

It is not unusual to observe in these children severe problems in interpersonal relationships. Much of this stems, in some children, from an *emotional bonding disorder*. This is characterized by an early disruption in the normal bonding process between mother and child—during infancy and early childhood. It results in a basic instability in feelings of belonging. People thus seem interchangeable, and there seems to be little emotional "fidelity" to specific people in their lives.

Feeling unloved and ignored by their parents and unable to muster any strong feelings for their peers, Cynthia and Ellen manifest disruptive behavior in the classroom. They often go so far as to provoke punitive responses from teachers and instigate retaliatory hostility from peers. To a counselor, they appear jittery, anxious, and unfocused. Their inability to concentrate further compounds their underachieving at school.

Though the children are able to make friends at school, they are unable to keep them for long. In part, this is due to their aggressive behavior and inability to share with others. Surprisingly enough, the girls behave remarkably different at home. They are mild-mannered and well-behaved; they appear terrified of their father, who metes out severe punishments. It may seem difficult to understand the great discrepancy between the girls' behavior at home and school. Though most episodes of poor behavior in school were reported to the parents, the girls were evidently not afraid of being punished by their father. We believe this is very interesting, especially since the girls' father is punitive for the smallest infractions at home. Systems theory can be helpful in explaining this seemingly contradictory behavior.

The girls, from a systems point of view, are acting out their father's unconscious wish, that is, to "even the score" by defying authority. It is surprising and interesting as well to note just how little effort the father has demonstrated in disciplining the girls for their poor school behavior.

In family therapy sessions, the parents have argued the merit of each other's preferred approach to discipline. Jeannie feels her husband is too lenient, too permissive, and, at times, too brutal toward the girls. He, on the other hand, accuses her of being too exacting and too strict, and of using traditional, outmoded values in child-rearing. Such conflicting parental signals confuse the children. This confusion, along with the tacit paternal "approval" for their disruptive behavior at school, adds intensity to problematic behavior at school. Ordinarily, the girls experience their father as distant and aloof. However, through their poor behavior at school, they feel his approval. It is as if the girls in their behavior are saying, "If being bad in school is the only way we can get your love and approval, we will continue to do bad things, though we disrupt the classroom and upset teachers by our behavior."

Many veterans with emotional problems have difficulty providing leadership values to their children. This is because these fathers have not been able to overcome their own bitterness toward a culture they perceive as having "left them alone in personal ruin with no support." This bitterness interferes with responsible parenting by preventing the teaching of exemplary interpersonal behavior, strong values, and self-discipline.

Ken, a combat veteran who married Sue after the war, was unsure of his role as husband and later as father: "You know, let's face it. Killing people, women and children and seeing all that I saw is not mine or anybody else's idea of what's normal. I have abnormal ideas and feelings about a lot of things. That shit that I went through, that went on in the 'Nam was some abnormal shit, man. It was really abnormal. I shouldn't have had to go through all that shit. It hurts, man, yeah. Look how fucked up I am now. I can't even be the husband I want to be. I want to be a good father to my kids. They're great kids, but I can't. I need help."

By 2 years of age, both of their twins suffered emotional problems, and were diagnosed as hyperactive and emotionally disturbed. By age 4 both children were well on their way to being learning disabled. They were unable to concentrate or pay attention in school and appeared to be frightened, unhappy, and troubled. Each manifested aggressive behaviors and each was dubbed by the school psychologist as a "behavior problem." In school, the children were a "holy terror"; at home, however, they were "like two little mice." Mutual parental dissatisfaction was very apparent, and struck a severe blow to the family system, adversely affecting the children. Family violence and hostility made an indelible imprint on their minds—of anxiety and terror.

It is clear that the well-being of children is compromised by the father's symptoms. Jim, the father of a boy and girl, ages 6 and 8, had been in heavy combat during the Tet Offensive. In order to survive psychologically, he had to numb himself to all feelings. He could not allow himself to respond emotionally to the things he experienced and soon his experiences became detached from his emotions. To survive with his mind and body intact, he could not respond to his environment. At home, Jim remembers having to leave his best friend to die, because as a medic, he was ordered to save those wounded who had the best chance of recovery. Today he is haunted by this memory. He is filled with intense guilt, often seeing his dying friend in his dreams and nightmares.

Jim has been married for 6 years to Mary. Suffering from PTSD for the last 8 years, he has numbing responses that make him seem emotionally aloof from his children; they thus question his love and affection for them, believing he wishes that they had not been born. Though the children have tried everything possible to engage him in fun with them, make him relax and give up his tenseness, they have not been successful. Consequently, they feel sad and alone.

The other important function of family life is the development of personal intimacy, growth, and satisfaction between parents. Numbing and denial play havoc on intimacy, setting up barriers to effective communication; creating a beclouded family atmosphere devoid of the lively warmth of emotional expressiveness. Jim's numbing also made his wife feel unloved and emotionally unavailable to him. With the birth of their children, however, he became increasingly isolated and "cold." Mary had thought that after marriage and especially after having children, Jim would feel better and "get his act together." But according to her, "I live with a total stranger. We never share anything. I believe that his problems stem from the 'Nam, but he refuses to discuss the war with me; he insists that he cannot talk about what happened to him over there because I wouldn't understand. He keeps everything bottled up inside and I just can't reach him, can anyone? I am about to give up. What about me? He doesn't care."

Prior to marriage, Jim had suffered a number of PTSD symptoms, particularly nightmares and other intrusive images. But these symptoms diminished after marriage. The relief was, however, short-lived, returning with the birth of their first child. He became jittery, tense, even desperate, causing him to withdraw from his wife and baby. She wanted to share her happiness over the new baby, but "he could not be found anywhere, emotionally." Jim's nightmares, or as he called them, "night terrors," understandably created a most potentially catastrophic, nocturnal atmosphere. He slept with two knives and a pistol under his pillow, and unintentionally attacked his wife during nightmares. He attempted to strangle her, calling out "you VC bastard." He often slept only 2 or 3 hours a night, and awakened the next morning "totally exhausted and irritable, jumpy," and ready to pounce on everyone. Mary would also wake up irritable and had to face the children, get them ready for school, and give them as much attention as she was able to muster, but sleepless and frightened. "I don't understand him now. He never explains anything. Just last night he had one of those nightmares. He was thrashing and moving about very violently in jerky movements. He struck me lightly with a knife, and struck me a few times in his dream. He woke up in a panic and soaking wet. He thought I was a VC and was running from being captured. So he was attacking me in the nightmare."

Severe deterioration in Jim's functioning followed the birth of his child, which was the specific triggering event. We have observed this phenomenon repeatedly over the years. The birth of one's child is especially difficult to the veteran who may have been responsible for killing children in Vietnam. Jim had killed a child who refused to stop and he blames himself every day in his mind. Some children carrying concealed explosives knew what they were doing in approaching American soldiers because they had been strongly indoctrinated that self-sacrifice was necessary to free their country of foreign oppressors. Very young Vietnamese children, of course, were unaware of the dangers and they paid the supreme price for their parents' struggle.

Jim had not known for certain that the approaching child was booby-trapped. What he remembers of the incident, after it was discovered that the child had in fact been booby-trapped, was a virtual "carnage" in which several civilians were killed. A village "infested" with VC had used the child to bait the GIs, who loved young children. After killing the child, Jim and his men knew they had been set up, and that the village was a hideout for the VC. This episode of killing left a number of other children dead, ranging in ages from 3 to 10. The birth of his child also resurrected the "bad" dreams of screaming children bleeding and dying. Like others who had killed children in Vietnam, Jim feared an unknown enemy would kill his own children in retaliation, a common fear among combat veterans.

Jim's guilt feelings isolated him from his own children, who consequently felt that he hated them. But his feelings reflected his self-hatred and inability to forgive himself for his "war crimes against children." A "bipolar perceptual and emotional conflict" causes the veteran to swing from perceiving his child as totally helpless and innocent, to perceiving the child as able and blameworthy. When perceived as helpless, the concomitant emotion is warmth, overprotectiveness (often in an aggressive manner), and nurturing. On the other hand, when the child is viewed as blameworthy, the emotion generated in the father is anxiety, vindictive anger, and withdrawal.

For some men like Jim, this stems from a basic "conviction" that children cannot be trusted; "they can kill you," as they did in Vietnam. The other side of the bipolar conflict is the veteran's conviction that all children are innocent and must be protected from "people like myself; people who could kill children." It is not that Jim is totally unaware of the difference between the past and the present, or between his children and the Vietnamese children, but rather he is stuck in the emotional quagmire of a painful past, relived repeatedly in the present.

This basic fear of children and distrust in their innocence and motivations often lead the maladjusted father to attempt either to overly control his children, especially male children, or allow them "to go wild," uncontrollably and without discipline. Some veterans' family systems are modeled after the regimentation of the military; the children are drilled, militarized, and punished severely for the smallest infractions.

There are also some veterans who secretly envy their child's innocence—the innocence they once had and lost in Vietnam. The more disturbed fathers tend to view their children from the aforementioned diametrically opposed viewpoints. This distorts the father–son or father–daughter relationship at times to the point of becoming delusional. For example, Jim has declared, "There are times I feel so sorry for my children. All

children suffer so much: they need their parents' protection, care, and understanding." These words exhibit Jim's irrational perception of his children. This belief in their extreme frailty, in turn, has induced fears and anxieties in their mother, Mary.

Mary could not understand her husband's "crazy talk about the kids"; it terrified her. This concern manifested itself in her clinging to the children, and them becoming increasingly dependent on her. This dependency is alarming to the veteran who seeks the gratification of his own needs of dependency; he may begin to resent the children for interfering with the satisfaction of these tendencies. He may thus become angry and punitive with the children and may even turn violent in his accusations of "what's really going on," meaning that his wife loves the children more than she loves him. An unsettling familial rivalry develops between father and children vis-à-vis the wife.

Frank, another Vietnam veteran with family problems stemming from PTSD, didn't seek counseling until his wife had threatened to leave him, a situation that in our experience is common. Often, though a veteran may be in pain and suffering for years, he does not seek therapy because of his basic fear of: (1) getting worse; (2) not being understood and becoming increasingly angrier; (3) reliving certain painful aspects of his Vietnam experience; (4) fear of being condemned by the therapist or counselor; and (5) fear of revealing inner torment and fears. Many men have to overcome these resistances in order to seek help.

Frank and Sue have been married 5 years and have a 3-year-old son, Chris. From the time of the child's birth, Frank became exceedingly agitated and violent with his wife, and over the ensuing 3 years had assaulted his wife repeatedly, fracturing her arm and ankle. She called the police, but later dropped the charges after Frank promised he would seek help.

During an early group therapy session with fellow Vietnam veterans, one of the veterans said: "Yes, I got a problem with my wife. There are times I tell her to get the fuck away from me—usually for no reason. It's just something that comes over me." Many men are unable to explain their hostility and violence toward their wives, because they are often extremely dependent upon them for emotional support. In fact, research has shown that veterans in good supportive relationships fare better emotionally than those without such support.[9] Merely being married is not enough: there must exist adequate emotional support in order to be of value to the veteran's readjustment.[9] Frank and Sue were fortunate. The treatment plan, which included "rap group psychotherapy"[10] and individual psychotherapy for Frank, helped him to overcome his angry feelings and fears and learn to better regulate his anxieties concerning intimate relationships. Sue learned to deal with her feelings and to realistically evaluate her marriage so she could better decide if she wanted to remain in the marriage. She was also helped in a "rap group psychotherapy" especially designed for Vietnam veterans' wives who wanted to develop self-knowledge and understand the nature of their own PTSD symptoms they had "acquired" through internalizing their husbands' symptoms. Sharing their experiences with each other proved a balm for these women. Sue was then able to rationally make the decision to leave her husband. She said she may consider going back to him but only if he changed his violent ways, and became more loving and able to fulfill her needs.

In Frank's rap group, one veteran confessed, "I never apologize to my wife for anything; I ask her to apologize to me." This highly negative attitude of some veterans toward their wives is undergirded by an unconscious need to control and "command around the wife the way they were commanded around in Vietnam." For some men, apology is related to weakness—to "giving in" to authority. From a psychological perspective, they need to become the authority themselves in order to avoid the devastating feelings of being out of control of their own inner world of emotional chaos. Moreover, to apologize is tantamount to giving in to their profound feelings of guilt and blameworthiness. That is, to apologize for anything, at any time, to anyone, means, in their minds, that they have something to be guilty for.

Most veterans are not aware of their destructive tendencies within the family. With good treatment it takes months, even years of intensive psychotherapy before the veteran can make the emotional "connection" between his current idiosyncracies, irrational thoughts and behavior to occurrences in Vietnam over a decade ago.

Drs. Victor DeFazio and Nicholas Pascucci, both specialists in treating Vietnam veterans and their families, have identified common patterns of behavior among veterans and their spouses. In their private practice and at the Vietnam Veterans Outreach Center in Jamaica Hills, New York, they have made important observations of these couples and families:

"Dependency plays a central role. The women are frequently older than the men. Most are divorced [from previous marriages] and have adolescent or preadolescent children (by the time they come for assistance). The women are usually quite concerned, clearly efficient, capable, and motherly. In their own lives they have often suffered a profound rejection and have a powerful position in the current marriage [to the veteran]. Most frequently, the men abdicate almost all responsibility and power (including financial) to their wives. They (the wives) tend to describe the early part of the relationship as usually warm and sexually gratifying. They . . . describe themselves as almost being 'taken aback' by the degree to which they become the central focus of their husband's lives . . . to the exclusion of almost everything else. An idealization [of them by their husbands] takes place which becomes difficult to resist."[11]

Love, in the context of PTSD, is difficult to achieve and maintain. Our observations of these couples show that during courtship and marriage the wife is often in emotional turmoil and confusion about her life. It is well known that men and women who are unhappy and are in psychological distress tend to find others who are suffering like themselves. The unconscious notion of finding and marrying someone who is similar to themselves in suffering tends to improve their own fragile self-concept, and increases their self-esteem. Women filled with anxieties about themselves and about intimacy and life in general, may find that they can achieve some significance by becoming a full-time caretaker to the veteran with low self-esteem. Such women can only feel complete, in the psychological sense, if they lose themselves—lose perspective of their own needs and self-worth—in the family role of caretaker of their husband and children.

In such families, the wife seems to fulfill every vital function. The veteran, often himself very immature psychologically, feels he had done all the work he needed to do in Vietnam 10 or 11 years ago, and *he* wants to be taken care of now. So the wife is left uncared for even during pregnancy and delivery, often without her husband's presence in the hospital at all. She performs all postnatal care by herself. There may also be no one who would help her since her husband may be overpossessive of her and discourage friendships. She remains 100% involved in the child's developmental needs, and at times is the one who goes to work to support her family. For some veterans only a nurturing maternal woman is able to restore within him a sense of being alive. Wives, in many respects, function as "life-givers" to their husbands and become instrumental to their emotional and psychic rebirth.

But in other cases, the wife–husband relationship can be described as "pathological" when a veteran unconsciously desires to be nurtured "as an infant," and the wife's personality characteristics produce a complementary role of being a "supermother." While the wife appears to be more able, under the surface she also is dependent. Together, they form a pathological bond, which may even appear mature and stable, but which in fact conceals the underlying emotional vulnerabilities. They are incapable of mature forms of intimate behavior because of being childishly needy. In attempting to resolve the pathology stemming from this kind of emotional entanglement, psychotherapy with a family therapist who is familiar with combat stress disorders would be most helpful.

Another marriage of turmoil is that between Ronald and Jeannie. She complains of her husband's anger, sexual dysfunction, and anxiety. He complains of her rigid style of discipline. A thorough analysis of the family system convinced us that both are playing out their own unresolved bitterness of the past. Jeannie was, in fact, a rigid disciplinarian; her parents had treated her punitively during most of her upbringing. Her current punitiveness with her own children created a *familial recapitulation* for her, in which she unconsciously attempted to master her own anxiety and anger toward her own parents for the way they treated her. In terms of Ronald, he grew up in a very democratic and loving family environment in which his parents were openly demonstrative in their affection for each other and their children.

The next logical question is then: "Why is he so abusive to his family if he grew up in a normal home? Isn't it true that veterans who have all these readjustment problems had unstable families with all kinds of problems?" According to the best and only wide-scale research on the readjustment problems of Vietnam veterans, those veterans who saw heavy combat succumb to stress reactions and disorders despite solid family backgrounds. (Heavy combat as opposed to light combat is defined as a relatively high frequency of engaging the enemy, and being exposed to dead bodies, being wounded, etc.) The war experience itself had an effect on the relatively uncrystallized identity of many soldiers, causing psychological and social *fixation* or *arrest*. As a result, they remained at the immature level of an adolescent, a condition adversely affecting their relationships with wives and children. Thus, the veteran father-husband's immaturity appears to be an important issue in family functioning.

In a family setting, immature individuals find themselves unable to be direct in expressing their true feelings; they are often too fearful of rejection, losing love, and other forms of anticipated "retaliations" for being "bad." And being bad often means feeling guilty about surviving, committing atrocities, or killing the Vietnamese. (We have noted a high degree of guilt feelings in black and other minority veterans, in particular, over killing people so much like themselves.[12]) The immature veteran also fears losing control over his feelings, slumping into depression, and making choices and taking responsibility for the consequences of those choices. He is often unable to perceive accurately and understand without undue distortions. Verbal and nonverbal signals and statements often miscommunicate his or her true intentions, resulting in further anger. It is thus not very difficult to see how an immature person(s) can cause havoc to the family environment. Both Ronald and Jeannie show these immature characteristics: for Ronald these derived for the most part from his Vietnam experience; for Jeannie, from her family experience.

This couple has been unable to make their relationship satisfying and growth-enhancing. Moreover, their immaturity, especially Ronald's, has made it virtually impossible to transmit clear cultural values with conviction to their children, who have thus been deprived of the necessary stability, security, models, discipline, and enriching communication that prevail in a thriving family.

Intimacy between husband and wife is very difficult to achieve when the husband has failed to complete the grieving for major losses in his life, particularly those that occurred in Vietnam. Ed and Nora are an example. When they sought help for their problems, it was his third marriage and they were discussing divorce. His violent outbursts began shortly after the birth of the first of their two children, Jeff and Joey.

When they met 6 years after his return from Vietnam, Nora was impressed with Ed's warmth, charm, and sensitivity. But she could not see the hidden aspects of his personality nor did she want to consider herself forewarned when he casually explained away the dissolution of his previous two marriages as due to "flying off the handle, at times." He had not discussed Vietnam with her or his former wives. Actually, he was not himself aware that Vietnam "had anything to do with how screwed up [he] was." He tended to blame his problems on the fact that his parents had been divorced when he was 7. Yet that did not explain the fact that he had been having severe nightmares related to his war experiences during the entire course of this marriage.

Ed has been unable to hold a job for more than 3 months. It is rather baffling looking at and listening to this veteran, who "seems to have it all together." And his supervisors and peers adore him for his wit, brilliance, and friendly and cheerful attitude in the workplace.

As his first two marriages broke up because of his violence and self-destructiveness, his third marriage is similarly being threatened. Ed seems to provoke rejection from his wife by his violent outbursts. She then refuses to cook for him, keeps the children away from him, and withholds sex for days and even weeks at a time. At those times, Ed seems to feel quite comfortable being estranged from his family, as if fulfilling a need for self-punishment and protecting himself from losing his fragile sense of identity and self-boundaries.

During therapy, he finally revealed that at those times he would feel strange, and the vivid memory would return of the time he made a promise to himself after his best friend died in his arms. This promise was similar to one reported by our colleague, Sarah Haley, of a Vietnam veteran who said he would never get close to a human being again as long as he lived.[13]

He harbored this memory as a shameful secret, keeping his wife distant and uninformed about his war experiences. When she would find Ed crying like a baby in the corner of the bedroom, she blamed it on his "rotten childhood," though she suspected that his "hair-raising" nightmares were caused by the war. She finally got fed up with repeatedly being accused of seeing other men, of having the children be rejected, of being repeatedly assaulted, and of being blamed for all his problems. Finding herself and her children suffering alone with anxiety and rage, she threatened Ed with divorce.

It takes a significant threat to the stability of a marriage to jar a veteran into seeking treatment. Most commonly, it is the threat that his wife will leave him, and in this case, Nora did exactly that, but with an attitude of love and concern. As her strength and courage had kept the family together and protected the children from turmoil, an article on the special post-traumatic problems of Vietnam veterans prompted her to seek help for Ed and herself. And they both received it. She expressed pent-up feelings of anger and was helped to understand the conflicts between being a wife and mother and her personal needs for love and satisfaction. They were both able to talk about communication and sexual difficulties, which included his problems with impotency. He was given special individual and group therapy to resolve feelings of anger, fear, and grief that had remained buried for years and interfered with normal expressions of love, affection, and sexuality. With new hope, they decided to remain together.

The disturbed family system involving two immature parents who both depend upon a specific child to provide them with parenting we refer to as the *child-as-parent* phenomenon. In such families, parents give up their parenting prerogatives in order to get love through "looking up" to their child for guidance and support. Within the family system dynamics, the child functions to keep the family intact by allaying familial anxieties. Without the parents' using him in this way, they would not be able to remain as a family, and he, unconsciously, understands this and offers himself as "sacrifice" on the family's altar of emotional primitivity.

The child-as-parent is a devastating responsibility for any child. The intense stress of overseeing both parents catches up with the child; he often becomes symptomatic and thus in need of professional help. Usually, it is a guidance counselor or a teacher who first notes the child's problems, which may have been hidden at home. The child-as-parent then becomes the "symptom bearer" for the family's emotional pathology. If the outside observers are able to "convince" the parents that their child needs help, an interesting, yet painful family phenomenon occurs. As the child gets better and begins to behave as a child, replete with his need for parental nurturance, the family system takes on a desperate, frantic picture. Actually, many such disturbed family systems, because of a profound aversion to change, strongly resist role changes. And their needs to maintain homeostasis at all costs often propel them out of family therapy in order to *save the family,* rather than *save the children.* For this reason most good clinicians refuse to treat children of severely disturbed family systems without treating the entire family. For experience has taught that without total family involvement, the child is ultimately taken out of treatment when beginning to get better.

Many family systems in trouble, as we mentioned earlier, tend toward homeostatic balance by "making" a family member the "sick one." More often than not, the family member with PTSD is "chosen." When Lou came to seek help for his PTSD, he had been a virtual prisoner in his home, barricading himself in the house by placing reinforcements across the windows and doors. If he ever ventured outdoors, it would be in his yard, which he often tried to avoid because "it reminded me of the bush in Vietnam." As a recluse, he preferred to work during the night at a warehouse in New York City to "avoid being tempted to hurt somebody." His wife and children viewed him as "the family nut," but after months of intensive psychotherapy, Lou began to recover from his traumatic mental symptoms. His violence was substantially reduced, and he seemed more able to regulate his intense rage, and more tranquility reigned in the home. But then the therapist noticed a very interesting occurrence regarding his wife, Nancy. She soon began "ranting and picking fights" with her husband. His surprise, fear, and anger over her provocation threatened to "send [him] back to the good old bad days of violence" in the family. "She's asking me to kill her. I think that's what she wants." Actually, Lou felt bewildered when his "killer-self" threatened to emerge so soon after just gaining control. Lou's former inappropriate practice of dressing his son up in Green Beret jungle fatigues, cap, boots, machine gun, and play grenades, was now taken over by his wife whose level of anxiety had risen to high, unbearable levels. The family system would not be able to sustain itself with the assault to its organization without the wife and children becoming involved in the treatment process. It was discovered by the therapist that Nancy had come from a family of violence, perpetrated by an alcoholic father she had grown to hate. Some of her psychopathology presented in the family setting was, however, understood by the clinician as coming from having internalized her husband's PTSD symptoms and behavioral styles after years of marriage to him.

What can be done to effect changes in troubled family systems of Vietnam veterans? Our experience has led us to believe that those who are successful in intervening with these families have been well trained in understanding and assessing complex family dynamic systems. For we view assessment of such "rigid family systems"[14] as important as the therapeutic process itself.

The procedures of assessment are those of "intrafamily impact analysis" (IFIA) and "extrafamily impact analysis" (EFIA). The former set of procedures focuses on the specific elements *within* the family system itself, while the latter focuses on the specific elements *outside* the family system. IFIA procedures determine: (1) The impact of the veteran's posttraumatic symptoms—degree and severity—upon spouse, son, daughter, parents of the veteran, and the family as a whole. (2) The impact of the family's (individual and collective) reactions to the veteran's behavior. (3) The impact of the veteran's behavior on himself as perceived by family members. (4) The impact of naturally occurring events such as births, deaths, marriages, divorces, dual-career strains, adolescence, stepparenting, etc. on the veteran and on the family as a whole. (5) The nature of the family atmosphere (humor, sensitivity, laughter, mood). (6) The "family management" operations—Who makes the decisions, how are they made, through democracy or authoritarianism? How are problems solved, by whom, how effectively? Nature of parental roles. (7) Family emotional life; that is, how are feelings expressed, and by whom? Are the feelings and their expression sanctioned in the family? (8) The "identified patient," or, who is the "sick one"? (9) Family communication style—how is it conducted? Are verbal and nonverbal messages clear? Are messages straightforward, or confused? Who is the family communicator—veteran, spouse, son, or daughter? (10) In what way is the family involved in the community? (11) How close is the veteran–wife pair? (12) The nature of the overall *total family system*. This includes the *extended family system* of the nuclear family: The children's aunts, uncles, cousins, grandparents, great-grand-parents, and other relatives representing many generations. It also encompasses the *augmented family system*, which includes long-time family friends and acquaintances. All these people are important to the nuclear family, and serve as a rich source of support—financial, educational, consultative, and spiritual. The proficient clinical assessor knows to pay strict attention to the role of these family structures, a concept that has been especially useful when assessing the veteran family systems of black, Hispanic, American Native, and Asian combatants.

In terms of EFIA procedures, the assessor determines: (1) The impact of job stress, job changes, unemployment, underemployment, and the working mother in the family system. (2) The impact of the social and political climate with regard to the Vietnam veteran. (3) The impact of specific social-political events on the veteran's symptoms, such as the return of the Iranian hostages, the invasion of Grenada, the wholesale massacre of American marines in Beirut, the hostilities in Central America, and so forth. (4) The impact of cultural agencies, school, and church on the veteran's life.

The family therapist is well aware that children learn values through the family. They learn to depend on others and support others. They learn to trust and to love, and learn how parents behave with each other. When children grow up and become parents, they live out their parents' behaviors which they observed as children. Overwhelming evidence reveals that patterns of behavior learned early in life remain influential. Hence, a Vietnam veteran's disturbed parental behavior may be reflected a generation later by his children's disturbed parental behavior.

The clinician makes an assessment to determine how much, if any, of current problematic behavior in the family is related to earlier conditionings of parents or to other catastrophic events outside of Vietnam. In the event that the wife was in a traumatic event herself, this is taken into account by the clinician in his overall *family system assessment*.

In working with the family of the Vietnam veteran, the family therapist assesses the nature of family life on holidays and special social events. This is especially important because holidays and social events have special meanings to most Vietnam veterans who served in combat units. For these veterans and their families, family life on holidays may be a most difficult time. In Vietnam, the VC had used "ambush psychology," attacking the compounds when GIs were relaxing on holidays. Sometimes heavy casualties were sustained, yet at other times, none at all. The basic objective of "holiday ambushes" was to harass American troops, keep them off balance, and induce terror. Ronald remembered these times in Vietnam: "I just don't know what would come over me at Christmas and Thanksgiving, and other holidays. A VC squad attacked us on Christmas and zapped a lot of guys, including Tony, my closest buddy. I'll never forget that; I'll probably never get over it, I guess. It's pretty spooky, because I may be sitting or standing, or anything else and I feel these funny feelings coming over me. I then get real uptight, angry, scared. I then withdraw and don't want anybody talking to me about anything or looking at me, either. I am very hard to deal with when I am like that, and I am sorry for my family. They deserve better than this; they really do. I really love them and I don't want to do anything to hurt them. But I just can't help it on holidays. I become the greatest turnoff to my family and my wife's family. . . .The holidays are spoiled by guys like me, especially for the kids. I am feeling much better now that I've been in treatment and attending the rap groups at the Vet Center in my city. My wife is getting some help too. Things are changing for the better."

There are many clinicians who have made headway in helping families move toward family cohesion who once lived as if in a combat zone. The members of the family grow to fulfill the vital functions of family life. Children begin to sleep well again, do well in school, overcome various school-related inhibitions. Furthermore, we have noted that husbands stop physically and emotionally abusing their wives and children. Their sexual relationships become more enriching. We have also seen wives grow and change, finding for themselves new options in their lives. Wives have found new inner strength even though often met with utter shock by their husbands.

During these times of change toward better mental health and improved family life, the family system is in flux, seeking a new, healthy equilibrium as it recovers from Vietnam.

Chapter 7 / SPECIAL VETERAN GROUPS: WOMEN AND THE ETHNIC MINORITIES

Women and the ethnic minorities represent special populations of Americans who served in Southeast Asia during the Vietnam era. We refer to these groups as "special" because of the uniqueness of their readjustment needs, which have significant gender role and cultural elements. This uniqueness is based, essentially, on their marginal status in American society. Both female and ethnic minority veterans have had experiences in the military that differ in fundamental, qualitative ways from those of white male veterans.

Like male soldier-"grunts," many nurses in Vietnam were young and away from home for the first time. Vietnam represented their first big job, after completing professional training in nursing. Most went to Vietnam because they wanted to provide good nursing care where it was needed—in Vietnam. Moreover, these young women identified with our "teenaged warriors," who were close to them in age.

Some women also hoped to find love and romance in Vietnam (or in the military), while others wanted to find a husband. Due to the taboo about fraternizing (most nurses were officers) with enlisted personnel, these women were limited in their choices of available men. In addition, most male officers in the Medical Corps were already married. For some nurses, the inner pressures stemming from their own human needs for romance and sexual fulfillment, in conjunction with the external pressure to "conserve the fighting strength," proved overwhelming. Like many men in the war, these women had grown up in rather protected family environments. Then, quite suddenly, they were plunged into a war, replete with its *innocence-destroying* influences. Like some men in the war, the nurse was ill-prepared to survive physically or mentally in a guerrilla war, but she did, at great costs though. The price of being in the war was the same for men: irritability, deep fears, anxieties, anger, and, for some, despair.

Unfortunate stereotypes were prevalent about the women in Vietnam who served in the military, especially in the war zone. Women were spoken of as whores, lesbians, prostitutes, dikes, and male-haters by some men—usually enlisted men who felt rejected by these "delightful round-eyed American women." Because American women were the only round-eyed women in Vietnam, they were highly prized romantic and sexual partners. Thus, men whose romantic intentions or sexual advances were denied, often felt this rejection very deeply. The stereotypes, then, to a great extent, were fostered by angry, rejected men. In Vietnam, it was fairly easy to "score" with Vietnamese women, some of whom were prostitutes; they were available.

Because American troops were conditioned daily attitudinally against the Vietnamese, it was difficult for many soldiers to view the nationals as human beings. Earlier in this book we discussed the process of transformation of the soldier from "good American boy" to "bad killer-machine." We posit that, during this transformation, the Vietnamese are also transformed within the soldier's psyche, from real people to "gooks," "dinks," and "slopes." With this almost complete dehumanization of the Vietnamese, it is no wonder that the American woman had such tremendous appeal. She was the only "real woman" to some of these men. This "conviction" that white American women were the ultimate in romance and sexuality, made rejection by them all the more painful and narcissistically injurious to the soldier.

The damaging stereotypes given to women in Vietnam adversely affected their self-esteem and self-concept. Negative interpersonal experiences in Vietnam created mental scars that persist in some women today. Women are finally beginning to talk about their Vietnam experience. "Breaking out of the long silence" is being accomplished by Vietnam nurse veterans such as Linda Van Devanter, whose new book *Home Before Morning* we recommend very highly to those interested in understanding the world of the combat nurse in Vietnam. Further, Jane Thompson and Rose Sandecki, national cochairpersons of the Women's Working Group sponsored by the Vet Center Program, have been instrumental in teaching the nation about the woman's experience of Vietnam and her unique readjustment needs.

In Vietnam, female nurses were exposed to the *carnage of war* daily. In addition, some had to make decisions as to who lived or died— a rather awesome responsibility for a young person. But this had to be done, and she did her job well. Deciding who lived and who died was the task of the triage (designating need for specialized treatment) nurse. It was she who decided whether a soldier brought to her was "too far gone" to be saved. Those wounded soldiers who she felt could be helped to recover were given medical attention and care, while those who seemed beyond the help of medical procedures were allowed to suffer and expire. To this day, many nurses talk of their disturbing memories about triaging decisions.

For women who served in the military in general, and those who served in Vietnam in particular, a number of critical issues set them apart from others in terms of adjustment to civilian life. We refer to their four-pronged psychosocial task as the "quadripartite identity challenge" (QIC). This is a composite of four distinct images the female veteran is called upon to resolve or overcome during the recovery process, in order to begin a rich and fulfilling life. These images include: (1) her identity as a member of a gender relegated to second-class status in American culture; (2) her identity as a "woman" in a rigidly traditional military system that regards women on the whole as inferior soldiers; (3) her identity as a "woman" in the combat zone, and attendant strong self-expectation to nurture others while denying or repressing her own needs; and (4) her identity as a "female Vietnam veteran" with PTSD.

For the black woman, we add to her adjustment challenge the factor of race—her identity as a member of an "outgroup." We thus regard the black woman as being faced with a "quintuple adaptational challenge" (QAC). We further believe that it would be virtually impossible to understand the enormous difficulty of female veterans' readjustment were these issues not placed in an appropriate, realistic, and honest perspective.

Female veterans have contributed significantly to the military effort in American wars, and have made great sacrifices. For example, during World War II, some women served as test pilots in unsafe, untested aircraft. Many died in crashes during these experimental flights. The list of heroic deeds and outstanding accomplishment of women in the military is yet to be told. These deeds reflect great commitment to service—love for country, fellowmen, their fellow Americans, and freedom. Women in the Vietnam War made great contributions under the most dire of circumstances.

During the Vietnam era, women comprised 2.1% of military personnel (or 197,513), 83.5% of whom served in Vietnam as nurses. According to Kolb's "Vietnam Veterans Fact Sheet,"[1] eight female nurses died in Vietnam. Nonmedical female soldiers in Vietnam served as secretaries, air traffic controllers, supply clerks, and other clerical roles in nonmedical occupations. There were also a number of women classified as DACs (Department of the Army Civilians). Though here we will focus on the nurse veteran's experience, it must be understood that thousands of women served in Vietnam in nonmilitary roles. Jeannie Marie Christie, who served with the Red Cross in Vietnam has pointed out that women served in the Department of Defense, United Service Organization, American Red Cross, Armed Forces Radio, USAID, CIA, MACV (Military Assistance Command, Vietnam), church-related volunteer groups (for example, the Mennonites), embassy staff, field service staff, clerical and administrative staff, Peace Corps, and International Volunteer Service. Christie claims that of the 33,000 women in civilian support positions in Vietnam, 25,000 had volunteered to go there.[2]

Though there is a paucity of research regarding the readjustment problems of female veterans, there is much supporting evidence to suggest that these veterans have had trouble recovering.[1] How did these problems arise? What sociocultural conditionings, individual personality traits, and/or biological predispositions may have intensified the stressors in the "war zone"? What were the *stressors-of-war* that were unique to the Vietnam nurse-soldier? These important questions are not easily answered. Although further investigation is obviously needed to shed more light on the inner and outer worlds of these veterans, we will attempt to answer these questions here.

Many Vietnam nurse veterans have been found to have posttraumatic stress disorder (PTSD). Like their male counterparts, other women suffer not from PTSD but rather from "posttraumatic demoralization syndrome" (PTDS)—a layer-upon-layer accumulation of stresses, without relief, beginning with Vietnam and the repatriation. These women often do not have the symptoms that "add up" to PTSD, but are nevertheless dull, anhedonic, anxious, angry, with painful memories and occasional "bad" dreams. For the diagnosis of PTSD to be made, however, a critical factor must be present: the "existence of a recognizable stressor that would evoke significant symptoms of distress in almost anyone."[4] A stressor is a "stress-event"—in the outside world as well as in the mind—that overrides the individual's natural coping capacities. In situations where a stressor is not recognizable, the diagnosis of PTSD cannot be made, even if certain classical symptoms are observed in the individual.[4] For some veterans, our concept of "posttraumatic demoralization syndrome" has been found to be a valuable alternative to PTSD in cases where the stressor is either unrecognizable or at best dubious. There are also a number of male and female veterans whose postcombat symptoms alone fall short of the PTSD diagnosis, even though they might have suffered a catastrophic event that is recognizable. Some stress events are exclusively extrapsychic (or environmental), while others tend to originate intrapsychically. In either situation, the clinician must ensure that a complete exploration of the nature of the stressor is made and the personality of the veteran is fully understood. Determining the "toxicity" of an external, but especially an internal, stressor is extremely difficult to do, since there are so many variables the clinician must consider very carefully.

In the specific case of female nurses suffering from repetitive occurrences of intrusive, haunting memories of Vietnam, as well as a numbing of responsiveness, what was the specific "recognizable stressor" responsible for these readjustment difficulties? We view the specific stressor unique to nurses in Vietnam as stemming from *three* specific sources, one of which is external and the other two internal. The first is the *war-induced* stressor (external); the second, the *relative maturity-induced* stressor (internal); and the third, the *sociocultural role-induced* stressor (internal). The first stressor (type I stressor) is identifiable in the nurses' daily experience of the *carnage of war*. Inescapably involved in this fast-paced world of suffering and gloom, nurses were witness to gruesome wounds and mutilations.

Many were witness to dismembered bodies. They "dealt with an unending stream of the bits and pieces of people coming across the tables to be put back together,"[5] writes Linda Van Devanter, a Vietnam nurse veteran whose book *Home Before Morning* portrays her personal experience in Vietnam. "Multiple traumatic amputations, massive abdominal wounds, chest wounds, spinal cord injuries, disfiguring head and facial wounds, and overwhelming burns were the order of the day."[5] They heard the chilling cries, groans, and sobbings of young men who were frightened and suffering excruciating pain. Many had to attend to soldiers with severe burns, sometimes covering the entire body. These same sights, sounds, and cries reappear today in the dreams of many nurses. To many of those exposed to the smell of burned human flesh, such a smell never seems to go away completely, being sensorially replayed in dreams of the night, or in flashbacks during the day.

The sophistication of American technology made transportation of the wounded to medical-surgical field hospitals in Vietnam easy and quick. Thus, there were times when nurses had to work around the clock—in 12-hour shifts—to attend to the large number of "wasted" bodies, frightened hearts, and minds tortured by deep anxieties. Nurses not only took care of their patients' bodies, but also attended eloquently and sensitively to their psychological and emotional needs. They spent time comforting, reassuring, and instilling hope in their patient-soldiers.

Nurses in Vietnam ranged in age from 22 to 25. Since the average age of the men was 19, the nurses' *relative maturity* evoked in many of them the added strain of feeling totally responsible for their patients' recovery and welfare (type II stressor). This stressor converged with the type I stressor to compound further the nurses' anxieties. Being older than the men made some of them bestow upon their patients motherly and sisterly devotion far beyond the call of duty. We believe that those nurses whose personalities made them more inclined to become "super-saviors" were most vulnerable to the type II stressor.

The third (type III) stressor emerged from the nurse's socioculturally-determined sex role. Sex roles spring in part from social expectations learned early in life, which are internalized (intrapsychically) during the individual's emotional and social development. These internalized expectations govern masculine and feminine behavior. Suzanne Keller, a sociologist at Princeton University, discusses some of the core elements of the female role in society:[6]

> [There is] an expectation that women will emphasize nurturance and life-preserving activities, both literally as in the creation of life and symbolically, in taking care of, healing, and ministering to the helpless, the unfortunate, the ill. Preeminent qualities of character stressed for women include sympathy, care, love, and compassion, seemingly best realized in the roles of *mother, teacher,* and *nurse.* [italics added]

Thus, as both a "woman" and a "nurse" in Vietnam, their feminine role in society was congruous with their professional role. We believe that this confluence of roles in Vietnam proved instrumental in inducing exceedingly high levels of stress. By the confluence of their sex role and professional role, many women felt "locked in" and compelled to do indefatigable, ceaseless work to save their patients' lives.

Nurses in Vietnam displayed genuine concern for the needs of their patients. They worked hard for long, painful, and physically exhausting hours because the situation demanded this level of commitment and herculean effort. But there is a point at which there is nothing left to give. Many nurses caught up in their societal role of nurturer experienced such intense internal demands on themselves that today they feel as if they have nothing left to give.

The confluence of these three types of stressor made the experiences of the nurse in Vietnam as potentially devastating to the psyche as those of the "grunts" in the field. For though nurses never killed anyone in battle, some did hold themselves blameworthy for the deaths of patients in their care. In fact, some nurses today feel guilty for having helped *both* American troops and the enemy troops, believing that their interventions caused additional killings on both sides.

Our experience reveals that nurses in Vietnam often identified intensely with some of their patients; the deeper and more intense this identification, the greater the sense of responsibility and grief at the death or permanent disability of the patient in their care. For many, the cumulative experience of dozens of deaths and other kinds of losses began to pile up in their minds as "additory trauma."* The concept of additory trauma—the mounting up of trauma upon trauma—is basic to understanding the profound sense of loss and "impacted grief"† that Vietnam nurse veterans still feel today. Each loss of a patient—especially those to whom the nurse "allowed" herself to become attached to—was experienced as either a "minitrauma" or a "megatrauma."‡

Evidence abounds that nurses in Vietnam had to numb their feelings for their own psychological survival. Some people believe this to mean that nurses were unable to have genuine feelings of caring, warmth, love, and affection for their patients and for their romantic partners in Vietnam. However, this is not at all the case. We believe that the nurses' relative maturity in psychological development gave them the apparent capacity to *numb* and *denumb* themselves selectively. Thus, this *selective numbing* made it possible for them to numb themselves to hideous burns, facial and head deformations, and mutilated bodies, but, at other times, to open themselves emotionally to patients they had invested with their special interest, compassion, and devotion. It is quite possible that the life-pre-serving, protective, and care-giving capacities of women—be these qual-ities cultural or biological—may contribute to the self-regulation necessary to function under traumatic conditions. The life-preserving qualities of women seem to "rise to the occasion" in traumatic incidents to preserve life and promote well-being. Of course, women, as mentioned earlier, are expected by society to do as much.

For a large number of nurses, the Vietnam experience was one of loss: losing patients, losing friends (due to rotations), and losing touch

---

* We use the term "additory trauma" to refer to the situation in which the multiple traumata impact on the other, creating a cumulative effect. In this psychic situation, the mind remains unrelieved from the earlier trauma.

† "Impacted grief" is a term coined by Dr. Chaim Shatan. It appears in his paper, "The Grief of Soldiers: Vietnam Combat Veterans' Self-Help Movement," *American Journal of Or-thopsychiatry* **43** (1973), pp. 640–653.

‡ We apply the term "minitrauma" to painful, catastrophic events that result in *relatively* mild mental effects—symptoms and reactions in acute (rather than chronic) forms. The term is the conceptual opposite of "megatrauma"—the relatively severe and chronic forms of posttraumatic stress reactions and symptoms.

with other people in the "shifting sand" of Vietnam. Out of this developed for some a deeply ingrained "terror of closeness." Many still experience depression over these unresolved losses. One specific loss common to many nurses is that of their capacity to maintain a trusting and receptive attitude toward men, women, and life in general.

Jean, a Vietnam nurse veteran, expressed to us her fears and anxieties about getting close to male friends. She links these feelings to the death of significant individuals in Vietnam. Patricia's problem in getting close to men, she believes, is related to the death of her boyfriend, a platoon leader, in 1969. Patricia's friends describe her as distant, but hard-working and diligent. Like many other nurses who served in Vietnam, Patricia is having great difficulty overcoming the rigid defense mechanisms she erected in Vietnam 15 years earlier. Unable to relax, she feels as if her life is "on a tightrope." She describes herself as "uptight, high-strung, and anxious." Sherri, another nurse veteran, says, "I have not come down off the Vietnam high as yet. I am still way up there, it seems. I get very bored very easily. I always have a need to 'keep on truckin' all the time. It would probably be nice to relax for a change. I still go around tensed, expecting some emergency to happen at any minute, in my many relationships with men, with my two children, with my boss, with everybody."

The high tension experienced in Vietnam has remained as though organically embedded in many nurse veterans. They, after all, had had to contend on a daily basis with an "unending flow" of emergencies, emergencies creating high anxiety, tension, and fear. Living life in a state of "emergency high-gear" required extraordinary mental and physical energy. Today these women live their lives with a tremendous sense of seriousness. Like these nurses, other Vietnam veterans have no interest or patience in trivial matters; in fact, they avoid or reject anything that has the appearance of fun. Instead, they focus on the serious, sober side of life. Intense, worried, but reflective, they are not given to spontaneous playful behavior. Matilda speaks about how difficult it is for her to be playful with her 5-year-old; she mentions her anxieties about mothering. As she put it, "I don't always know how much to give and how much to hold back. When I feel I am giving too much, I am inclined to get angry and resentful and then become withholding. Crazy thoughts go through my head, 'Will I lose my child?' 'Is she going to grow up alright?' 'Will she be taken from me?' I know these thoughts are crazy, but I have them anyway; they can be very disturbing to me at times."

The survivor's guilt that a combat nurse feels is here referred to as "responsibilitizing guilt." In her words: "I am guilty for not having been able to save [the soldier] from dying"; "I am guilty for giving medical aid to those VC and NVA bastards I was forced to treat, because they just went back and 'wasted' American boys"; or, "I am guilty because I volunteered to go to Vietnam to have helped that boy come home alive, not in a body bag." In essence, responsibilitizing guilt means the nurse feels personally responsible for not having been good enough, for not having known enough, for not having done enough to have saved the patient. Needless to say, many nurse veterans exhibit all the classical and nonclassical signs of posttraumatic stress disorders that are present in their male counterparts.

Just as for other Vietnam veterans, nurses have been bitter and resentful at the "dysreception"* that met them upon their return from Vietnam. Female veterans are, in fact, angry. They are angry because they gave all they had, and no one seemed to care; angry because their inner world of torment will not go away; angry because they left so much of their own vitality in Vietnam; and angry because they had to send so much of themselves back home in body bags. They feel helpless and unloved, even though there are those who want to help and love them. Feeling hurt, they are angry because they are unable to ask for help. So conditioned to helping others, they long ago lost sight of their own human needs. Perhaps the most frustrating and generating much anger is their difficulty in falling and remaining in love, or even maintaining satisfying relationships with men or women.

Some nurses have a strong desire to marry, settle down, and raise a family. Despite this, they may paradoxically react to such a prospect with repulsion. Remembering having cared for wounded and dying soldiers in Vietnam, they fear that raising children will once again drain them of every ounce of themselves. Many do not want to ever be so depended upon

---

* The term "dysreception" was coined by one of us and appears in: Erwin Parson, "The Reparation of the Self: Clinical and Theoretical Dimensions in the Treatment of Vietnam Combat Veterans," *Journal of Contemporary Psychotherapy* 14 (1984), pp. 4–51.

again. In addition, many women feel unable to *surrender* emotionally to a relationship. They feel that they must always be in charge and on guard; and they tend to habitually scrutinize because of the dread that "I mustn't make a mistake, not this time; I must be sure." Some of this defensiveness also stems from a deep feeling of being unlovable and unworthy of unrequited love and affection from others. Other nurses were so "programmed" and conditioned in Vietnam to be the giving one in a relationship that now they want relationships in which they are fully in charge. They seek out helpless and ineffectual men as husbands and lovers who will be completely dependent on them. Involvement with men who require endless nurturing is one pattern that characterizes their relationships.

In another pattern, these women desire to be totally taken care of by men. It's payback time. Deep within her, the nurse veteran needs to *undo* some of the "harm" she brought on some GI she had "failed" to help adequately in Vietnam. Because of deep self-lacerating guilt and fear over not having done the right thing in tending her patients, such a woman may abdicate the caring role, and unconsciously seek out a man who will take care of her instead. To allow a man to take care of her may be the equivalent in her mind of undoing the caretaker's role that brought her such pain and low self-esteem. Whichever pattern the nurse follows, she often reacts with periods of heightened ambivalence: she gets close, then backs off; she might feel happy, then, unexpectedly and unexplainably, becomes angry, moody, and morose.

Issues of child-rearing are to the female veteran similar to those of the male veteran discussed in Chapter 6, "Family Life after Vietnam." Some nurse-mothers feel easily drained by their young children's demands, and some resent having to meet their children's needs. Others appear as if they have indeed given all they will ever have to give another human being. Though many want to be taken care of, they also paradoxically want to escape from anyone offering kindness and understanding. Unable to adequately give or receive love, many remain single, get divorced and never have children. The reasons for these decisions and behaviors are many and complex, and vary from one woman to another. Basically, we believe that many Vietnam nurse veterans have made these decisions because of what we call a "generic block to intimacy and closeness." This blocking relates to a powerful unconscious desire to avoid pain—

the pain that comes from getting "too" close to other human beings. Blocking human closeness avoids human losses by avoiding human relationships.

To date, there has been only one study on female nurses who served in Vietnam. A 97% rate of participation in this study revealed the nurses' readiness to discuss personal war experiences. Conducted in 1982 by Jenny Schnaier,[3] it has some methodological limitations but contains important information on these veterans' mental health adjustment. Based on its sample of 87 women, the study shows that significant war related problems continue to plague these veterans today. Posttraumatic symptoms stemming from the war include: suicidal thoughts in 27.6%; feelings of alienation in 19%; and feeling depressed between 15 and 30 times per month in 19%. Though almost 50% had sought mental health services for postwar readjustment problems, only 43% of those who sought mental health services brought up Vietnam in their therapies as an important possible source of their current problems. In addition, many women expressed distrust, skepticism, and cynicism toward governmental agencies.

With regard to each woman's perception of the relative benefit or harm of her Vietnam experience, Schnaier's study found that 45% felt Vietnam had been a positive experience, while 32% rated it as a negative experience. Whereas the latter response is not at all surprising given the nurses' extraordinary exposure to violence, death, and suffering and given the "dysreception," the former is.

Interestingly enough, despite the suffering and loss that characterized Vietnam, some women came away with some very special experiences. Some had become mature human beings there. Others attributed the enhancing of their personal and professional growth to their Vietnam experience. Even some of the women who suffer most from PTSD symptoms were able to "salvage" something positive out of an otherwise negative situation. Actually, we do not find to be surprising that more women in the sample viewed Vietnam as a positive experience. We trust that the newly congressionally mandated national assessment study of Vietnam veterans will shed new light on these and many other issues pertaining to female veterans.

Upon their return from Vietnam, many nurses sought jobs that would keep them enmeshed in their psychological quagmire. They sought work in emergency medical settings and crisis centers because of their great unconscious need to continue their "super-savior" role. This type of behavior and dynamics represents a kind of *reliving in vivo*. They are able to "keep busy" while feeding their residual fantasies of saving everyone.

Dr. John Russell Smith, in his paper entitled "Personal Responsibility and Posttraumatic Stress Reactions," has described the case of M, a nurse who served in Vietnam:[7]

> M, a Boston nurse who had served in Vietnam, described her current difficulties in a recent interview. She was haunted by troubling thoughts of Vietnam and described her inability to stay in bed at night without the light on. Since her return, she indicated that not a week had gone by without recurrent thoughts about the decisions she had made in Vietnam. She gave the example of one night, when, with a short-handed unit, she became the triage officer whose duty it was to assess the gravity of injuries, and to select, given the limited treatment resources, those soldiers too severely wounded to die. As ostensibly neutral non-combatants, despite their vigorous objections, medical staff was required to treat both Americans and any wounded North Vietnam prisoners. Torn over an oath to care for the injured, she followed common practice and selected Americans with even minor injury for treatment while leaving North Vietnamese prisoners, with severe but treatable injuries to die.
>
> Despite objections, American and North Vietnamese patients were often placed on the same ward. The nursing staff loyal to their American charges, were often reluctant to care for the Vietnamese. One evening, M volunteered to change dressing on a severely burned Vietnamese for whom no one else would care. As she was changing the bandages and cleaning the wounds, the prisoner suddenly grabbed a pair of scissors and lunged at her. Narrowly escaping, she called for a pair of military guards "to take care of" him. The military guards quickly hustled him off the ward. A short time later, they returned to assure her that he would no longer bother her and that he had been taken care of. She has a recurrent nightmare about this incident.
>
> Because of a recent flashback experience she no longer carries scissors. On this particular day in the operating room, a fellow nurse announced that she was reaching into the pocket of M's uniform for a pair of scissors. As the nurse did so, M panicked, turned and struck the other nurse.
>
> Until her interview, she had never spoken with anyone about the earlier incident. Though highly regarded by her peers, she feels ashamed

and inadequate about her performance as a nurse in Vietnam. Afraid to look into the future, she refuses to look at the past, feeling that if she did, she would start crying and never stop.[11]

As we can see from the above account, M's Vietnam experiences continue to interfere with her life and happiness in very significant ways. Intense fear and panic remain with her as painful and internally disorganizing as the day she was attacked by the NVA prisoner.

More methodologically sound research on the special readjustment needs of female veterans is important. The Congress has recently determined that a national needs assessment study of Vietnam veterans is essential. It will be the first to include female veterans in its sample. This initiative, we trust, will further elucidate the complexities of the readjustment process in female nurse veterans.

Any useful psychotherapy with the Vietnam nurse veteran will have to be sophisticated enough to take into account her sociocultural role as a "woman," her identity as a "woman" in a rigid and traditionally male military system, her identity as a "woman" in a combat zone, and her posttraumatic stress reactions and/or disorders. It is hoped that mental health providers will become fully aware of and sensitive to the QIC dynamics to better address the readjustment needs of this special population.

The Black Vietnam Veteran

Historically, black Americans have always served their country well; they have fought in every American war. For the most part, their motiviation in serving came from an ardent desire to prove themselves as worthy citizens. They believed that since military service ranked so high among American ideals, their participation would earn them the respect, personal freedom from discrimination, and benefits accorded other groups of Americans. Though it may be that some blacks had different motivations for military service, respect and its accompanying benefits were the overriding reasons for serving in the military for the majority of black Americans.

Up to the latter part of the 1960s, most black Americans believed that racism and discrimination could be overcome by service in the military. However, after 1967 black leaders spoke out against injustice and discrepancy of having a black man fight in a foreign war against people of color.[8] Black people spoke out, moreover, against racist practices against black Americans. They made it clear that sending black men to fight for someone else's freedom, while they themselves were still under the yoke of racism and oppression, was contradictory. This "Creed–Deed" contradiction, in conjunction with the "Service–Exclusion" contradiction—or requiring blacks to fight while still oppressed—was eloquently articulated by Dr. Martin Luther King, Jr., in terms of a powerful paradox[9]:

> We are taking young black men who have been crippled by our society and sending them 8,000 miles away to guarantee liberties in Southeast Asia which they have not found in Southwest Georgia or in East Harlem. So we have been repeatedly faced with the cruel irony of watching Negro and white boys on TV screens as they kill and die together for a nation that has been unable to seat them together at the same school. So, we watch them in brutal solidarity burning the huts of a poor village, but we realize that they could never live on the same block in Detroit.

Soldiers are in the business of killing: this is the job for which they have been trained; this is their obligation. Though the soldier has been taught to kill, most need some personal philosophy that can offer meaning to his actions on the battlefield. According to Dr. Charles Moskos, in his paper "Why Men Fight: American Combat Soldiers in Vietnam"[10]: "Whether motivated by patriotism or a belief that he is fighting for a just cause, the effective soldier is ultimately an ideologically inspired soldier."

The period between 1965 and 1967 was characterized by high ideological inspiration among our soldiers in Vietnam.[11] During these years morale was high, and most soldiers believed they were fighting for a just cause—defending freedom abroad to safeguard America and the free world. However, from 1968 to the end of the Vietnam War in 1975, demoralization, confusion, and anger grew rampant among the men. Extreme political apathy and a lack of direction and clear mandate, eroded the ideological bedrock of the earlier period. This erosion interfered with the passing down of ideals to the later soldiers deployed in Vietnam.

During the late 1960s, most soldiers, drafted or volunteering for service in Vietnam, were not as interested in winning the war as they were in returning home alive. Some may ask: "If the war was such a negative experience and the would-be soldier was so uncommitted to fighting in the first place, why then did he go to Vietnam?" The complexity of this question, like any other question that involves the motives and behaviors of a large number of people, defies any easy explanation.

Actually, many men made a conscious decision *not* to be drafted. There are numerous accounts about the extent to which some men went to avoid being drafted. Some paid their physicians to produce false reports of their unsuitability for military service; others went to Canada or elsewhere abroad. Still others were able to use their affluence and political influence to avoid military service. As pointed out in the *Report of the National Working Group on Black Vietnam Veterans*[12]: "Many of the most affluent members of society who did not fail their physicals were able to secure deferments or able to secure special assignments as officers in the Air Force, Navy, and Coast Guard to avoid Vietnam combat. The fighting in Vietnam was thus on the shoulders of a disproportionate number of blacks and other minorities," as well as on the shoulders of indigent white Americans.

Evolving forth from the Johnson Administration's War on Poverty initiatives, "the Department of Defense devised a means of inducting individuals who were previously ineligible for military service. This effort was formally known as *Project 100,000*."[13] The Project intended to draft at least 100,000 youths who might otherwise have gone to prison or been totally excluded from an opportunity to secure a better economic future for themselves. Though this program appeared to have been motivated by noble and humane ideals, its implementation proved harmful to minorities and to indigent white Americans.[14] For the combat skills given these inductees could not be transferred to meaningful civilian occupations.[12]

Those men who chose to go to Vietnam went for the following reasons: (1) patriotism; (2) familial pressure and a tradition of military service; (3) to follow in their father's footsteps by military service; (4) unconsciously attempting to undo the death of a father, uncle, or brother in World War II or Korea; (5) the anticipated excitement of war; (6) to develop and refine their masculine identity; (7) to escape boredom; (8) to help find direction in their life; (9) to open avenues to a secure future; and (10) they felt they had no choice but to serve, because of limited options owing to their lower socioeconomic level. Many have thus referred to the Vietnam War as a war of the lower classes.

We believe that the black soldiers' capacity to develop *ideological inspiration* in Vietnam was undercut by a number of significant factors. One was the stigma associated with fighting an unpopular war, which meant being twice rejected—first by black Americans, then by society at large. Black soldiers also felt conflicts about fighting against a poor agrarian people, so much like themselves. The Vietnamese nationals were perceived by many as a vulnerable racial minority fighting off a Superpower; thus, black soldiers came to admire the Vietnamese's resilience and resolve to fight and survive. Much of this admiration stemmed from his own experiences as a black struggling against racism in America—against the *same* Superpower. For many of these black soldiers, the Third World status of the Vietnamese created within them a powerful emotional bonding with the Vietnamese.[15] Such bonding led to a profound inner conflict when they had to kill the Vietnamese. Underlying this emotional link with the Vietnamese, was the process of psychological identification, which one of us has referred to as "gook-identification," defined as "the conscious and unconscious emotional identification with the devalued, maligned, abused, and helpless aspects of the Vietnamese people, by the black soldier."[15] Killing the Vietnamese, then, was experienced by the soldier as killing and destroying aspects of himself.

Scientific support for the *black–Vietnamese* dynamics described above is contained in a new study reported by Drs. Yager, Laufer, and Gallops. These scientists investigated among a number of other variables, the symptoms of black and white veterans *who participated in abusive violence (atrocities) against the Vietnamese.* They were interested in learning whether symptom differences would be found between these black and white veterans. Analyzing their data, the authors stated: "What struck us most forcefully was the discrepancy between *whites' and blacks' feelings toward the Vietnamese*"[16] [italics added]. In general, they found that whereas blacks' attitudes toward the Vietnamese were marked by positive feelings (e.g., "I think those people was just trying to survive" or "I couldn't get used to the killing, and I'd have nightmares and dreams"[16]), whites' feelings were negative (e.g., "Killing a gook was nothing really. It didn't bother me at all"[16]) Some have asked: "If blacks felt this way, how could they have committed atrocities against the Vietnamese?" Our response is that every young soldier who fought in combat was caught up in the psychotic reality of the terrorism of this guerrilla war. And atrocity is an inherent activity in any guerrilla war. Blacks were caught up in this as any other soldier. They participated in atrocity, just as they participated in other aspects of the war. Blacks were expected to be good soldiers, and a good soldier did as he was ordered to do, or did what the immediate situation required. In our experience, most black veterans who report having committed atrocities against the Vietnamese, did not seem aware that they were engaged in acts for which they would suffer guilt at a later time. As James points out, "When I was over there I was so confused, I didn't know what I was doing. I am not making excuses for myself and what I did, but I must say that if I was as rational as I am now, I would not have done any violent acts against the Vietnamese. But it's too late now. When you're in war, you're in war. You do what warriors do: they fuck people up; that's it! Now that I am back, now I feel guilty, but I wasn't guilty then, because of the craziness of it all. Some of us were so numbed out anyway, we couldn't ever feel nothing. Morality and compassion were thrown out of the window."

This black–white disparity of feelings for the Vietnamese is not intended to suggest that there were no blacks who despised or hated the Vietnamese, or that there were no whites who had positive feelings for the Vietnamese. The point we wish to make is that black and white soldiers in Vietnam may well have experienced their combat involvement in a different way, and that this difference may have great relevance for how one understands the unique readjustment plight of black Vietnam veterans. It is clear to us that the war experience was different in general for blacks and for whites. Black soldiers' identification with the Vietnamese made them more vulnerable to developing higher levels of posttraumatic symptoms, as theorized by one of us in 1981[14] and now substantiated by research evidence.

In 1968, following the assassination of Dr. Martin Luther King, Jr., black soldiers became fed up and angry. More than ever before, they questioned why they were fighting in Southeast Asia when in fact they would not be safe even in their own hometowns. "It made no damn sense," said "J.J.," a black combat veteran. "I didn't want to fight anymore. For what?" The Communists took advantage of Dr. King's assassination by broadcasting over Radio Hanoi a number of messages aimed at demoralizing "the brothers." In Wallace Terry's *Bloods: An Oral History of the Vietnam War by Black Veterans,* Richard Ford III, a black Lurp with the 25th Infantry Division, describes this period[17]:

Right after Tet, the mail helicopter got shot down. We moved to Tam Ky. We didn't have any mail in about three weeks. Then this lady by the name of Hanoi Hellen come on the radio. She had a letter belonging to Sir Drawers. From the chopper that was shot down. She read the letter from his wife about how she miss him. But that didn't unsettle the brothers as much as when she came on the air after Martin Luther King died, and they was rioting back home. She was saying, 'Soul brother, go home. Whitey raping your mothers and your daughters, burning down your homes. What are you here for? This is not your war. The war is a trick of the Capitalist empire to get rid of the blacks.'

The assassination of Dr. King was a trying and painful time for black soldiers in Vietnam; and the pressures exerted by the Communists through Radio Hanoi seemed to threaten to overthrow and overrun their confidence and loyalty to America. But these soldiers resisted the "invitation" of the Communists to defect. Regarding this issue, Wallace Terry states in his Introduction to *Bloods,* "The loyalty of the black Vietnam War veteran stood a greater test on the battleground than did the loyalty of any other American soldier in Vietnam; his patriotism begs a special salute at home."[17]

After Dr. King's death, a wave of racial hatred spread among the troops. Blacks no longer acquiesced to the status quo of racism. They resisted discriminatory practices from their white superiors and peers. This new sense of black nationalism produced an intense reaction by whites. From Binkin and Eitelberg, "Black consciousness fed white racism."[13] Some soldiers—both black and white—resorted to violence, creating a war within the war. And, as always, violence spawned violence. Racial slurs, "fraggings," and race riots were instigated by both sides. Provocative whites burned KKK-type crosses and flew the Confederate flag.

The racial rift divided certain units into two armed camps: "all blacks" and "all whites." Racial violence sparked by the American response to the Civil Rights movement and enflamed by the assassination of Dr. King, made this period in American history different for the black soldier than for any other racial or ethnic group of Americans who served in Vietnam. Black rage created dangerous confrontations with officers and peers. Militancy—for any cause, for any reason—in the military, except in combat, is unthinkable; however, blacks' fury and determination were so strong and pervasive that normal military codes of deportment were overlooked and violated by black soldiers. The military fought back: "dissident" blacks were given administrative discharges. Though not quite a dishonorable discharge, this is a type of discharge given under less-than-honorable circumstances. In general, blacks were given a disproportionate number of these discharges.[18]

Back home from Vietnam, the black veteran found that unemployment was higher than when he had left. To his utter shock and dismay, he discovered that his military combat experience had no value for civilian employment. Years earlier in 1966, Project 100,000 was started by the Department of Defense to "rehabilitate" the nation's "subterranean poor."[13] Central to the Project's objective was to offer the nation's indigent youths a chance for a better future. Between 1966 and 1969, the program recruited approximately 246,000 youths, the majority of whom were black. Because of their limited education and skills, these inductees were placed in dead-end military occupations, without a future.

With a less-than-honorable discharge (widely called "bad paper" discharges), unmarketable skills in the workplace, and high unemployment, the black returnee became distraught, mortified, and very bitter. For those returning with severe drug and alcohol problems, social services were often nonexistent, inaccessible, or insensitive to his experiences both in Vietnam and back home. For these veterans and for those with high levels of posttraumatic stress reactions and disorders, there was little if any treatment available to rehabilitate and return them to the (bleak) job market. During this time, jobs were fewer for all Americans; however, for those who were unskilled, unemployment and underemployment were severe problems.

Ultimately, the black veteran had to deal with a three-pronged problem, which one of us has referred to elsewhere as the "tripartite adaptational dilemma"[14] (TAD). Thus, the black veteran is faced with readjustment challenges in three areas: (1) his identity as a "black-American—descendant of slaves; (2) the stigma of having served in Vietnam; and (3) the adverse psychological effects of combat stress (postcombat stress reactions or posttraumatic stress disorders). Today, for psychotherapy to be effective with this group of veterans, all three aspects of TAD need to be addressed. In our experience, the counselors and therapists that have been the most successful with black veterans have prepared themselves personally and professionally for this transcultural work of helping the black Vietnam veteran.[14]

The most successful counselors and therapists, moreover, have educated themselves in two specific areas: (1) African-American history, including the slavery era and the Civil Rights movement; and (2) the psychological and social effects of combat trauma and other catastrophic event(s) on the mind and personality of black Americans. Additionally, when necessary, successful clinicians have consulted with other professionals who are competent in clinical interventions with black people. Inherent in the black veteran's identity as a "black" American is his *bicultural* nature—the black male/female veteran is *both* African *and* American. Dedicated professionals have kept this point in mind throughout the therapy process.

The following two profiles illustrate the kinds of readjustment concerns plaguing black Vietnam veterans today:

> Bruce is a black Vietnam veteran who served during the Tet Counteroffensive of 1968 in South Vietnam. He was involved in the defense of the city of Hue and saw "lots of action" along the DMZ. He lost 12 buddies during his 12 months in Vietnam. During search-and-destroy missions, and during firefights with the VC and the NVA, he killed a relatively large number of VC and NVA troops. After these missions, Bruce became depressed and very angry: "I shouldn't even be here killing these poor people; they are only trying to survive. No black guys should be killing Vietnamese people. They didn't do us no harm. I feel bad for being suckered into committing these crimes. Now I have all kinds of nightmares and real bad flashbacks. I can't get close to nobody. I just want to be left alone. I am real uptight, depressed, lonely, and filled with rage. I feel I want to kill somebody most of the time. I just don't like living this way." He carried his guilt back home after the war. It has caused problems in his marriage. He's now divorced for the second time, and though he wants to marry again, he is also aware now that his past lack of success may be related to unresolved issues from Vietnam. "I need help with Vietnam, so I can have a better life."

In Bruce's case, the treatment strategy involved taking into account four areas of difficulties during the course of his treatment. Since his immediate problems seem to revolve around Vietnam, the recommendation is to begin by exploring memories of Vietnam; second, examining more closely his level of current functioning in relationships and work; third, exploring issues of identity related to being a "black" American; and fourth, exploring issues around the stigma of being associated with the Vietnam War and, moreover, being rejected by America for having answered the call to serve in that war.

> William is a black Vietnam veteran who served in a noncombat support role in Nha Trang during 1968 and 1969. He did not see combat directly, but he was close to intense fighting and was fully aware of all major and minor battles and firefights. A number of rocket and mortar attacks had been made on his compound, on the average of two per week. On six occasions he witnessed soldiers on his compound killed by rocket rounds. William has not been able to hold a job since coming home in late 1969. He complains of nightmares depicting "wasted and mangled bodies," and his being chased by a VC with a big rocket in his hand—"for me." William has never been married, even though he had lots of girlfriends in high school and prior to going to Vietnam. He said, "I'm just not the same person anymore. I get into a lot of fights. I like playing with weapons. I am tired of hurting people. I want some help. You know, I am from a good, religious family. I was brought up the right way by my parents. They never fought at all; no problems, no nothing like that. But look how I turned out. I can't believe it myself. I am ashamed of myself— about the things I didn't do in 'Nam. I just feel I should have been doing something to help those poor people who were killed on the compound and those getting killed in the bush. I have no job, no place to stay. Man, I am really hurting. I also have this young girl who I like a lot, and I know she cares for me, but I feel like a cripple inside; I can't open up to her; I can't get close to her. When I do, I get panicky, and I draw back. I want to give her a lot of myself; I want to get to know her and to have her know me too. I just can't. Another thing, not having a job and not having my own place, makes me ashamed around her; it's like I am not a man." William also discussed his drug and alcohol problems both in the past and in the present.

An interesting question arising in William's case was whether to diagnose his symptoms as PTSD. The clinician needed to determine not only the "existence of a recognizable stressor"[4] (i.e., serving in Vietnam), but also whether the identified stressor was sufficiently pernicious to "evoke significant symptoms of distress in almost anyone."[4] The fact that William did not engage the enemy in direct battle nor was placed in direct line of enemy fire might lead some clinicians to decide he did not strictly meet all criteria for the PTSD diagnosis. This is a fact since the structure and intent of the DSM-III* is to reduce variability among those who make diagnoses, by featuring specific criteria ("criterion-referenced") involving the presence, number, and duration of specific symptoms.

In this case, the clinician believed that William's constant state of fear and anxious arousal in Vietnam—seeing dead bodies, not knowing when the next shell would hit, not being able to run, hide, or fight back (as in an "ambush")—along with a significant number of PTSD symptoms-especially the nightmares and the great alteration in his pre- and post-war personality functioning—led to a diagnosis of PTSD. Regarding black veterans as a group, they may tend to succumb to stress reactions and symptoms, without having been in combat.[19] The reasons for this are not clear, though some speculative and hypothetical assumptions have been made elsewhere.[14]

William's treatment was planned to include three phases. First, the counselor, feeling that he could help William, reassured him that he could be helped, and proceeded to describe the entire treatment plan. (It is during this initial phase of the treatment that the therapist or counselor also articulates to the veteran his understanding of the problem, and what the veteran could reasonably expect during the course of the treatment.) In the second phase, William's immediate needs were addressed. He was helped to secure food stamps, a place to live, and a part-time job in a store in the community; he was helped in submitting to the VA Regional Office for his benefits and for possible compensation for a service-connected disability. Third, William was also assisted, during the third phase of the treatment, in working through his traumatic experiences in Vietnam. Not all black veterans require the first two phases of this three-pronged treatment approach, though from our experience most black veterans seeking readjustment services do.

* *The Diagnostic and Statistical Manual of Mental Disorders*, 3rd edition, American Psychiatric Association. This manual is the official document widely used to make diagnoses. Its significant shortcomings in the diagnosis of PTSD are now well documented.

In Bruce's case, because he was functioning at a much higher level psychologically and was self-sufficient, phases 1 and 2 were unnecessary. Treatment with Bruce began at the third phase level, during which time issues of Vietnam were fully explored as well as his pre-Vietnam experiences: and techniques were taught to help him relax; deal with issues of identity; and find meaning in life.

THE HISPANIC VIETNAM VETERAN

Hispanics have a glorious, lofty, and peerless history of military service in this country. Hispanic soldiers have always felt great pride in their effectiveness as soldiers in war. However, much of the blacks' negative experience in terms of discrimination was also true for Mexican-Americans and Puerto Rican soldiers. The Hispanic soldier's day-to-day experience of Vietnam depended on a number of factors including his geographic origin, cultural values, and degree of acculturation and assimilation into American society. Another important factor for the Hispanic was language. Though Mexican-Americans ("Chicanos"), for the most part, had little or no problems with the English language, Puerto Ricans appeared to have had more difficulty during military service because of the language barrier, especially if they were from Puerto Rico. Most Puerto Ricans who were highly acculturated (from New York, New Jersey, and Boston) had an easier time than their countrymen from Puerto Rico. In fact, those from rural Puerto Rico experienced perhaps the *most* stress of any minority group during the militarization process, from basic training onward. Between entering the military, experiencing discrimination, being away from the familiar, and not knowing the English language—not understanding what was expected of him—the rural native Puerto Rican experienced the most severe form of "culture shock."

The Puerto Rican from rural areas found that going to Vietnam was a "double culture shock"—entering the non-Spanish speaking world of military life and entering Vietnam, a land of different culture, language, and customs. Because of his relatively limited exposure to diverse linguistic, conceptual, cultural, and geographic experiences, the usual problems and stresses of war were compounded for this soldier. However, on another level, according to Edwino Rivera Ayala, Director of the San Juan

Vet Center ("Centro De Veterano"), the soldier from rural Puerto Rico found Vietnam—its terrain, vegetation, and climate—similar to his homeland. He states, "I have met some veterans who have not come out of Vietnam mentally because there are a lot of things on this Island that resemble Vietnam. They are still thinking they are in Nam, hiding, not coming out to see people. Some of these veterans experience nearly continuous flashbacks because of the resemblance between Vietnam and Puerto Rico."[20]

Urban native Puerto Ricans had still a different experience. In many respects, Vietnam was a culture shock for them with its heavy foliage, rough terrain, and "bush" countryside—the very features of Vietnam the rural Puerto Rican soldier found to be familiar.

Most Hispanic soldiers, like blacks, identified with the Vietnamese nationals as a tough people trying to survive against a Superpower. Their own struggles with discrimination and systematic exclusion made the identification easy to establish and personal. The relatively dark skin and hair texture of Mexican-Americans and Puerto Ricans were similar to those of the Vietnamese. Thus, many Hispanic soldiers experienced an emotional bonding with the Vietnamese—as did black soldiers[15]—which tended to make killing them so much more difficult, and resulted in much more guilt and personal remorse.

Traditionally, Mexican-Americans have identified themselves as warriors, and have performed extremely well over the years in the military. As Dr. Gregorio Pēna III, a Mexican-American psychologist, points out, "Historically, war has been good to Hispanics in this country; it brought people out of the fields to bear arms and they distinguished themselves . . . . No other culture in this country is so well-decorated and has been so well-recognized in the field of battle as Mexican-Americans."[20] Like black soldiers, Hispanics wanted to prove themselves as valiant warriors. And they did. Puerto Ricans in Vietnam wanted to fight in the spirit of the "65th," an all-Puerto Rican fighting unit renowned for storming up a dangerous hill overlooking Chorwan during the Korean War. And they, along with Mexican-Americans, brought much deserved respect and credit to Hispanics in the Vietnam War.

Like most other Vietnam veterans, Hispanic returnees were disappointed, frustrated, and bitter over the rejection and revilement that met them in the United States as well as Puerto Rico. Many Puerto Rican veterans have reported hearing the same negative stereotypes of the Vietnam veteran in America and Puerto Rico.

Like other minority Vietnam veterans, Hispanic returnees found conditions in the United States and in Puerto Rico to be worse than when they had left. Jobs were much harder to find. In fact, very high unemployment still characterizes both Hispanic veteran populations. From a psychocultural perspective, Hispanic men expect themselves to be the head of their families. Their wives expect this of them as well. Being employed and able to provide for their families is so deeply rooted in their culture that unemployed Hispanic veterans may suffer from significant psychological problems involving their self-concept and self-esteem. Consequently, for the Hispanic veteran, being unemployed cuts away and attacks not only some aspect of his self-concept, but assaults "viciously" his self-as-a-whole. The Hispanic male's feeling of well-being is directly linked to his mental, physical, social, *and* economic capacity to be in charge—at the head—of his family. Thus, having to depend on "handouts" or the "goodwill" of friends and relatives, or on welfare checks—unlike prevailing stereotypes would lead one to believe—was shameful to the Hispanic male's conception of self.

Recent research findings[19] reveal that black and Chicano Vietnam veterans suffer more stress symptoms than do white veterans. For these veterans, a combination of *de facto* discrimination and their stress-related problems has prevented them from fulfilling their culturally defined role as provider and protector of their families. It is clear that being unemployed—jobless and penniless—has a devastating impact on most men's self-esteem and self-evaluation—regardless of race, culture, or class. This has been borne out by Harry Maurer, an investigating journalist, in his book, *Not Working*. Maurer reports the personal stories of unemployed men and women of various ages, religions, and ethnic and racial groups. He examines the "human damage" experienced by these individuals[21]:

> Unemployed people have been robbed of something, and they know it. The bewilderment they often express is like that of the homeowner who returns to find rooms ransacked, valuables and beloved objects missing. The sense of violence and invasion, the feelings of fear and loss and helplessness descend with the same stunning force when a worker is deprived of work. And the loss is much greater, because work . . . remains a *fundamental human need*. [italics added]

When working is linked to profound issues of the self—deeply rooted in the psychocultural matrix of the personality—unemployment takes on a more devastating and stunning force. For the man whose cultural values require him to head his household or suffer personal psychological "ruin," being unemployed is a most severe blow to the self and to well-being. Thus, we often observe that Chicano, Puerto Rican, and black veterans who seek assistance stress their need for a job. It is only later—perhaps much later—that purely psychological matters can be attended to more directly with these veterans.

Posttraumatic stress reactions and disorders stemming from service in Vietnam afflict proportionately more black and Chicano veterans than white veterans. These veterans have symptoms of flashbacks, nightmares, high levels of anxiety, depression, sleep disturbances, and concentration and memory impairment, just as in the larger population of veterans with mental symptoms and readjustment problems. However, minority veterans, especially Hispanics, may experience their stress symptoms with a greater degree of subjective discomfort, because of the vulnerability deeply felt in relation to their sense of psychological, spiritual, social, and economic emasculation. Posttraumatic stress symptoms are exacerbated by the absence of a personal sense of masculine control in these veterans.

Contributing to the intensification of symptoms and inner distress, moreover, is their cultural requirement that men should not ask or cry for help. Emotional expressiveness is not condoned by the culture of the Hispanic. It is viewed as a sign of weakness, not of manhood and control. *Controlarse* (control yourself) is a basic cultural mandate. "As Latino, as a Hispanic, Puerto Rican, you grow up believing men aren't supposed to cry; you're supposed to hold your feelings within . . . we are taught not to show even in the most extreme circumstances. . . .[T]he macho thing was war. I remember the first serious cry I had when I was in Vietnam and I remember my thoughts then were, 'If Pop saw me crying, he'd get mad.'"[20] These are the words of Angel Almedina, Director of the Manhattan Vet Center, a Puerto Rican Vietnam combat veteran from New York City.

We believe that the Hispanic veteran is faced with a three-pronged readjustment problem we call the "tripartite adaptational challenge" (TAC). He is called upon to: (1) deal effectively with his *dual-cultural* identity (Hispanic and Euro-American); (2) overcome the stigma of having served in Vietnam; and (3) overcome the adverse effects of PTSD and related reactions and readjustment difficulties.

The following two case histories demonstrate some of the important issues that Hispanic Vietnam veterans present to the therapist or counselor when they seek assistance for mental, interpersonal, and social readjustment problems.

> Eduardo sought help for nightmares, flashbacks, and "problemas con mi familia" (family problems or problems with my family). In addition to his anxiety and general discomfort in being in the presence of "a foreigner" having only come to New York 3 years earlier with his wife and children, he was very uncomfortable with his use of the English language. He was embarrassed about having to have his 10-year-old son act as interpreter. He explained his alienation from his family and the personal pain and anguish this had caused him since he came back from Vietnam. He had always had a great relationship with his parents, siblings, and other relatives. With a voice filled with much trepidation, loss, and great regret, he said, "I don't have that anymore."
>
> Eduardo served in Vietnam from 1968 to 1970, and saw considerable combat in some of the most heated and devastating battles in Vietnam. At 38 years of age, married for the second time, unemployed, and with many familial difficulties, this Hispanic veteran sought assistance in restoring his psychological control over his symptoms, but more importantly, in restoring his self-confidence and self-esteem as a responsible and worthwhile human being—husband, father, and provider, at the head of his family.

Though the therapist's assessment of Eduardo revealed a chronic PTSD, he first moved toward addressing the veteran's immediate problems. Aware of the Hispanic *cultural ethos,* which stress respect and dignity, the therapist immediately replaced the veteran's son as interpreter.* He had seen that Eduardo, as a veteran, a man—a Hispanic man, had felt his dominance and control slipping away to his son during the interview. Eduardo was deeply embarrassed and humiliated in the presence of the therapist, who he viewed as an outsider and foreigner—in many respects, an intruder. By replacing the son, and thus showing Eduardo that he was aware of his discomfort, the therapist alleviated Eduardo's discomfort,

---

* A bilingual therapist is highly preferred in any transcultural treatment with Hispanics. However, when such is not available, the next best situation would be an interpreter—in certain types of therapeutic interactions.

while offering him reassurance that he was understood. The therapist, moreover, summarized to Eduardo what he had heard and understood during the initial interview. This articulation in English of his inner self and feelings further helped Eduardo feel understood, and finally he allowed himself to relax. He felt respected and understood.

The Hispanic veteran needs to feel dignified and respected (*respecto*) in his early interactions in counseling or therapy. Many Hispanic veterans leave the initial session never to return, since the therapist failed to give respect and understanding. *Machismo* is also a vital aspect of Hispanic ethos. Male superiority is important to the Hispanic. The therapist, then, must be aware of his or her own values and feelings in this area. A therapist who believes strongly in the equality of the sexes and is unable to suspend this belief during therapy may be unable to work effectively with this population. Often, those therapists who become very judgmental "run the client out of the treatment," prematurely.

In Eduardo's case, the therapist proceeded to intervene in a concrete and immediate manner by contacting available community human services, unemployment office services, veterans benefits office, etc. Meeting these immediate needs made it possible for the therapist to focus on Eduardo's mental symptoms—his anxiety, depression, flashbacks, nightmares, and sleep disturbance. Eventually, steps were taken toward integrating Eduardo's wife, children, and parents into the therapy. (In most successful treatments with Hispanics, the family's involvement is crucial.) As *confianza* (trusting relationship) developed in the treatment, Eduardo was well on the way to recovering from Vietnam and finding tranquility and increased self-esteem.

> Juan is a Mexican-American Vietnam veteran who served in heavy combat in Vietnam during 1969. His chief complaint to the counselor was his belief that God was now punishing him for what he had done in Vietnam. He also expressed deep concern about his inability to hold a job as well as his "giving in" to PTSD symptoms. "I felt very strange when I got back from 'Nam; my family didn't know me. That really bothered me and bothers me now, a lot." Because of his actions in the war, he felt he had violated his loyalty to God and his family. Juan found it hard to discuss his Vietnam experience, and actually "downplayed" the importance of Vietnam, though he ambivalently made reference to the war as having adversely affected his relationship to God and his family.

For Juan to be helped, the therapist needed to understand the all-encompassing nature of Catholicism to Juan. Though it is not unusual for a veteran of *any* war to tell a counselor or therapist about the "sinfulness" of killing, this lamentation takes on much greater significance with the Mexican-American Vietnam veteran. In their cultural ethos, loyalty to God and to family are core issues. Juan, a deeply religious man when he went to Vietnam, believes God has forsaken him because of his "bad activities" there. He believes that his readjustment problems are a result of God's displeasure with him.

Another central issue attended to by the therapist was Juan's shattered sense of *macho* (manhood). Like most other Vietnam veterans we have treated, Juan struggled with the self-esteem-devastating perception that he had "given in" to postcombat symptoms. Juan felt "less than a man for not being strong enough" to withstand the bad memories and experiences of Vietnam.

That Juan downplayed the importance of Vietnam provided the therapist with one side of his ambivalence, and was understood as a "ditch effort" to preserve his self-esteem from total evaporation. For if Vietnam was the source of his mental and spiritual demise, then not making it important to himself and to the therapist was his way, psychologically, of "shoring up" his fragile and tenuous self-concept. In this case, the therapist did not "force the issue" about Vietnam, but, during the sessions, was very alert to the many diverse derivatives of the Vietnam experience that Juan talked about indirectly for several months.

When Juan was ready to discuss his experiences in Vietnam in greater detail, he did so. Juan was appreciative of the therapist's sensitivity. One of his greatest fears before seeking assistance with a mental health professional, was that he would not be understood, and that "some Anglo therapist was going to rip my guts apart about Vietnam right away."* Like most minority individuals seeking mental health services, Juan did not expect to be understood and anticipated being "put down" by the professional. The therapist's cultural sensitivity preserved Juan's self-respect by paying attention to his self-concept of *macho* and related concerns.

---

* In a recent lecture, Gustavo Martinez, Assistant Director for Program Management (of the Vet Center Program), stated that therapy for the Hispanic veteran is *an invitation to crack.*

THE NATIVE AMERICAN VIETNAM VETERAN

More so than any other minority group of veterans, Native Americans come from a culture in which being a warrior is regarded with dignity and respectability, even today. Although Africans were brought to America from a warrior society, hundreds of years of varying degrees of acculturation have attenuated this ethic. However, for some of the tribes of the American Native, being a warrior remains a central part of his identity and sense of well-being.

In Vietnam, Native soldiers appeared to feel at home with the land, vegetation, climate, and the lurking dangers within the jungles. Most Natives are taught from a very early age to be warriors. The chance to serve in the Vietnam War, and especially as a Marine, was seen as an opportunity for dignity and honor. For many American Natives, however, the experience of entering the military, especially from rural areas and the various reservations, brought on a clash of value systems. But regardless of whether they were from a reservation or from a large urban area, their experiences depended on their degree of acculturation to the values of American society. Their experience was also dependent on whether they were members of one of the approximately 300 existing tribes in the United States, and whether they adhered to *traditional, bicultural,* or *reconstituted traditional* values. Traditional values are those exclusively of Native culture. Bicultural values bridge the Native value system and that of American society. Reconstituted traditional values are traditional Native values that have been "lost" by an individual but are reaffirmed later in life.

Contrary to the "dysreception" experienced by most Vietnam veterans, Native Americans received many honors and strong social and spiritual support. As pointed out by Native American Harold Barse, a Vietnam era combat veteran and Outreach counselor at the Oklahoma Vet Center: "Returning veterans received a lot of support from family and tribal members when they got back to the reservation or tribal area where they originated. Like many Vietnam veterans . . . those Indians who returned to strong support groups fared better than veterans [Natives] without such reinforcement."[22] Concerning the religious meetings and rituals, as well as the great celebrations given by the returnee's tribesmen: "Our families were there to greet us when we got home; they provided a soldier dance, prayer meetings, peyote meetings, stuff to make us feel good . . . to recognize us for our experiences and to honor us for the sacrifices that we made. . . . [We knew all] the people would come out in their tribal garb and dress and they'll honor you. . . . That [took] a lot of the sting out of Vietnam."[22]

As scientific evidence [19] indicates for other groups of veterans, strong support systems prevent or reduce the incidences of significant stress reactions to war. However, some Native Americans did have significant readjustment problems: those who had long ago forsaken their traditional cultural roots (for the most part, the "bicultural" Native veterans) and had isolated themselves from their tribes. This was also true for Natives who had grown up in urban cities, without the benefit of tribal communities.

Like other minority Vietnam veterans, most Natives have to this day found it difficult to secure jobs. Though the Native work ethic differs from that of most other Americans, these men do want to work, and their sense of well-being often depends on whether they are successful in finding employment. Thus, many of these Natives soon became more bitter. As it was, they had grown up bitter over white domination and oppression. They had always been angry over broken treaties, over being tricked and swindled out of their lands, over the malicious and false stereotypes given them, and over the ecologically ruthless treatment of their lands. They had not forgotten that Natives had lived in this country as early as 40,000 years ago.

In addition to a long list of grievances against the American government, Natives felt they had been used once again by the white man—to fight against the Third World people very much like themselves. They viewed the Vietnamese as a people defending their land against foreign aggressors, just as their own ancestors had done in America. Playwright Bruce King, an Oneida combat veteran, has commented: "They [the Vietnamese] were the same kind of people [as us]—a Third World people. We made the connection that in Vietnam, we [Natives in the Armed Forces] were involved in the same kind of colonization process that was carried out by whites in this country."[23]

Some Native Vietnam veterans, especially those who live in urban areas and others who have "left the ways of the tribe," suffer from post-traumatic stress reactions and disorders. Those who early in their lives experienced tribal conditioning in the warrior ethic and later tribal ceremonies devoted to healing, are far less subject to PTSD. Much research is needed to clarify these issues and to understand how tribal ceremonies have helped the Native veteran overcome the adverse effects of Vietnam. Dr. Tom Holm, professor of American Indian Studies at the University of Arizona at Tucson, has said[23]:

> The psychological value of these and other tribal ceremonies cannot be over-estimated. Nearly every Indian Society in America possesses rituals of renewal and restoration and, although they are often ignored as products of mysticism, they serve specific functions. Ceremonies like the Sun Dance, the Green Corn Dance, the Blessing Way of the Navajos and the stomp dances of the Creeks, Seminoles, and Cherokees reaffirm group cohesion, reassert the individual participant's value in the community, and attest to the tribal obligation to the Creator. Whether or not the individual fought in an unpopular war matters little, because the purpose of the ceremony is to restore the tribal bond.

The following case history illustrates the issues that therapists working with Native American veterans must keep in mind:

> Tom is a Native American veteran who served with the Marines in Vietnam in 1969–1970. He grew up on a reservation up to age 12, when his family moved to a large city in the Northeast. Drafted at age 19 he went to Vietnam a year later and extended his tour of duty to two years in Vietnam. His chief complaint is "feeling at odds with my own culture." Tom expressed his concern that his parents, grandparents, and other extended family members had "turned their backs" on him. He missed the closeness he once enjoyed as a young child, and stated that his mental symptoms of depression, anxiety, and bad dreams contributed to his withdrawing from his family, friends, and from tribal unity and values. Tom seemed to need his parents' and grandparents' Native values after returning home, but he had been reluctant to face members of the tribe. Actually, Tom felt he had "turned [his] back on [his] culture, not the other way around." He felt he could be healed were he to find tribal acceptance once again.

When Tom had been a boy growing up on the reservation, the only people who his parents had gone to in time of trouble were family and other tribal members. If this did not work out, they would then go to the medicine man. Tom was from a "traditional" family structure, which had become "bicultural" when he reached the age of 12 or 13. Tom now wishes to "reconstitute" his traditional tribal heritage and reaffirm those values of his past. He feels he would be able to put Vietnam behind him if he could restore tribal well-being within himself.

Tom was referred to the nearest Vet Center where counselors were aware of and sensitive to Native American tribal values. The Native American creed maintains that: "Because veterans have been to war, it is believed that they should not only be honored, but also purged from the taint of battle and restored to a harmonious place within the community."[23] Western traditional methods of treatment are often ineffective with the kinds of issues presented by Tom. For him to give up the pain of Vietnam, he had to involve himself in "completing the circle of healing" by songs of honor, the Gourd Dance, chants, prayers, and ceremonies by his tribesmen.

> Joe, a Native American veteran, suffers from a variety of readjustment problems. He grew up in a large city and served with the Marines in Vietnam. Though he grew up in a "bicultural" family system, he was keenly aware of his ethnic identity. He has always wanted to be both Euro-American and Native American, since his father believed that if Joe was to succeed in America, nothing less would suffice. After Vietnam, Joe made a good adjustment until 11 years later, when in his own words: "My life came crashing down to the floor. You can't get no lower than that." He lost his first job, family, and resorted to alcohol to help him deal with his PTSD symptoms and disappointments in life.

Therapists and counselors who have worked successfully with Native veterans are those who have learned to relax, demonstrate respect, and acquire competence in the cultural ethos of these veterans. Obsessive-compulsive, perfectionist types have proved completely ineffective with this population. Unlike other minorities, Native Americans resent taking advice from therapists. Many perceive suggestions as orders from people in authority.[24] Thus, to be truly helpful to Joe, his therapist had to be cautious about being too verbal. He had to listen more than with most other ethnic groups, avoid being authoritarian, and show due respect.

Dr. Edwin Richardson, a psychologist who has written extensively on Native Americans, advises fellow therapists: "Relax, settle back, and enjoy the [Native American] client. It is best to start off with a soft voice; if you must stare, focus your gaze at the floor or the desk, and listen."[24]

He recommends that the therapist learn by observing,* and attempt to develop a relationship based on honesty and directness, marked by an accepting, nondeceptive, and noncondescending attitude. Moreover, the therapist, he feels, should be eclectic and adaptable, and concentrate on problems rather than on personalities. In terms of useful techniques, Richardson further recommends to the therapist that he be nondirective, especially in the initial phases of the therapeutic interaction, at which time the therapist uses: (1) silence; (2) acceptance; (3) terse restatement of what the client has said; (4) short statement of clarification; and (5) short summative restatement of issues presented by the client.[24] More directive approaches are more difficult since the therapist may be viewed as overbearing and forceful. However, once a relationship of trust and mutual respect has been established, more leeway is granted.

THE ASIAN VIETNAM VETERAN

A number of Asian-Pacific Americans served in Vietnam during the Vietnam era. Most of these soldiers likely came from highly structured traditional families, in which the concept of patriarchy established the supremacy of the father in the family. In such a family system, the father's authority is unquestioned, and the son is expected to be dutiful and obedient, carrying out his highly structured role in the family. The son's expression of strong emotions is discouraged, and his individual needs are subservient to the welfare of the family. Hence, this unquestioning attitude toward authority may have protected him as a soldier in Vietnam from the degree of inner chaos, disorientation, and conflict that most other soldiers felt. Moreover, his unflinching obedience to authority made him less of a disciplinary problem to military field leaders as compared with other groups of American soldiers.

Ironically, though Asian-Americans and the Vietnamese have a common Asian background, many Asian-American soldiers felt less conscious conflict in warring against the Vietnamese than other minority groups. This, we believe, is because of the Asian's powerful traditional family

* With most other groups, the therapist learns, in large part, by asking specific questions.

values which stress the importance of doing the best possible job under any circumstances—favorable or otherwise. Doing the best possible job meant adhering to what the military authorities demanded of the soldiers in the field, while keeping feelings and emotions out of the picture. Since fighting and killing the Vietnamese was sanctioned by the authority of the United States government, internal conflict was kept to a minimum. This is not to say that *all* Asian soldiers did not feel some repugnance, shame, guilt, and some conflict in killing. Rather, in general, their cultural values may have served to cushion extreme reactions.

When one examines the Asian cultural value system closer, it becomes apparent that guilt, shame, and conflict are determined and regulated by the degree of success achieved in glorifying the family name by peerless service. Such success is determined by controlling emotional expressiveness, subserving individual interests and accomplishments in the war to the overall mission and meeting expectations of those in authority.

Though the external stresses of the war were as problematic for Asian soldiers as for most soldiers, it appears that his culture-based *fatalism* may have proved adaptive to surviving in Vietnam—both psychologically and physically. Fatalism is the belief that all events are determined by fate, and the acceptance of all events as inevitable. We, as clinicians with years of experience in treating Vietnam veterans, have not seen many Asian Vietnam veterans for readjustment services. In part, this is because, as a group, Asian-Americans prefer to disavow their emotional problems and repress them. Thus, when these veterans do seek assistance, their problems may have reached an advanced stage.

However, the fact remains that though many Asian families maintain strong traditional values, the influences of American culture have made an impact. Within the ranks of later generations of Asian-Americans has emerged a subgroup referred to as the "Yellow Power Movement."[25] These Asians rebel against the notion of complete parental authority and domination, and are averse to the white American stereotype characterizing Asians as the "model minority." Their main intention is synthesizing the best of their Asian culture with the best of the dominant white culture of the United States. We would conjecture that this small minority of the Asian population, with its distrust of authority and of the United States government, was more susceptible to PTSD than their more traditional counterparts. Though most Asians prefer to maintain "low visibility," many of the more activist Asian men have expressed their anger and frustration over having been used in Vietnam.

The complexity of what many consider to be the hard-working "model minority" is evident in the following two case histories:

> Tim, a Chinese Vietnam veteran, served as an officer in Vietnam. His major complaints are depression, shame, guilt, and anxiety over his sense of failure in life. Though he has always done well in school and in the military, his father had never praised him, always demanding that he strive harder. Later during the interview Tim presented another set of symptoms: headaches, pains in his joints, and other physical problems. Tim had grown up in New York. He is the oldest of three children—two males and one female. At age 37 Tim has two boys and is married to a Caucasian woman. His marrige, after Vietnam, brought great resentment from his parents, especially his father, who felt he was letting his parents down by admitting to himself and to others that he had mental problems. Though he felt "somewhat nervous" after Vietnam, he does not attribute his current problems to Vietnam. Currently, he is employed at a prestigious business firm as an accountant. Even though he is successful by most standards, he feels he is a failure, and that he should attain much "higher things" for himself and family.

Though Tim had married a Caucasian woman and was somewhat involved in the Asian-American activist movement, his therapist was keenly aware of Tim's strong traditional family values. And though Tim has a "dual-cultural" frame of reference, his strong traditional values were the source of his mental—and physical—symptoms, for a thorough physical examination failed to produce any basis for his physical complaints. The therapist understood that, like other minorities, Asians tend to somatize psychological conflicts. It was much easier for Tim to discuss physical symptoms than mental ones. Focusing on somatic symptoms helped him "save face," whereas were he to discuss mental ones he would suffer shame. Particularly for the Asian, mental symptoms and problems are dealt with within the family structure, not with outsiders (like therapists and counselors). That Tim had sought mental health services went totally against his traditional cultural values, and the resultant shame and guilt over having "sold out [his] family" was a critical issue explored by his therapist.

Though the therapist's questions produced the suspicion that some of Tim's symptoms were related to service in Vietnam, Tim chose to focus on other issues in therapy. Thus, for a while, explorations centered on Tim's conflict between deeply rooted traditional values and particularly loyalty to his family, on the one hand, and his personal desires on the other hand. After several months of culturally sensitive therapy, the therapist's earlier hunches that Tim's current problems may be linked to Vietnam, were revived. He felt that Tim's "all-of-a-sudden" interest in traditional Chinese values may reflect unconscious, "subterranean conflicts" stemming from even deeper traditional human values—that is, against killing. However, this was only a hunch. The therapist continued to explore those inner conflicts that were culturally based within the veteran's conscious awareness.

As time progressed and as trust deepened, Tim seemed able to talk about his experiences in Vietnam. As a platoon leader, he had led his men into a village suspected of being a VC stronghold. Approaching the village, a barrage of AK-47 fire hit his platoon, leaving four men dead. The remaining platoon members "went beserk" and began shooting up the village, killing a number of VC and civilians. The therapist helped Tim to understand that, although his traditional values do mean very much to him, Tim was most concerned and in conflict over what had happened that day in the village. He was helped to make "the connection" between his current obsession of his sense of failure and his deep sense of having *failed* to protect his men from being killed, and at having *failed* to protect so many innocent civilians. In time the therapist was able to help Tim to see that his guilt over having abandoned traditional values related to his guilt, sense of responsibility for the acts his men had committed over a decade earlier.

Though Tim did not have a full-blown PTSD, he nevertheless had significant conflicts about his actions and inactions in the war that needed to be explored, at his pace, when the time was right. Premature discussion of Vietnam would have been insensitive and would have caused a "shutdown" on Tim's part. Since Asians are culturally taught to "keep the lid on" strong feelings, forcing the veteran to "divulge" painful memories is, in essence, "an invitation to crack"[26] Encouraging him to recollect the tragic experiences of that day in the village would have brought on strong feelings that would have resulted in panic, and in the subsequent rupture of the therapeutic relationship. After a number of intensely emotional sessions, Tim was able to work toward dealing more effectively with his conflict over his two systems of values. As time went on, Tim made the unambivalent decision to seek a synthesis of both value systems—toward a bicultural identity as a Chinese-American.

Sam is a *sansei* (third generation) Japanese-American veteran who served in Vietnam in 1970–1971. He complains of PTSD symptoms that interfere with his ability to hold a job and attend adequately to his wife's and children's needs. Sam grew up in a *nisei* (second generation) traditional family. Describing himself as rebellious against traditional authority for most of his life, he has had so many heated arguments with his parents over the years that they have disowned him. Since his wife threatened to leave him if he didn't do something about his life, Sam had nowhere to go except to a professional therapist. As a Vietnam veteran he also expressed anger over having to go to Vietnam and "kill all those Asians like myself. I was a fool for going. I should have remained home and fought for our rights as American citizens." He felt he was "a terrible human being, and a terrible husband and father." He also said, "I need help now, I really do. I have no job, no money. I have rent to pay."

The therapist immediately moved to address Sam's concrete needs such as food, transportation (to look for a job), veterans benefits, and employment. In Japanese-American culture, the terms *enryo, ha zu ka shi, ie,* and *hi-ge* are of fundamental importance.[27] *Enryo* is a concept that refers to proper cultural role behavior. It involves "mainly deference and obsequiousness in order to avoid confusion, embarrassment and anxiety. The blank stare, the noncommittal answer, and passive group behavior reflects *enyro.*"[27] *Ha zu ka shi* describes a central theme in Japanese-American cultural conditioning and mental development; namely, "others will jeer and laugh at you, embarrass you, and you will disgrace the family." *Ie* refers to the Japanese family system, as "a corporate entity that exists through time. . . . [It] is a continuum from past to future whose members include not only the present generation, but also the dead and those as yet not born."[28] *Hi-ge* is the term used to convey the cultural expectation that children refrain from egocentrism and self-praise. This does not, however, prevent "traditional families from being competitive."[27]

As a sansei, Sam had rejected these values in favor of American cultural values. Caught up in the throes of this conflict, he reports that he has been very rebellious, confused, and irritable for most of his life. Unlike Japanese soldiers from traditional families, Sam internalized the Anglo system of values, which offers some freedom to question authority. In retrospect, Sam remembers that in Vietnam he had anti-authority feelings toward the United States government, his military leaders, and his parents.

Sam's therapist was aware that even though the two older generations of Japanese describe the sansei as "fully Americanized," in actuality they still had strong traditional influences in their lives when compared to whites with regard to the need for order, deference, and succor (the sansei scored higher than whites on these). In the areas of aggressiveness and dominance, the sansei showed less need for these traits than whites.[29] Thus, even though a counselor may be working with a sansei Vietnam veteran, he still must be very aware of cultural elements.

We view the Japanese Vietnam veteran's quest for readjustment as a "tridimensional identity challenge" (TDIC). This challenge requires the Asian veteran to deal with: (1) the intergenerational/bicultural identity conflict (in being influenced by issei, nisei, and sansei relatives and peers and the larger society); (2) the Asian/Vietnamese identification (which was a source of danger and distress because they were occasionally fired upon by American troops); and (3) the mental and physical symptoms associated with postcombat readjustment problems.

Recovering from the Vietnam experience is a most complex task and challenge for any veteran who decides to take a hold of his life and change it. The therapist similarly faces a difficult task in restoring the confidence and morale, in enhancing the value of life, and in healing the broken bonds for these veterans. Therapists who have successfully accomplished these tasks have studied in depth the cultures that shape these veterans' perceptions, reactions, attitudes, and values. They have devoted time to studying the music, religions, and way of life of the various ethnic groups. They have learned that minorities, in general, do not respond to abstract approaches; they prefer things to be made clear, concise, and concrete. They are not quick to respond with self-disclosures. Only by understanding the societal and cultural matrix in which the veteran's responses to posttraumatic combat reactions are embedded, can interventions with female and minority group veterans be successful.

In line with these therapeutic goals, the Vet Center Program has established special Working Groups on black, Hispanic, American Native, Asian-Pacific, handicapped or disabled, and female Vietnam veterans. These Working Groups have as their objectives the enlightening of Program staff and officials, as well as the Veterans Administration itself, as to the gender and cultural elements in Vietnam veterans that call for unique as well as common therapeutic approaches, policy changes; and new initiatives.

According to Vet Center Program statistics, for the 6-month period of October 1983 to March 1984, Vet Centers served almost 18,000 black veterans, including 388 females; over 4600 Hispanic veterans, including 56 females; over 1000 Native American veterans, including 11 females; 380 Asian veterans, including 10 females; 84 Alaskan veterans, no females; and 42,421 (or 56.4%) white Vietnam veterans, including 840 females. In this Ethnic Categories Report, 8771 male and 47 female veterans refused to furnish information as to their racial-ethnic identity. Overall, 1352 women and 73,817 men were seen by the Vet Center program. Male veterans comprised 98.2% and female veterans, 1.8%. New initiatives have been taken to increase the number of women seeking services at Vet Centers. The National Women's Working Group has been instrumental in assisting Program and policymakers to devise a system of services more congruent with the needs of female veterans.

Chapter 8 / THE PROBLEMS OF SEEKING AND RECEIVING HELP

Combat veterans have been conditioned to fight, be courageous, and not admit defeat. This has made it hard for them to accept their problems and ask for help. This applies not only to those Vietnam veterans with the relatively minor symptom of recurrent traumatic dreams, but to those with serious self-destructive symptoms, particularly when combined with the outward appearance of relative normality. Consequently, the first problem facing the Vietnam veteran needing help is that his self-defeating actions often disguise his wish for help. He often appears to be either inching forward on a tightrope, nearly blocked in midcourse by despair, or tottering on the brink of falling. This dilemma of needing but fearing help was described by a Vietnam veteran seeking treatment. Repeatedly in trouble with the law, and unable to enjoy any of the normal activities of family life because of his self-punishing symptoms, he was finally forced into a treatment program when threatened with divorce and the possibility of a prison sentence for his attacks of rage. He admitted: "The only reason I have come to the hospital is because my wife will leave me if I don't. She can't handle it when I hit her and I don't want to do it but it happens anyway. And if she left me I wouldn't have any more reason to live anyway. I pick fights with people all the time and I don't know why I'm still alive. I hate everybody and I hate myself because I've hurt so many people. I don't have any goals for myself because I can't see any light at the end of the tunnel."

Another Vietnam veteran was eventually propelled into treatment because of the threat of being prosecuted for assault. He was subject to aggressive outbursts, sometimes under the influence of drugs or alcohol, and sometimes while dissociating into a different "personality." He recalled one such incident: "About a year before I came in the hospital, a big guy where I worked kept provoking me. I warned him to leave me alone but he didn't believe me. He weighed about 300 pounds and no one dared to take him on but he went too far one day. I can't really remember exactly what happened but they told me that I picked him up by the throat and held him over the edge of a three-story building and threatened to drop him. I guess they thought I acted like a crazed killer and they called the police within five minutes. A few months later, I almost killed a man again but I don't remember anything. That really scared me. I had no choice other than to go to the VA hospital for help or I'd be in prison."

Even with the best of help, Vietnam veterans with PTSD symptoms seldom improve rapidly or easily and treatment is often lengthy though rarely complete. Those who enter a treatment program face potential risks, particularly if it means entering the hospital. Knowing about these potential risks beforehand may help them be better prepared to begin and remain in treatment through difficult times. The first risk is the possibility of only partial recovery. For many, this may make it seem not worth the effort to enter a treatment program, particularly for those looking for wonder drugs and magical results.

Then there is the risk of losing a tenuously held job or marriage. The unfortunate fact that Vietnam veterans have difficulties sustaining employment often means that few employers will have patience with their unpredictable behavior problems nor wait for them to return from the hospital. On the home front, the embittered wife who feels that she is finally free of the burden of responsibility for her husband's welfare, may leave him in the hands of mental health professionals and divorce him. If she has good intentions but little patience, she may not be able to withstand the long period it may take for her husband to recover from his detachment, his disregard for affection and love, and his inability to handle responsibility.

Thus, the Vietnam veteran who still has his job may fear that entering the hospital for several months will most certainly result in his losing it, and in our experience, that happens only too often. It is also very likely that an employer will not hire or keep a Vietnam veteran in his employ if he requests time off for even several hours a week while participating in an outpatient program.

Similarly, the veteran with a stable marriage may fear that his absence from home, while entering a hospital treatment program, will cause his wife to lose interest and leave him, which sometimes happens. It is also not uncommon that this fear of loss is hidden by an openly expressed, though irrational, fear that his family is in danger, which reinforces a strong, aggressively protective wish to stay home and guard his wife and children. This irrational attitude is frequently related to postwar guilt feelings about abandoning friends in Vietnam. For example, Ira, a married veteran with children, suffered the loss of many of his close friends in Vietnam and felt considerable guilt about surviving. He entered a treatment program and received only partial help. Remaining 2 months, he asked for a discharge, saying he was afraid something might happen to his family. In spite of his belief that he would be able to return home and be a protective husband and father, he returned to the program 2 weeks later with frightening unresolved aggressive symptoms. Fortunately, after his return, he felt a need to stop concealing his past and was able to talk more openly about a number of very disturbing memories of buddies getting killed, which he had avoided before.

The veteran entering treatment sometimes feels the risk that if his personality changes, his wife will lose respect for him. Kirk felt comfortable with his aggressively protective attachment to his wife but became very anxious when encouraged to display openly his affection, which he had never done in his 14 years of marriage. He volunteered: "I have never told my wife I love her and and I can't. That's not me. I'd feel phony and less than a man. She ought to know I love her anyway. If she can't accept me the way I am, I'd just as soon she leave me now. She would probably leave me for sure if I tried to change."

Fortunately, this veteran's wife was very committed to their marriage, her interest was sustaining to him during his difficult process of change, and she, moreover, received emotional support from a group comprised of veterans' wives. However, her resilience was only made possible by her having been forewarned that her husband's improvement would likely be preceded by periods of depression and anger; he would remain emotionally distant from her before he could be more sensitive to her needs and expressive of his affection.

Some Vietnam veterans fear that the changes necessary for a breakthrough could be so dramatic as to result in a complete psychotic breakdown. Neil, a Vietnam veteran from the South Bronx, entered a hospital treatment program after "surviving" a number of years under conditions similar to those of a combat zone. The only reason he began treatment was because his common-law wife opposed his criminal activities and insisted he seek help. Living alone in a vacant apartment building without water or electricity, he was surrounded by thieves, drug pushers, and drug users. His only means of survival was taking money at gunpoint from other drug dealers and occasionally dealing himself.

In spite of the obvious self-destructive nature of this life-style, he was uncertain that he could live any differently or fit in anywhere else. Even though he had grown up in a more conventional home, after 2 months in the treatment program he yearned to return to the "combat zone," which was similar to his Vietnam experience. He particularly feared his increasing depression and accompanying fear at the prospect of changing: "I don't know if I want to stay in the program any longer. When I got here, I knew there was something wrong with me but I didn't know what. Now I know what it is and I don't like it. If I stay any longer I don't know who I will become. I know I don't want to become just another phony American. And I'm really afraid that if I don't leave now, I could go crazy."

In developing trusting relationships with people, the veteran may grow to feel exceedingly vulnerable. This same veteran was quite resistant to his therapist's suggestion that he would have to take the risk of trusting those who were helping him: "In the South Bronx where I live, nobody trusts anybody else. I'm used to that and I feel safe. If you trust someone, you might get a knife in your back." More than once, he considered dropping out of the treatment program rather than face painful grief and guilt-ridden memories that could only be touched upon after developing relationships a great deal more trusting with the staff.

Another risk that Vietnam veterans face is experiencing more acute emotional pain after recalling disturbing memories and emotions that had previously been blocked. For example, a veteran who had been in a hospital treatment program several months finally disclosed to one of the staff nurses a memory of which he felt profoundly ashamed. During the next 2 months, he became irritable, isolated, and withdrawn from that nurse, who did not understand the reason for his distancing behavior. The communication barrier that developed exacerbated his angry feelings. Eventually, an important step toward resolution was taken at a meeting wherein each of them began to wear away the barrier, and the veteran said: "When I told you those things about me that I didn't want anyone to hear, I felt vulnerable and I didn't want anyone around me anymore." Through this admission, both understood the origins of the barrier and were able to resolve it so that the veteran felt somewhat less isolated and guilt-ridden.

Veterans fear that revealing past experiences may bring upon them the rejection of friends and counselors; they also fear it could lead in the latter case to their prosecution for war crimes. (This is unlikely, given the legal privilege of confidentiality during psychotherapy.) It is not infrequent, however, for a Vietnam veteran to leave a treatment program before he has received the help he needs rather than talk openly about "secrets" that have caused him terrible feelings of shame and guilt. To a veteran who has harbored his own secret for so many years, it seems that his is worse than anyone else's could conceivably be. Dean, who had been an outstanding high school student, dropped out of a hospital treatment program only to return 2 weeks later to make a "confession." While in the field in Vietnam, he had taken a foolish chance that brought enemy fire toward his squad. As a result, he was wounded and his closest buddy was killed trying to rescue him from where he lay. This "confession" became both a relief and a burden since talking about it openly activated his guilt feelings more strongly; he consequently projected onto his therapist that the therapist had lost all respect for him.

Despite such fear of rejection, most Vietnam veterans would more likely share their most guilt-ridden memories with a counselor than with another patient. When a group of veterans were asked why this was so, they replied: "We value the friendships of our 'brothers' more than the friendships of the staff. So if it doesn't work out to tell a staff person, we haven't lost as much as it might if we tell another vet."

Many fear that reviving their experiences of war will unleash their "killer instinct." In a similar vein, many have a healthy fear of hurting those whom they depend on. Most of them are likely to do anything to avoid a situation in which they could lose control and hurt someone, including leaving treatment if they feel there is no alternative. For that reason, a Vietnam veteran receiving treatment should expect his therapist to be alert to this possible though unlikely risk of being the target of a rage attack. The patient can expect his therapist to ask him to talk about the anger, if possible, which will generally keep it from being expressed physically. Veterans can expect to have their therapists establish firm guidelines, prohibiting violent actions and spelling out the consequences if they do occur. If the therapy is being provided in a group setting, the therapist will expect support from other veterans to help any one of their group who appears to be on the verge of losing control.

Perhaps the most difficult barrier for nearly every Vietnam veteran to surmount, is to eventually give up the desire for revenge. For if he learns to give up harboring resentment and feelings of revenge, he will no longer be the walking time bomb some describe themselves to be. This will eventually pave the way for him to become comfortable with normal feelings of anger so that he can recognize it within him and learn to express it safely. Having decided not to physically strike out, a veteran can learn alternate ways of controlling himself when feeling vulnerable. This may mean temporarily finding a place to be quiet and alone, using words rather than actions, and learning to assert himself productively and in a positive way.

Finally, a Vietnam veteran may risk becoming depressed and even suicidal, particularly after revealing painful memories. For example, Dave had grown up in a conservative churchgoing family. During one therapy session he described his vicious outbursts of rage toward Vietnamese civilians and his torturing of a VC prisoner. Following this "confession," he became withdrawn, edgy, and found his relationships with his wife and children deteriorating, and then seriously contemplated suicide. Only after several months of ongoing therapy did he feel some relief from his guilt and curb his self-destructive behavior toward his family.

Getting better means taking directions from authority figures, among whom are doctors, psychologists, social workers, and nurses. This can be a frightening experience evoking angry feelings, particularly if it reminds veterans of Vietnam and conflicting feelings about power, leadership, and responsibility. Vietnam veterans often fear power and responsibility, having felt betrayed by leaders who they trusted in the past. During the process of recovery, they eventually become cognizant that it is also their own power that they fear; at this point they begin to feel more vulnerable, depressed, and angry. One ex-Marine described his own fear of power at the prospect of taking on responsibility for others. He uttered: "I have been in positions of responsibility so much in Vietnam and it resulted in guys getting killed, that I don't ever want to make decisions that involve other people any more and I don't want to help any other Vietnam veterans who are in this group with me."

The patient's fear of power and responsibility often places him in a Catch 22 situation; he comes to dread the thought of remaining or being discharged from a treatment program. For if he appears to be improving, he will be saddled with the pressure of having to perform and take responsibility. This may thereby cause depression, sleeplessness, bad dreams, and irritability. Unfortunately, these symptoms are sometimes misinterpreted by the professional. He may view them as regressive insofar as a patient's wishing to remain dependent, when, in fact, they are an understandable fear of responsibility that often accompanies improvement. Thus, professionals should be aware of the growing pains that accompany improvement.

Another problem Vietnam veterans face undergoing treatment is the pain of accepting the world as it is. Sometimes this is synonymous with accepting situations that are not always ideal; even accepting the unpleasant reality that an impersonal government will not likely become more humane or that the American system of government will not always impart justice fairly; or that not all of society will ever completely accept Vietnam veterans and their problems; or that change is slow in coming. When a veteran's considerable impatience interferes with his acceptance of these realities, he is in danger of perpetuating a cycle of victimization. This unremitting identification with being a victim will leave him repeatedly suffering from PTSD symptoms as well as disappointment and anger.

In addition to accepting the world, getting better means self-acceptance; acceptance of continuing to experience unpleasant dreams, anger, and bad memories; acceptance of difficulties with ordinary relationships; acceptance of problems with sexual relationships. Many have trouble in relationships with women, particularly when they attempt a short-term sexual involvement. They are better off considering that this kind of relationship may not be the best for them. They are well advised giving up this kind of self-destructive sexual relationship with women and replacing it with other, more constructive kinds of relationships. Long-term friendships are more likely to be constructive and do not run the risk of creating feelings of disillusionment, abandonment, and rejection should they break up. When Vietnam veterans ask, "What do you do with women besides have sex?" we suggest the following: "Women are people, like you are and it would be best if you take enough time, which we believe to be at least nine months, of talking and sharing feelings before considering sexual relationships. A love relationship which includes sex, requires a great deal of groundwork first and that means patience. But it is worth waiting for. It can sustain you through a lot of difficult times."

Finally, getting better means to cease being a victim and to become fully committed to finding a purpose for living once again. It means discovering meaningful and loving relationships. An ex-Army sergeant, for instance, had become alienated from his father after returning from Vietnam. Once he resolved his guilt about surviving his buddy's death, he said: "Ever since I came back, my father and I haven't gotten along. I can't even spend any time with him at all any more without our getting into a fight and it has been very depressing and I haven't had any purpose for living. Now I think I have found a purpose which I've avoided for years and that's to reconcile with my father." Self-acceptance is related to finding a purpose, often a reconciliation with loved ones and a reconciliation with one's self. As a Vietnam veteran chaplain said to a group of veterans: "The key to resolving the guilt about what you did in Vietnam is reconciliation. If you can reconcile yourself and accept that part of yourself that you have hated, you will have achieved a significant step toward getting over guilt and self-rejection. Getting better means resolving guilt and accepting forgiveness."

Once a Vietnam veteran considers seeking help, he may wonder what avenue of treatment would be the easiest to follow. At the present time, his most likely route to getting proper help begins with one of the 137 VA Outreach Centers in the country, although he may also visit one of the 172 VA hospitals or seek help from a private counseling center.

During the early and mid 1970s he had few places to go for such help. If he went to the VA outpatient clinic, alcohol and drug treatment program, or general psychiatry inpatient unit, he might receive some treatment for current problems in his life, but his chances of becoming disillusioned and disappointed by lack of effective treatment for symptoms of PTSD were high. Hospital treatment at that time was generally ineffective, mainly because of the lack of a proper diagnostic category. Between 62% and 77% of Vietnam veteran patients treated on general psychiatry units were not recognized as having posttraumatic symptoms and received a diagnosis of schizophrenia, borderline personality disorder, alcoholism, or drug dependency.[1]

Since treatment was determined by the diagnosis, Vietnam veterans who were labeled schizophrenics were treated with antipsychotic medications. Those who were labeled alcoholics were treated in alcoholic treatment units. Those with antisocial characteristics were often labeled sociopathic or borderline personalities and were rarely helped since they were considered thoroughly manipulative, unpredictable, and distrustful of therapists.

During the 1970s, many hospital staff personnel, in their failure to understand Vietnam veterans' problems, sometimes responded to their angry denunciations of the VA with comments such as: "Vietnam veterans are just a bunch of character disorders. They don't want to get well. All they want to do is drink up a storm and live here."

If a veteran left and returned a second time, personnel again were likely to respond with, "Why do you want to come into the hospital again? I suppose you got drunk and had a fight with your wife. If you can't make it out there, you're probably coming back because you want to get disability compensation." Upon successive readmissions, a Vietnam veteran might even be greeted with, "Do you want to use this place as a home? Guys like you take up all our time and don't give us an opportunity to get on with our real work."

During the past 5 years, however, the VA has begun to recognize that its real work is to help America's veterans with symptoms related to the battlefield. That recognition began after Congress voted to provide funds and President Carter signed Public Law 96-22 on June 13, 1979 for development of the Vietnam veterans' Outreach Program. The director of the program, Dr. Arthur S. Blank, has stated: "The . . . nationwide network of Vietnam vet centers—collectively termed Operation Outreach—in all 50 states, Puerto Rico, and the Virgin Islands . . . treat veterans with a broad range of individual counseling, group counseling (rap groups), and family counseling, as well as offer assistance with problems in employment, education, and VA benefits."[2]

As a result of this program, 91 small counseling centers were placed in communities across the country, staffed by four counseling personnel in each. That number has since grown to 137. Many individual VA hospitals have also responded to the need to help Vietnam veterans. Nationwide, 11 have developed specialized treatment programs and others are in the process of developing them.

The 11 special hospital treatment programs, called "Stress Units," "Traumatic Stress Treatment Programs," "PTSD Treatment Units" or "Inpatient Specialized Treatment Units" (ISTUs) have an average bed capacity of 26 and a 3- to 9-month average treatment time. Approximately 600 Vietnam veterans across the country can be treated each year in these Units although just as many are admitted for short periods of time and receive minimal benefit from the experience. There are also a number of other VA hospitals and VA outpatient clinics where therapists have developed a specialized interest and expertise in providing them psychotherapy.

Not all of the approximately 800,000 Vietnam veterans suffering from PTSD need treatment in a hospital; no available statistics accurately cite how many do. And nearly all of the 11 inpatient programs have a lengthy waiting list averaging 6 months before admission, making it somewhat difficult for a Vietnam veteran to get immediate hospital treatment. However, they will be admitted more quickly when referred by a VA outpatient clinic or Outreach Center. Outreach Center counselors may be called to help a Vietnam veteran in crisis, and are able to get them hospitalized more easily. An upper Midwest Outreach counselor told us that if it weren't for the VA hospital in his city and the psychologist from that hospital who provides him with consultation about counseling difficult patients, his job would be much more difficult. If he must respond to a threat of suicide, physical violence, or a veteran's deteriorating mental condition, his consultant will arrange to have the Vietnam veteran admitted immediately if necessary. But because his hospital does not have a specialized PTSD Treatment Unit, the Outreach counselor will likely get the veteran back from the hospital relatively soon following the crisis and will continue the counseling process on an outpatient basis. Provided the veteran has a stable home environment and a source of income and his counselor is skilled, he may make continued improvement, although he may have new crises requiring hospitalization again.

The demand for hospitalization of Vietnam veterans is related to the increasing awareness of the disabling symptoms of PTSD, and is sometimes complicated by an immediate need for basic safety and shelter. Darryl, who has a master's degree in literature, described himself as sleeping in a tree in New York's Central Park for a month since he lost his job. During that month, he had been mugged twice and nearly killed by his attackers. Another Vietnam veteran, recently divorced, had become afraid of his own attacks of rage and preferred isolation, sleeping in a tent on a relative's property in Connecticut. With the changing weather in November, however, that life-style became impractical. Hospitalization kept him from freezing to death in his tent and, moreover, provided him with treatment for his PTSD symptoms.

The shortage of treatment facilities has often created political pressure upon VA hospitals to open up new specialized treatment units. Although political pressure has often worked to force a new program to open, it has been without adequate cooperation from local hospital administrators. The lack of administrative support may stem from the disbelief that Vietnam veterans need special treatment, extra facilities, and additional staff. Even after starting a new program, impatient administrators may fail to support it through growing pains, often taking 2 or more years, or may not realize the need for a well-trained and dedicated director and trained personnel.

Qualified professionals can be found to staff specialized PTSD treatment programs when hospital administrators decide to commit themselves to support them. However, those professionals must be dedicated and willing to see a new program grow and flourish. There can be rewards for those staff who involve themselves in the work. As a nurse on a specialized hospital program said, "I know that a lot of the nursing staff who work on other wards in this hospital don't like Vietnam veterans and can't understand why I do. But I have found this work the most rewarding thing I have ever done. Once you have gotten through being tested out by them, Vietnam veterans are very loyal and responsive to anyone who wants to learn about their problems and really want to help them."

For specialized mental health workers to be really effective, they must combine professional competence with integrity and humanness. They obviously need basic professional training, but also need to supplement it with reading the available PTSD literature, attending special PTSD training meetings and workshops, having informal discussions with other mental health professionals in the field, and listening to Vietnam veterans themselves without passing judgment. We, as therapists, have found videotapes effective in our own learning and research. One of us has videotaped about 40 hours of interviews and therapy sessions with these veterans. After reviewing them, we found the process very helpful.

We believe and emphasize that it is the personal encounter of the therapist with his patient—the Vietnam veteran—that is more important than adhering to traditional psychological formulations. We hold that the therapist must be an emotionally sensitive, experiencing, and empathic person who is open-minded to learning about the veterans' experiences. In our experience, we emphasize that because veterans' reports of guilt-ridden events, such as killing and sadism, provoke considerable anxiety within therapists, traditional therapy methods may be ineffective. We thus urge therapists to be aware of their own personal struggles about the Vietnam War and share their own feelings with other therapists or supervisors. At times it may also be appropriate for therapists to share reactions and attitudes with Vietnam veterans in "rap groups."[3] Psychologist Dr. Robert Shapiro has described the importance of developing a strong working alliance with these veterans. However it is also important for therapists to maintain enough objectivity in order to avoid overidentifying with their patients' feelings of victimization.[4]

Tom Williams, a Vietnam veteran who became a psychologist, suggests that professionals who were veterans of Vietnam may have an advantage over other therapists. They can more rapidly establish trust and facilitate disclosure of war-related experiences. Yet, there is also the problem that Vietnam veteran counselors face potential "burn out" if their own traumatic dreams and memories are reactivated by the stories they hear or if they begin to feel overburdened by the responsibility of helping all their fallen comrades.[5]

During the relatively short history of the special treatment programs for Vietnam veterans, there have been few statistics available to determine success. In our opinion, only approximately 50% of those veterans who enter a treatment program with the desire to get better, maintain lasting improvement. Long-term outpatient treatment may be more favorable but hospital treatment is less so. For example, the research director of a highly regarded hospital program at one VA Medical Center told us informally that over a 6-month period, 11 of 25 Vietnam veteran patients left the program prematurely because of alcohol or illicit drug use. Of the remaining 14, 3 reported no improvement. These statistics do not tell us why some veterans recover and others don't; however, preliminary evidence and subjective reports suggest that the success of the treatment is related to a number of factors, the psychological approach used during treatment being one of the most important. Thus, it remains a frequent challenge for mental health professionals to tailor the most effective treatment approach to each specific individual veteran seeking help, whether it be crisis intervention, hypnotic uncovering of a traumatic memory, or long-term intensive psychotherapy for bringing about a major posttraumatic personality change.

Some do not respond to treatment or maintain the improvement they have made because there exists no stable, growth-producing, or nuturing environment for them at home or work. For those without a family or spouse, some form of a stable environment must be maintained if they are to sustain their level of improvement. We have known, in fact, a number of Vietnam veterans who have made significant recovery without professional help but only because of the presence of a steady job and a committed and loving wife and family. Those without family, job, vocational training, or other environmental support such as regular meetings with other Vietnam veterans, have much less than a 50% chance of sustaining whatever gains they may have made. Those with no jobs waiting or no job prospects at all become discouraged and demoralized, particularly if they feel they are failing their families.

While follow-up statistics are not readily available on the success rate of those without good supports at home, the veterans themselves are pessimistic about their chances of recovery if those supports are not present.

Paul witnessed 30 patients admitted and discharged from the program he was in. He recounted: "I can count on the fingers of one hand those who I know have made it out there after they left this program. And those are the ones whose wives have not left them. I don't think I can make it out there if I leave the program. No one is going to give me a job. I have no wife. And when I leave here, it will be just like leaving 'Nam. Only worse." Fortunately, he was in a hospital that began organizing an aftercare program to provide sheltered employment, semistructured housing (with other Vietnam veterans discharged at the same time) and follow-up psychiatric treatment for those who desired it.

In some cases the absence of support at home and stable employment have been considered such stumbling blocks to progress that treatment programs have focused primarily on resolving them. The Menlo Park VA Hospital in Palo Alto, California, which keeps 90 veterans for an average stay of 4 months, has strongly encouraged community activity as part of its program. This helps the veterans feel they are contributing in a meaningful way.[6] Another program, not under the auspices of the VA, began in the early 1970s in the San Francisco area. It has been described by veteran-counselors Chester Paul Adams and Jack McCloskey as emphasizing the development of work patterns and job skills within vocational training programs. For 4 weeks, veterans do the routine operations of a farm in exchange for board, room, and services. The next 4 weeks are dedicated to preparing the veteran for seeking employment or for beginning vocational training in an urban environment. The last portion of the program promotes the development of alumni support groups for those graduating from the program.[7] Such programs are rare, however, and we still do not know their success rates.

There are other potential pitfalls in therapy such as different expectations in terms of recovery between therapist and the patient. If a great disparity exists, progress toward recovery may be seriously impaired. The veteran who does not present the therapist with clear goals for his own recovery may face disappointment when, after a period of treatment, he feels no better. Similarly, the therapist who is not aware of the full severity of the veteran's difficulties may expect complete recovery in a brief period and become disappointed if the problems continue or become worse. Both patient and therapist ought to be aware of the range of severity of PTSD symptoms, the process required for recovery, and the time it may take.

We know of one Vietnam veteran with above-normal intelligence who, after a year in a hospital program, had improved to the point that the staff personnel expected that he would soon be able to leave the hospital and get a job. But when he angrily resisted, both the staff and he grew disappointed. The staff, nonetheless, accepted his decision to stay. During that extended period, he uncovered additional traumatic memories and emotions related to violence and the death of friends. This enabled him to "work through" and understand better the relation of these experiences to his enormous fear of taking on responsibility.

"Expectation dissonance" or a disparity in expectation of progress between staff and patients can also occur in regimented treatment programs in which patients are expected to move from one phase of treatment to another at a specified time. If at the end of the final phase of the program, not every veteran is ready for discharge, a frustration emerges for both patient and staff.

The problem of "expectation dissonance" occurs so frequently that staffs must find ways to resolve it. One possible resolution is to provide posthospital continuity of care with the trusted therapist. A second possible resolution might be time flexibility; permitting veterans who need more time to remain in the program. This approach is more likely to succeed when the staff is cognizant that different patients are in different phases of recovery and they require more individualized treatment. A third resolution is for veterans to repeat the program as often as necessary after making partial gains toward recovery. They could return to a stable home environment, and then feel free to return for further treatment if symptoms recur or in the event of a crisis. A fourth resolution is a flexible treatment program wherein both treatment personnel and patients can arrive at mutually agreed-upon goals. A good treatment outcome should be possible when the goals are broad enough, realistic enough, and specific enough to be measured, and the treatment is to be carried out by accomplished personnel.

A complication that makes treatment more complex is the multifarious aspects of the diagnosis of PTSD. This diagnosis is often complicated by a patient's having PTSD in association with another problem. The professional would then have to determine the relation of all the diagnostic complexities and their origins.

A veteran whose PTSD symptoms are complicated by chronic or cyclic depression, may have suffered serious losses, not only of friends in Vietnam, but of friends and family before and after the war. To help him complete the grieving process, he may need, in addition to psychotherapy or counseling, specific medications for his depression.

Other patients who suffered considerable turmoil or family instability prior to Vietnam, have reacted most profoundly to any experience of loss, betrayal, or abandonment. These veterans, sometimes receiving a label of borderline or narcissistic personality,[8,9] have the most difficulty establishing meaningful relationships, including therapeutic relationships. Their considerable fear of losing anyone fuels their desire to resist developing intense bonds with even their therapists, which blocks their chances of improvement. Vietnam veterans with such difficulties, may fluctuate from grandiose feelings of omnipotence to profound fear and depression. The combination of individual and group psychotherapy, particularly in a hospital setting, works best for such patients. They will have more personal contact with the therapist and will be subjected to peer pressure in groups of other veterans who can actively help them to contain their self-destructive behavior.

For veterans whose treatment is complicated by unpredictable behaviors and memory loss, it is important ot recognize that they may have yet other complicating diagnoses. For example, Tim, a 48-year-old veteran, reported frequent personality changes. On one occasion, he found himself in a strange town and did not know how he had gotten there. Sometimes people told him that he acted strangely, but he had no memory of what he had done. While his traumatic experiences in Southeast Asia and other symptoms verified the diagnosis of PTSD, his psychiatrist found that he also had two other diagnoses: borderline personality disorder and temporal lobe epilepsy (a type of convulsive disorder). He was placed on specific anticonvulsant medications to control the personality changes, referred to a Vietnam veterans treatment program, and referred to a qualified therapist for long-term psychotherapy, a preferred treatment for his personality disorder.

The diagnosis of schizophrenia is today rarely confused with PTSD, although Vietnam veterans in the 1970s were frequently given that diagnosis erroneously. However, there is a small minority of Vietnam veterans whose recovery seems blocked because of persistent intrusive images, disorganized thought patterns, and an inability to sustain relationships with people. Such patients may suffer from a degree of psychotic thought disorder and generally require specific "antipsychotic" medications to improve thought organization ability and reduce the frequency of intrusive imagery.

There are a variety of problems facing both prospective therapists and their Vietnam veteran patients. Legal problems, unstable marriages and jobs, fear of change or becoming worse before getting better, inadequate treatment facilities, untrained therapists, and mixed diagnoses all contribute to the difficulties. Despite all these impediments, approximately half of those Vietnam veterans seeking professional help make steady improvement toward a recovery from PTSD and healthy, fruitful life.

Chapter 9 / RECOVERY PHASES

Recovery from the stress of war moves slowly through a number of phases. Most veterans complete these phases without professional help while others become locked in one, or vacillate from one to another and require assistance in order to progress. To understand the complexities of these phases is mandatory for the Vietnam veteran and those assisting his recovery.

The following five phases of recovery have been commonly described.[1,2,3]

1. *The emergency or outcry phase.* The survivor experiences his life being threatened and responds with fear, helplessness, and an accompanying physiological "fight–flight" activation of pulse, blood pressure, respiration, and muscle activity.

2. *The emotional numbing and denial phase.* The survivor protects himself by burying the experience in his mind.

3. *The intrusive-repetitive phase.* Traumatic dreams, images, and emotions intrude into the survivor's consciousness and sleep.
4. *The reflective-transition phase.* The survivor develops a larger personal perspective on the traumatic events and becomes positive and constructive; he thinks more about the future and is less fixed on the past.
5. *The completion or integration phase.* The veteran has successfully integrated the previously traumatic event with his prior life experiences to restore a sense of equanimity and continuity. Now able to put the war into its proper perspective, the veteran sees the war as merely a past memory.

To complete all phases of this progression obviously requires a great deal of personal effort on the part of the veteran and is more often achieved through professional help than without it.

Psychologist John Russell Smith, a Vietnam veteran, has suggested a similar view of the recovery process. But in place of the higher-level phase, Smith has described two partial recovery phases: "sealing over" and integration; and a third and final recovery phase: atonement.[4] "Sealing over," which enables a veteran to put disturbing memories out of his mind, is made possible by the "sanction" or approval of the American public; this occurred for the young men in World War II. Sanction provided an overall purpose and meaning for the soldiers in that war, relieving feelings of guilt or need to justify their involvement. World War II was clearly a war in which Americans participated in order to save the world from Nazi Germany's destructive use of power and prevent the Japanese from controlling the Pacific.

The sanction of their country enabled World War II veterans to live productive and meaningful lives in most cases because they were not burdened with any collective or national guilt and could, for the most part, "seal over" their traumatic experiences. For those individuals who "sealed over" emotionally disturbing traumatic memories, recalling and talking about them over the years helped veterans integrate the memories as they became less disturbing.

On the other hand, since Vietnam veterans lacked the moral sanction of their country, many are left with the burden of national guilt on their shoulders and have never regained a sense of meaning in their lives. Some individual veterans, however, have experienced partial sanction from the acceptance of family members, friends, or other veterans, allowing them to "seal over" their combat memories and emotions.

In a recovery phase beyond "sealing over," Smith has described integration as a time when a Vietnam veteran finds personal meaning through finally accepting responsibility for his individual actions. This is not an easy phase and requires his recognition of both the good and bad aspects of his war experiences in order to "weave each strand of the experience into the overall fabric of his identity."[4]

In a final recovery phase that Smith labels "atonement," veterans find "At-One-Ment" with experiences they had previously rejected. Or they may finally feel at one within themselves or with forces much greater than they, such as their entire community, nation, and even religion. The pursuit of atonement may lead to a resolution of guilt and self-acceptance, described by Smith in the following example of a Vietnam veteran who accidentally killed his lifelong friend: "For years after his return [from Vietnam] Billy could not forgive himself for the death of his friend. Daily, he made a detour around the town where his buddy was buried. Billy's judgment of that act was frozen and locked into a value system which allowed him no forgiveness. Several years later, he had come to accept the fact that he had slipped in a moment of panic, accidently killing his friend. It was only when he could drive to the cemetery, kneel in front of his friend's grave, say he was sorry and accept forgiveness for himself that he could go on with his life."[4]

While it has generally been thought that men and women who complete the recovery phases successfully have received therapy, there are some who have achieved such results from life experience alone.

Dr. Dan Conlon, a Minneapolis physician and a Vietnam veteran, illustrates his own experience of traversing through these phases. He had been exposed to many traumatic experiences, including death and killing. After returning to civilian life and his medical practice, he had considerable problems with nightmares, irritability, and periods of depression. He recalls going through the denial and numbing phase—a phase he had seen in his own patients. "I'm seeing the similarities between people involved in divorces, involved in the grief reaction with sudden death of loved ones, grief from news of cancer and loss of a limb, etc. The divorce syndrome looks very similar to the posttraumatic stress disorder. . . . Are . . . we . . . talking about the same thing in different settings?"

He then experienced a degree of sanction, which helped him feel okay about his work in Vietnam for a time: "Unfortunately both myself and my men were all volunteers in hazardous duty apart from our assigned tasks during our stay. At the time it all seemed very worthwhile and we were all on a high, feeling that we were doing something heroic for our country 'above and beyond' as they say. The medals we got helped a little but they look cheap to us now."

Nevertheless, with the support of his wife, friends, and religious faith, he was able partially to integrate and "seal over" the most disturbing aspects of his agonizing experiences and continue his active career as a family practitioner. But not without some struggle: "I've resumed my 'Clark Kent' identity as a family physician . . . as though nothing had happened . . . . I've been carrying the Vietnam experience around in my conscious and unconscious mind since I left Vietnam in January 1968. Hardly a day has gone by that flashbacks . . . and confusion about that experience hasn't popped into my mind. But I have conveniently, until just lately [during 1984] shut out all deep thinking into my Vietnam adventure. . . .I have managed to somehow sublimate all my thoughts and doubts and frustrations concerning my involvement in Vietnam . . . [and] convince myself that nothing really happened to me of significance during my 365 days. But I know it did. I have felt it was unhealthy to be preoccupied with the past."

He goes on to say: "Drawing the whole experience to a meaningful conclusion would somehow make it okay. . . . Recently my thirteen-year-old handed me a stack of envelopes-unopened—dated 1968 that I got from my buddies and some of the Montagnards (Vietnamese mountain people) after coming home. I was so fed up with the whole thing I guess I just threw them in a pile and forgot about them when I got back. Only now am I able to read them, and they had a great emotional impact on me even now."

Finally, beginning the integration and atonement phases, he has begun writing a book and recently taught a course called "Vietnam—Retrospect" at his alma mater college.

Clearly, there are many Vietnam veterans who have not been able to traverse the recovery phases in such a remarkable way as this veteran.

Many of them remain fixed in one or more of the phases and require professional help in the form of psychological therapy to be able to move forward. Much of what has been learned about psychotherapy began in 1971 when the Vietnam Veterans Against the War (VVAW) organized "rap groups" and asked psychiatrist Robert Lifton[5] for help in leading them. With the help of Chaim Shatan[6] and other colleagues[7] these groups continued successfully for two years.

Dr. Lifton found that the group members frequently suffered from the self-condemnation of "self-lacerating" guilt. However, when they were able to talk openly about their war experiences and guilt feelings, they began to make progress. Eventually, self-lacerating guilt gave way to "animating guilt" that enabled them to take responsibility for their past actions and experience a new degree of personal liberation. These veterans became interested in helping others, particularly other Vietnam veterans; they often pursued further education and developed skills at writing, counseling, and public speaking. Through such activities, they experienced a renewed sense of personal integrity.[5]

In addition to resolving guilt, an important task of the rap groups was to help the members resolve feelings of "impacted grief," as Dr. Shatan describes: "The 'post-Vietnam syndrome' confronts us with the unconsummated grief of soldiers—'impacted grief' in which an unending, encapsulated past robs the present of meaning. Their sorrow is unspent, the grief of their wounds is untold, their guilt is unexpiated."[6]

Since the early 1970s there have been many others who have become involved in the research and application of principles of treatment for Vietnam veterans. Most have found that while therapy often helps them improve, survivors rarely are ever completely free of the imprinting effects of the traumatic events, beginning with the emergency arousal and initial outcry, for example, of phase 1; a time marked by vulnerability and terror acquired from a soldier's brush with death. Vietnam veterans with phase 1 symptoms continue to suffer from startle reactions and panic attacks, triggered by dreams and reminders of the event. Because of these physiological responses to memories, it is not difficult to understand why so many of these men complain of physical problems associated with parts of the autonomic nervous system: the heart, stomach, urinary tract, genitals, muscles, nerves, and blood pressure.

Researchers, such as Drs. Kolb and Mutalipassi at the VA Medical

Center in Albany, New York, have conducted research that found these symptoms to be a result of conditioned responses to trauma. They exposed veterans to noises simulating battle, and found that they responded with muscle tension, rapid heart rate, increased respiration, and increased electrical conduction on the surface of the skin. From these findings, they developed successful treatments using prescribed medications that not only subdued such conditioned physiological responses but the accompanying anxiety as well.[8,9] It has also proved useful to teach veterans relaxation techniques, meditation, or biofeedback training for controlling their autonomic nervous system and muscle tension. Weight lifting and jogging are additional ways of maintaining muscle tone and releasing pent-up emotional tension.

Some veterans with PTSD have reported other physical symptoms such as recurring dizziness and loss of balance, particularly in stressful situations. When we asked patients with PTSD if they ever suffered from dizzy spells or loss of balance, approximately 50% said they have had such episodes. One psychiatrist theorizes that these symptoms often reflect a disturbance in brain functioning due to the patient's profound fear of change and loss.[10] If this should be the case, a patient with these symptoms should only be treated with regular therapy to uncover and resolve that fear.

A Vietnam veteran often will develop a new physical symptom, a change of dream content, or a spontaneous recollection of a specific traumatic memory associated with an earlier recovery phase as treatment progresses. This is often made possible by the development of a trusting relationship between therapist and patient, permitting the previously blocked memory to begin to surface. If the memory is disguised in the dream or only partially recalled, it may be more fully uncovered through treatment techniques such as hypnosis. As reported earlier, a Vietnam veteran was treated for 15 months and hypnosis was used only when the patient developed a new symptom, the most unusual being a sudden numbness and tingling in his face. A hypnotherapy session discovered that agonizing traumatic events created the symptom. During a hypnotic trance state, he reexperienced the distressing memory that had been partially blocked. He saw himself being shot at point-blank range and felt the pain again of the bullet penetrating the bridge of his nose and piercing through his temple. After being ably supported through this reexperience, he fully regained his memory and the numbness and tingling in his face disappeared.[11]

Sometimes a new injury will cause physical symptoms related to a traumatic memory. For example, Lee suffered an injury to his neck in a fall. When the pain persisted, we believed that it partly represented a physiological memory, and suggested a hypnotherapy session. This approach was successful and permitted him to recall vividly a "blocked memory" associated with fear, guilt, grief, and his experience of nearly dying from a violent wound. He experienced complete but only temporary (24 hour) relief from pain following the session.

Vietnam veterans with phase 2-specific symptoms suffer from emotional detachment and numbing, full or partial amnesia, and little pleasure in daily living. If they are recent victims of traumatic experiences, they may respond to therapists who confront their denial, by evoking hidden horrifying memories through hypnosis, psychodrama, Gestalt therapy, and other "uncovering" techniques.

However, there are veterans fixed in this phase for years, who do not respond to such treatment approaches. Their major psychological defense is a persistent and profound hypervigilance that gives the appearance of a paranoid orientation to the world, as Drs. Herbert Hendin and Ann Pollinger-Haas have observed.[12] These veterans can often be intimidating to other people who sense the presence of smouldering rage. Unable to permit themselves to experience fear or other emotions, they are often consumed by feelings of vengeance, and are prone to periodic aggressive outbursts. They also have major conflicts pertaining to power; they view power as a destructive force and thus distrust people in authority, including therapists. Though Vietnam veterans stuck in this phase have associated their own use of power with destruction, they still attempt to control all events in their lives, but often do so in a self-destructive way.

Long-term treatment in group and individual therapy has been recommended for Vietnam veterans whose personality traits involve problems with anger, destructive use of power, and fear of vulnerability. They are in need of trusting therapeutic relationships, which can sustain them through the months and sometimes years it takes to change. Through such relationships, gradual acceptance of relative states of helplessness and vulnerability begins to emerge, enabling them to proceed through subsequent phases of recovery.

We believe that it is very important for group leaders or individual counselors to remain personable and not detached from their veteran patients. They must also be able to tolerate outbursts of anger and understand the relationship of anger to other emotions. Dr. Arthur Blank has stated: "It helps a lot in groups for the leader to make distinctions clearly amongst various emotions related to anger—hatred, rage, jealousy, envy, paranoid suspiciousness, bitterness, contempt, fear, anxiety. . . . There is often a relationship between anger and grief. Tears are sometimes felt unconsciously as clean anger—tears of rage may be extremely helpful, and crying from anger may be something to welcome as a part of important growth in a group or individual. There are other kinds of crying—relief, joy, frustration, a sense of contact and authenticity, sadness. It is good to be able to sense the anger involved sometimes in crying, though you may never say much about it."[13]

Yet the process of change for Vietnam veterans whose anger covers over their sense of vulnerability is slow. They frequently become defensive and test out how potentially powerful they or their therapists are, often for at least the first 6 months until trust develops. Psychiatrists Frick and Bogart have reported on their experiences of leading a group during the third through the sixth month when the members reported on many of their violent experiences, felt vulnerable, and then distrusted the leaders' possible misuse of their power over the group members. The psychiatrists, in turn, felt intimidated by the group members, sometimes retreating from them or even feeling like retaliating. When they found themselves doing so, they believed it was important to be honest and to also admit mistakes if they made them. "We sometimes had feelings akin to those of war prisoners being interrogated by their captors. We struggled with our feelings of intimidation, keeping in mind that these men had actually killed and were at times genuinely suicidal. We recognized our own rage . . . and accepted part of it as realistic and appropriate. On the other hand, their criticisms were sometimes quite accurate; it was necessary to be aware of our mistakes."[14]

Veterans who are less angry, emotionally numb, and guarded suffer from a predominance of phase 3—intrusive-repetitive—symptoms, as researcher Dr. Mardi Horowitz has described.[15] They reexperience disturbing memories, images, dreams, and emotions of fear, guilt, and grief. These symptoms are generally reenactments of the original traumatic experience; the unconscious mind attempts to replay the experience so as to master it. Certain therapeutic approaches can help the survivor undo, or master the associated fear, and help him eventually to understand the nature of his symptoms. These approaches include hypnosis, dream interpretation, and guided imagery—the use of imagined "pictures" to remember unpleasant memories. However, there are Vietnam veterans whose intrusive symptoms are so repetitive and disturbing that specific treatments are designed to control them. For example, psychologists John Fairbank and Terence Keane of the VA Medical Center in Jackson, Mississippi, have studied the effectiveness of a specific therapeutic approach called "flooding" for recurrent nightmares, intrusive images, and frightening flashbacks. In a very pleasant state of relaxation, the patient, along with his therapist, is exposed to traumatic scenes and sounds. After a period of eight sessions, anxiety-related images, flashbacks, and nightmares gradually diminish.[16]

Similarly, we as therapists have suggested that veterans with recurrent disturbing dreams practice holding the images in their minds as long as possible. This approach sometimes has a paradoxical effect and leads to a spontaneous reduction and disappearance of traumatic images.

Other less structured techniques have been used, with varying degrees of success, to end the distressing recurrence of traumatic images. For example, counselor John McQueeney[17] at Bay Pines, Florida, has taught Vietnam veterans the technique of repetitive dream rehearsal and modification, a method that has also been reported on by other researchers.[18] He instructs a patient with a recurrent dream of being ambushed to rehearse mentally a change in the dream, allowing him to take a different path from the one leading to the ambush. With an attitude of expectation when he goes to sleep at night, he soon learns to awaken from the frightening dream and immediately change the outcome; when he goes back to sleep, his mind will then choose the safe path. Eventually, the dream stops recurring.

Other therapeutic approaches have also been helpful for the veteran. For example, if a veteran is living in an unstable environment or has experienced a recent major loss in his life, he may need his time and daily routines completely managed until the crisis has passed. Voluntary hospitalization at such a time may be helpful to alleviate his family and job responsibilities, providing him with extra rest, and permitting him a relative state of dependency on staff personnel. During this time, he will be prescribed medications if necessary, will have a therapist, and be able to participate in a supportive group of patients with similar problems.

Dr. Horowitz, who has advocated "phase oriented" psychotherapy, has described the symptoms of trauma victims, which often vacillate between extremes of symptoms typical of phase 2 (denial–numbing) and phase 3 (intrusive-repetitive). Survivors who avoid recalling emotionally painful traumatic memories benefit from supportive therapists who can give "tolerable doses of awareness" while helping to maintain a balance between extremes of either group of symptoms.[19]

During our counseling experience, we have found that the educational aspect of treatment is of supreme importance in all phases. Learning about PTSD from articles and books and from a knowledgeable therapist is very helpful. But this education about the nature of PTSD symptoms ought to include the understanding that the veteran is not the only person suffering from them. For that reason, we also use educational groups, which provide support and shared knowledge from one another. In our educational group sessions with patients, we have gone so far as to focus on topics of educational value and elicit discussion about questions such as: What are the common PTSD symptoms? Why do Vietnam veterans use drugs? Why do Vietnam veterans have problems with power? What are the definitions of words like secret, conscience, anger, helplessness, receiving help, love, and trust? After completing the groups, veterans not only have developed considerable trust in their knowledgeable group leaders but have received a "cognitive anchor" that will help them continue through subsequent phases of the recovery process.

Educational groups take on therapeutic overtones and develop specific phases and dynamics of their own, similar to other therapy groups. One of us conducted a successful educational-therapeutic group lasting 16 sessions. It spontaneously evolved into four phases:

First, the members began to break through their emotional detachment and share vivid traumatic experiences, current problems with jobs, problems with relationships, drug and alcohol abuse. Second, during a phase of revelation of the brutalities of war, they described acts of violence, combat-related deaths, killing, their loss of moral values, and their feelings of victimization. Third, they focused on the depression related to feelings of being dead or partly dead. They also concentrated on their loss of values and their insensitivity to others. Fourth, they began to grieve together and earnestly help each other manage to become survivors rather than victims.[20] These sessions seemed to encapsulate similar phases, although spanning a relatively short period of 6 weeks, to those found in long-term individual,[21] combined individual and group,[22] and long-term group therapy,[23] making the time spent very profitable indeed.

Not only outpatient therapy but therapy provided within a hospital setting, in special PTSD Units, seems to proceed through phases. For example, the VA Medical Center PTSD Unit in Northampton, Massachusetts, has a treatment program with three phases. During the 20 weeks of the program, the initial phase focuses on stabilization of symptoms and helping participants feel comfortable enough so that they can be less guarded. The middle phase focuses on confronting and helping participants uncover hidden problems, grieve, accept the traumatic things that happened to them, and learn to become more comfortable with family interaction. The third or transition phase focuses on helping veterans develop useful skills and preparing them for responsible social interaction.[24]

Perhaps the treatment most widely used by patients and prescribed by their doctors, even though not necessarily most helpful in the long run, is chemical. Medications can be very effective in controlling many of the target symptoms of phases 1, 2 and 3. Vietnam veterans using alcohol and certain drugs, particularly marijuana, have known for years that they can temporarily suppress most target symptoms. In an article published in 1980, psychiatrists reported: "The acute administration of alcohol relieves many of the symptoms of classical traumatic neurosis. It is effective in inducing sleep and suppressing anxiety and can ease muscle tension and sometimes depression, irritability . . . agitation . . . [and] terrifying dreams." They also reported that when patients withdraw from alcohol, they will likely have the same symptoms.[25]

We have found that 66% of Vietnam veterans seeking treatment for drug and alcohol addiction suffered from recurrent dreams and traumatic imagery one or more times a week, for which they used "downers" such as alcohol, sedatives, or minor tranquilizers. Sixty-six percent were found to suffer from emotional detachment, risk-taking behavior, and aggressive outbursts and used substances to control these symptoms. Thirty-three percent used marijuana to control aggressive outbursts and 33% used alcohol or stimulants such as cocaine, Ritalin, or amphetamines to heighten emotional experiences.[20] However, it has also been commonly found that Vietnam veterans who continue to use alcohol over a period of years have more problems with intrusive traumatic images and unpleasant memories, particularly a few hours after stopping their drinking. Furthermore, those who have had aggressive outbursts are more likely to get into fights after they have been drinking even a small amount of alcohol. For that reason, we advise all of our patients to abstain from alcohol. Those who do not are at risk to lose control over their aggressive tendencies.

Yet, many veterans claim that marijuana does not worsen their symptoms but rather suppresses them. Psychiatrist John Yost, who had helped soldiers in Vietnam, is now involved in treating Vietnam veterans. He reports that many used marijuana as a self-medication to control anxiety, recurrent traumatic dreams, and flashbacks.[26] Although not advocating its use, many psychiatrists, hearing similar accounts from their Vietnam veteran patients, may not condemn marijuana use unless their patients are admitted to the hospital. Interestingly, they usually discover their patients will spontaneously stop using marijuana as a self-medication as their symptoms diminish through therapy.

Hospital-based treatment programs do no permit the use of alcohol or nonprescribed substances, including marijuana, at any time, whether on the premises or on weekend passes. And many veterans find abstinence from marijuana to be extremely difficult. As a patient said, "Marijuana mellows me out and keeps me from losing control. When I get so angry that I'd just as soon kill someone, I just smoke a joint and it calms me down; it's better than what I get from the doctor." Some newly hospitalized patients strongly object to the rule of being discharged when evidence of marijuana usage is found in their urine tests; they complain that the staff does not understand the anxiety of giving up their former methods of controlling PTSD symptoms. Thus, while mental health professionals ask their patients to give up using such substances, veterans ask their psychiatrists to be patient while they learn new ways to cope.

Medications have become a mainstay of PTSD treatment in many cases, particularly for hospitalized patients. They are used to control specific target symptoms, but should be discontinued as soon as the symptoms are controlled through other therapeutic means.

Valium and other similar tranquilizers of the "benzodiazepine" group have been prescribed widely for veterans with PTSD symptoms. They hold several dangers, however. Patients often develop a tolerance, and soon find themselves needing increasingly higher doses of the drug, and will even frequently develop a dependency on it. Moreover, many veterans who have used one of the "benzodiazepines" to control rage attacks, find themselves becoming more vulnerable to aggressive outbursts rather than remaining tranquil. Furthermore, if a Vietnam veteran discontinues taking one of this group after constant use, he might be plagued with withdrawal symptoms such as seizures, anxiety, restlessness, muscle tremors, and sleep disturbance. Doctors have sometimes prescribed one of the "major tranquilizer" group, such as the "phenothiazines" or Thioridazine (Mellaril), Mesoridazine (Serentil), or perphenazine (Trilafon) for the veteran with more severe symptoms of confused thoughts, agitation, severe recurrent flashbacks, and sleep disturbances which do not respond to other medications. Yet there is a risk here too of side effects, the most common being rigidity and abnormal muscle movements. Hence, they should be used sparingly.

Recent research has found a group of medications called the "adrenergic blockers" helpful for some Vietnam veterans with PTSD, particularly those who suffer conditioned physical reactions to fear such as rapid heart rate, increased respiration, and the "sweats." Two of these medications, clonidine and propranolol, prescribed in high doses, have been found to relieve the symptoms and also improve some veterans' sense of self-esteem.[27,28]

Those veterans suffering from disturbing dreams, depression, and sleeplessness have responded quite well to antidepressants such as the "tricyclic" group, trazedone (Desylrel), one of the "monoamine oxidase inhibitors" such as phenelzine (Nardil), or carbamazepine (Tegretol), normally used as an anticonvulsant medication. As a result, some patients using them under a doctor's care, may have fewer panic attacks, depresed states, anxiety, and nightmares. Other patients, with blocked memories and emotions, have recalled traumatic experiences and distressing emotions within a few days after beginning phenelzine.[29,30]

Vietnam veterans suffering from rapidly changing emotions sometimes feel more regulated after taking lithium. Recent research has also found that lithium has sometimes helped patients who are frightened of losing control over aggressive outbursts.[28]

Continuing research may point to increasingly more specific treatment of PTSD symptoms. For example, one of us has conducted preliminary research involving measurements of skin conductance (electrical energy on the surface of the skin) as an indirect indicator of brain functioning. Preliminary findings show that trauma victims use each side of the brain differently, either to recall or control the memories of traumatic events.

In some trauma victims, the right side of the brain may store traumatic memories while the left side of the brain may control them.[31] Researcher Dr. Claude Chemtob has made similar preliminary findings using more direct measurements of brain activity.[32] Perhaps trauma victims experience the posttraumatic defense of emotional numbing or detachment with a temporary physiological barrier between the right and left sides of the brain. Possibly, intrusive, disturbing memories result from a breakdown of that barrier. Our beginning research also suggests that if a victim who suffered a recent traumatic incident relives the agonizing experience during hypnosis, the structure of the physiological barrier may be altered. For instance, we measured a patient's responses 2 weeks after a severe beating when he suffered recurrent frightening dreams, fear, and depression alternating with emotional numbing and each side responded in a different way. Two months later, after receiving hypnotherapy and group therapy, his acute symptoms were markedly improved and the measurements suggested that both sides of the brain were working together once more, suggesting that he was no longer using physiological and psychological defenses to control intrusive unacceptable emotionally charged memories.

Since over a century ago, it has been known that hypnosis can be used to enable a victim to reexperience a disturbing traumatic event, after which time he or she appears to be free of posttraumatic symptoms, although sometimes only temporarily.[33] Hypnotically induced recollections are merely reenactments of the original traumatic experience, but in contrast to the uncontrolled nature of posttraumatic reenactments ("flashbacks"), those that occur during hypnotic treatment are controlled.

Historically, the word "abreaction" was used to describe the hypnotically induced, emotionally charged reliving of the traumatic event. The hypnotherapist guides the patient through the horror of the experience and helps him to remember it in a way that is less disturbing for him later. The hypnotic reexperience reduces the patient's compelling need to repeatedly recall the emotionally disturbing traumatic event, since it eventually becomes integrated into the conscious mind.[34]

Hypnotic abreaction, used earlier to treat World War II veterans shortly after developing symptoms,[35] has not been found as effective for the delayed symptoms typical of Vietnam veterans. Consequently, there have only been limited reports of successful application of hypnosis as a treatment. Instead, we, like some therapists, have found that intensive psychotherapy, with no more than occasional use of hypnosis, has more healing power because it permits the therapist a more active empathy and "sharing" of patients' guilt or grief-ridden experiences. As Sarah Haley, an experienced social worker and therapist, has described, this may be a painful experience for the therapist, who may be "dragged, kicking and screaming for release, down every jungle trail, burned-out village, and terrorizing night patrol."[36] Nevertheless, the veteran experiences a positive change within him because of the continuing presence, love, and understanding of the therapist.

Nevertheless, hypnosis has been used and apparently effectively in the hands of certain professionals. In one study, it was effective as part of a 6- to 9-month-long treatment program when video recordings of the abreaction were replayed at a later time for the patient when he could view them in a normal state of consciousness.[37] In this way, the hypnotized patient was able to observe his prior emotional experience and could understand it better.

We have found that recollections of traumatic experiences, induced not only by hypnosis but by other techniques as well, generally promote the recovery process.[38] This is particularly true when the trauma victim vividly recalls the event and reexperiences not only the original emotion associated with the experience, but also other emotions such as guilt and grief[39] that had been blocked at that time and since. Those most likely to benefit from this method are recent trauma victims still suffering from acute emotional distress, Vietnam veterans suffering the effects of a recent and unrelated emotionally disturbing event, or Vietnam veterans developing new symptoms or emotions associated with the original trauma.

Ted, a Vietnam veteran, was admitted to the hospital after his wife suddenly left him. The enormity of his feelings of loss for his marriage triggered a flood of memories and emotions related to a painful loss that occurred in Vietnam. During one of the first therapy sessions, the therapist asked him to talk about his experiences in that country. When he did, the memories released strong emotions of grief. The therapist then asked him if he saw a picture of the specific traumatic event eliciting such an emotional response in his mind, and if so, whether he could describe it in detail. The veteran, now grieving nearly uncontrollably, began to relive vividly, without the help of hypnosis, the traumatic experience of nearly being killed in Vietnam.

It is more common that a Vietnam veteran's emotional recovery will be enhanced dramatically when he relives an emotionally charged traumatic event after first developing a trusting relationship with the therapist, sometimes taking 6 months or more. Then, a change in the nature of the patient–therapist relationship may become the emotional pathway to a unique traumatic experience. In the case of one Vietnam veteran, the 12th month of the therapy process was marked by his developing anxiety about being a victim at about the same time that the therapist suggested that he would benefit from being a hypnotic subject. The anxiety was associated with dreams wherein he was a victim enveloped by flying blood and brain fragments from a dead VC soldier. During the hypnotic session, the therapist asked the veteran to go back in time and relive any past experience associated with his dream. The veteran began to relive a very traumatic experience of shooting an enemy soldier at point-blank range in the head and feeling fragments of the brain hit himself over the head and face.

Every Vietnam veteran has a unique group of traumatic memories, each of which should be specifically uncovered and treated.[16] Some veterans have been subjected to scores of traumatic experiences and as they proceed through the phases of recovery, they are likely to relive different traumatic experiences and associated emotions at various times. A dramatic example occurred during the last 5 months of an 18-month-long therapy process. Within the span of 5 months, the Vietnam veteran relived, during hypnosis, five different traumatic experiences, each associated with a different and more intense emotion related to fear, anger, grief, and guilt.[11]

We have often found, however, that veterans may recall different traumatic memories more readily when specifically exposed to precipitating events. As we mentioned earlier, when a group of hospitalized Vietnam veterans traveled together to a cemetery for the funeral of their friend who had committed suicide, considerable emotions and memories relating to death were evoked. As one of them said later, "I started crying at the cemetery and I couldn't stop. I wasn't just crying for [his] death but for all the dead buddies I left behind in Vietnam. And that was the first time I have cried since I got back."

While the pathway to a traumatic memory is the patient's common emotion at the time of therapy and at the time of the original trauma, his abreaction of the past traumatic experience is not the path's final destination. That occurs only when the patient and therapist can traverse the problems and interpersonal difficulties, including those with the therapist,[40] and then to find in the event a new meaning so that the patient can make the emotionally charged experience an acceptable memory.

Recovery is a process that may take many years for combat veterans, sometimes occurring spontaneously and at other times with the help of treatment. Yet, whether spontaneous or through treatment, getting better follows a progression of predictable phases. For those receiving treatment, medications, relaxation training, educational approaches, desensitization, psychotherapy groups, and hospital treatment have been used at specific times with varying success, particularly for the distressing intrusiverepetitive symptoms, rage, and emotional detachment characteristic of the early phases.

Paramount to the recovery process is the therapeutic relationship between veteran and therapist. Whether occurring in individual therapy, group therapy, or hypnotherapy, this relationship provides the nucleus for the recovery process. Particularly for those veterans who have developed longstanding personality changes following their return from Vietnam, their trusting relationships enable them to reveal hidden traumatic memories and emotions more easily. Specific techniques, including hypnosis, can be used at such times by the therapist to elicit vivid recollection and "abreaction" of traumatic events and later to help the veteran understand their relationship to specific posttraumatic symptoms.

Bringing to light the hidden traumatic memories associated with different emotional states of fear, anger, guilt, and grief is crucial in giving a momentum and direction to the recovery process. Finally, it is most important for the patient, with the help of the therapist, to integrate his past experiences, find meaning, new ways of coping, "atoning," and new directions for his life.

Chapter 10 / FINDING READJUSTMENT SERVICES FOR VETERANS AND THEIR FAMILIES

There has been in recent years an emerging positive relationship between Americans in their respect and regard for Vietnam veterans and the veterans in their self-determining, active role in society. The establishment of Vietnam veterans organizations for personal renewal, social and community action, and economic development is enabling the Vietnam-recovery process to become a reality for all these men and women. Vietnam veterans organizations include Vietnam Veterans of America, Vietnam Veterans Against the War, United Vietnam Veterans Organization, National Association of Concerned Veterans, Vietnam Veterans Leadership Program, Vietnam Veterans of Massachusetts, Inc., Nam Veterans Association of Cape Cod, Com Vets and Vietnam Era Veterans of Maine, in addition to many others around the country. These organizations are filling a deep void in the lives of many veterans.

Recent popular musical productions, artistic shows, popular songs, poetry, off-Broadway dramatic productions, movies, TV serials, best-seller books, and popular and professional journal and magazine articles, in addition to the 1982 dedication of the National Memorial of Vietnam Veterans in Washington, D.C., all point to an emerging positive regard, sympathy, empathy, and appreciation for Vietnam veterans and their sacrifices. Older, traditional veterans organizations such as the Disabled American Veterans (DAV), American Legion, and Veterans of Foreign Wars (VFW), and the more recent Black Veterans of All Wars (BVAW), American Jewish War Veterans, among others, have begun to take notable initiatives on behalf of veterans of the Vietnam War. Of special note are the relatively early contributions of the Disabled American Veterans (DAV) to the general welfare of Vietnam veterans. It was DAV that administered a number of Veterans Outreach Centers in various parts of the United States, and sponsored the now-famous comprehensive study of the readjustment problems of Vietnam veterans—the *Forgotten Warriors Project*. These initiatives by DAV predated the current federally supported Veterans Outreach Centers, known as "Operations Outreach." The American Legion currently champions the cause of Vietnam veterans in the areas of economics and employment, and in understanding the intricacies of Agent Orange poisoning. Other traditional organizations have contributed funds to assist Vietnam veterans in a large number of social, economic, and political concerns.

Legislative initiatives at federal and state levels are continuing to demonstrate some awareness of the special readjustment needs and problems of Vietnam veterans. In many cities throughout the United States, memorials to those who fell in Vietnam abound. For example, in New York City, Mayor Edward Koch has established the New York Vietnam Veterans Memorial Commission, with a number of task-oriented committees on administration, design, programs, communications, and finance. The objectives of the commission are to raise funds to support both a "Living Memorial" (job and career development programs for Vietnam veterans) and a monument in honor of those New Yorkers who died in the war.

Special legislation for job training, education, "Agent Orange" compensation, small businesses, etc. offer Vietnam veterans some options in their lives, and these go a long way in helping some to relax their defensive posturing against themselves and their world. As clinical specialists in mental health, we remain convinced that what most Vietnam veterans desire in their lives—more so than most other things—is the opportunity to serve. This ardent desire to serve others is exemplified by myriad situations in which these veterans participate in volunteer agencies that serve veterans, other underserved populations, and the nation as a whole. Thus, therapists, counselors, medical specialists, rehabilitation counselors. job and career development trainers will find their efforts incomplete if Vietnam veterans in their care are not adequately prepared for service to their fellowmen.

Yet for quite a long time, finding readjustment services for Vietnam veterans was and is still sometimes extremely difficult. Human service delivery systems have been remiss for many years with regard to the Vietnam veteran and his family. It is rather surprising that a sparsity of services exist despite the fact that Vietnam veterans were identified by the President's Commission on Mental Health in 1978 as a grossly underserved population. There are, we believe, two reasons for the reluctance or resistance of mental health agencies to develop useful readjustment services for Vietnam veterans and their families: the widespread belief that only the Veterans Administration is responsible for serving veterans; and the national stigma and the stereotypes associated with Vietnam veterans. Both have interfered with the development of research efforts to improve sorely needed services for these men and women. Vietnam veterans are consumers of health and mental health services. As citizens of this country, their needs should be addressed as forthrightly and as vigorously as any other population of Americans, particularly those targeted by the President's Commission on Mental Health as underserved. The time has come for federal agencies (other than the VA), state agencies, and local facilities to seriously reevaluate their service policies and practices to ensure that they are not unwittingly excluding this relatively large population of men and women from their services.

Unfortunately, many clinicians—psychiatrists, psychologists, social workers, therapists, and counselors—have, for the most part, turned their backs on Vietnam veterans as did much of American society. Like society at large, human service providers have had emotional difficulties in dealing with Vietnam veterans. Often from their judgmental pedestals, they have viewed these veterans as "losers," "baby killers," "hopeless," "unreachable," and even "untreatable." Furthermore, service providers, reflecting society in general, have misunderstood the Vietnam veteran, and been unable to separate the veterans' human needs from the ills of the Vietnam War and the political climate at home. From our experience as clinicians, consultants, and supervisors, we know that it is virtually impossible to make an accurate, unbiased assessment of needs when the consumer is already viewed as for example, "drug-crazed" or a "frenzied lunatic." It is not hard to see how the negative stereotype of Vietnam veterans has precluded and continues to preclude the establishment and development of services that would meet their readjustment needs.

Historically, there seems to have existed a sort of "mutual antagonism" between Vietnam veterans as consumers and agencies as providers of services. For the most part, these veterans have felt "estranged" from their therapists, whom they believed did not understand their needs and problems. Therapists, on the other hand, because of their own unresolved feelings about Vietnam, would totally avoid that subject. Such active avoidance communicated a clear message to the veteran: "You may not talk about that terrible place, and certainly do not tell me about the bad and horrible acts you guys committed while in Vietnam. Keep them to yourself. They are not welcome here." Such encounters were often scarred by a judgmental condemnation of the veteran, leaving him with increased feelings of bitterness, rejection, and with the "conviction" that no one cared. After such encounters, these veterans often lost all hope that anyone could help them. Compounding this, the veterans often came to view the professionals as "corrupted" in ways they did not understand. In the words of Julius, one of countless men and women who sought services for war-related problems with little or no success:

> When I got back from the 'Nam, I knew I needed psychotherapy or something like that. I just knew that if I didn't get help I was going to kill myself or somebody else. I just was unable to hold it together for myself and for my wife and two kids. I came back with a drug problem; and because I couldn't work, we were placed on welfare. I hate welfare. Here I am a real man—or am I a real man? When I was in Vietnam, I did a lot of heroic things and have the medals to show for it. I felt like a man over there. At a clinic in the past, the worker told me I needed some therapy, and recommended I see a doctor. I asked her why she couldn't see me. I was then told that my kind of cases are too confused and complicated for her, even though she had been a social worker for 13 years. See, she thought I was

the sicky because I went to Vietnam. This conclusion was made even before she really asked me why I was seeking help. It was automatically assumed that I was a basket case, a hopeless case. I went to see this doctor; he barely looked at me. I felt he "saw me coming" and knew all about my sickness. I was the "sicky" to him. He just kept on asking me all that bullshit about how many children I had killed and was I guilty and depressed about it. He asked how it felt to kill people. He also kept on asking me about my brothers and sisters. But he never asked me about what my experiences were like in Vietnam. He never did. I saw him for treatment for about a month— about three visits, but I quit because we weren't getting anywhere. We weren't communicating at all. During this time I had a lot of flashbacks in the daytime; lots of "bad" dreams in the nighttime. No rest; poor sleep; and he didn't know what to do or say to me. He just kept on giving me more and more medications. I could've set up my own pharmacy. I needed someone to talk to about my problems, my real problems, not some bullshit about my childhood. I needed someone who wanted to help. The clinic later referred me to another shrink. I think she was a social worker or a psychologist; I am not really sure. She was no different. I guess she thought she was being honest with me, by telling me that she was not a veteran, was not in Vietnam, and did not know what was wrong with me. She also told me that she had no experience working with Vietnam veterans, and that I should go to the Veterans Administration for help, since, after all, that's what they're supposed to be about. She apologized, and said she was sorry; but she wasn't as sorry as I was. I needed help, and was now feeling that I was hopeless, that I would just die in my misery and pain.

This was just one of those rejections, all over again, another fucked-up experience with a shrink. Two years ago, I made another try to get some help at another agency close to where my mother lives. I was also told to go to the nearest VA. I was given some dope medicine, and I never came back. I kept getting angry and angrier; I felt I was being handed a line of shit by these doctors. I also became scared that there was something really wrong with me now. I just didn't want to go to the VA for help. If I wanted to go there, I would have gone. I just felt uncomfortable going to the VA. I blame the VA for my going to 'Nam anyway; I wanted no part of it.

It was only in the last 3 years when my wife made an important phone call to a local Veterans Outreach Center that I started feeling

I had hope, that something could be done for me. I received the help that I have always needed. Finally, I found it easier to hold a job and take care of my family. My nightmares are not as frightening or as frequent as they used to be. Things are better now; I am learning to trust people and give more to my wife and children.

Historically, the most important event marking the advent of readjustment services for Vietnam veterans began in 1971 when the Vietnam Veterans Against the War (VVAW) believed it would be beneficial for their members to meet in groups and discuss their common experiences. Although this was in some respects an attempt to start a self-help movement among Vietnam veterans, the VVAW, a political activist organization, sought trained therapists to sit in during the group meetings.

One of the therapists, Dr. Robert Shapiro,[1] has described some rather interesting and important aspects of these groups. Foremost, the veterans wanted control over the structure and procedures governing each group's activities. They insisted that the meetings take place "on their own turf," at their headquarters. These conditions were to ensure that their effort was not going to become just another failure of "shrinks" at treating veterans with traditional, irrelevant techniques. The veterans avoided calling the therapists anything that suggested they were being treated for mental problems. The veterans were referred to as "veterans" and the therapists, "professionals."

There was considerable flexibility in the way these groups were structured. In great contrast to traditional group psychotherapy where patients are expected to regularly attend sessions scheduled at prescribed intervals, members of "rap groups" attended whenever and for as long as they desired. Held once a week, the rap sessions would last from 2 to 4 hours, sometimes without leaders. Altogether, several hundred veterans and some twenty therapists participated in this VVAW project, which also included individual psychotherapy and occasional weekend workshops on specific topics such as how long veterans would remain "veterans," the problems of intimacy, and the "John Wayne" image.

Therapeutic goals and the length of time required to meet those goals varied with each veteran. For example, if one found relief after making a "confession" of war atrocities before a group of sympathetic fellow veterans and empathic professionals, two meetings might be sufficient. If he was in a crisis situation, he remained in the group long enough to resolve the crisis. For a more complete understanding of his miseries, the veteran attended for as long as necessary to meet his individual needs.

Although these groups were intended for veterans to help themselves, the presence of group leaders (that is, the professionals) whom the veterans liked and trusted was important to their success. Several factors facilitated the rapid development of positive relationships between the veterans and the professionals. First, the therapists shared the veterans' anti-Vietnam War sentiments. Consequently, the veterans felt supported in their political views by the therapists, who were part of "the system" that angered them. Second, by sharing very personal and emotionally charged memories, the group members often developed intense relationships with the therapists. Third, the informality of the rap groups minimized the therapists' role as authority figures.

The experience gained by the leaders in terms of learning how to approach the veterans' deep-seated rage and distrust of people in authority, and the format of these groups, particularly as it pertained to the aspect of leadership and the flexibility of group structure, became a blueprint for the development of later therapeutic groups begun as an integral part of the service structure of today's Vietnam Veterans Outreach Centers ("Vet Centers") throughout the United States, Puerto Rico, and the U.S. Virgin Islands. Within such groups, leaders are not analytical in their interventions, and are committed to participating rather than controlling the rap group process. Leaders who have contributed to this process have found it so inherently worthwhile that a number of them have become advocates for the veterans, particularly since many veterans have felt vulnerable and helpless in dealing with "the system."

Most therapists or counselors—experienced or inexperienced, Vietnam veteran or nonveteran—have had to struggle with the intensity of group members' distrust of authority and resistance to share their painful memories of the Vietnam experience. The most effective therapists are those who recognize their own limitations and are open to learning from their patients and from more experienced clinicians.

An understanding of the following points is essential to providing services that are of real benefit to Vietnam veterans and their families:

1. Some Vietnam veterans are highly motivated to change their lives, contrary to the stereotype of the lazy, unmotivated veteran.

2. These services must give the veteran a sense of hope and control over what happens to him or her in the treatment group.

3. The services must protect the veteran from feelings of being trapped, while offering him a sense of security.

4. The structure of the services must be flexible—in duration of sessions, in integrating community-based services, etc.

5. The services must be rendered in such a way as to not give the veteran the feeling he is mentally "sick" or related stigmata.

6. Therapists and counselors need to respect the veteran's personal objectives and goals of treatment.

7. Self-disclosures, on the part of the therapists, are critical.

8. Nonjudgmental, empathic response is of paramount importance.

9. The treatment atmosphere must be informal, and the therapist would do well to downplay his role as "authority."

10. The therapist must be prepared to assume an advocacy role for the veteran.

11. The therapist must be constant and steadfast and sure of himself or herself.

The nationwide specialized readjustment services, are referred to as the "Vet Centers." Vet Centers were mandated by Congress in mid 1979 and implemented by the Veterans Administration in late 1979. They differ from VA Medical Centers, since they are on a much smaller scale, are staffed primarily by Vietnam veterans, and have an informal atmosphere. Collectively, these Centers are referred to as "Operations Outreach," and comprise a new service to a group of men and women who were alienated from most human service agencies, including the VA Medical Centers. This new program of services featured 91 "storefront"-type facilities, whose informality was most congruent with the veterans' life-styles. In 1981, because of growing public interest, the number of Vet Centers nationwide rose to 137; and, in 1984, Congress passed legislation adding 51 new service units nationwide. Vet Centers are located throughout the United States, in Rio Piedras–San Juan, Arecivo, and Ponce, Puerto Rico, and in St. Thomas and St. Croix of the U.S. Virgin Islands.

The mission of Operation Outreach is to assist those men and women who served their country during the Vietnam era, designated as the period between August 1964 and July 1975. Men and women who were honorably discharged as well as those whose discharges are designated "less-than-honorable," are eligible for services at these Centers. In particular, its purpose is to help them in the difficult task of reconstructing their lives to the particular level of adjustment each veteran needs, from which he or she can grow and mature toward self-actualizing goals. Vet Center Program planners, attempting to circumvent the veteran's profound alienation and anger toward "the system," reasoned that if Vietnam veterans were to be reached at all with these services, they would first have to be *outreached*. Hence, the basic Program philosophy essentially is: "since you seem reluctant to seek services in traditional places, we will seek you out and offer you services that go with your life-style and specific needs."

The specific services offered by the Vet Centers are considered under the general rubric of "readjustment counseling." Readjustment counseling involves psychological counseling and psychotherapy for the individual, or in a group, rap group, family, couple, multiple family, and multiple couple modalities. An important aspect of readjustment counseling is educating the veteran on the nature of combat stress (or PTSD) and other related problems. The veteran, his wife, or partner are given a "minicourse" geared to help them understand the impact of Vietnam on the veteran and on his relationships with his wife, partner, and children.[2] In addition to readjustment psychological services, Vet Centers offer crisis intervention, referral and follow-up services, and assistance with legal problems, upgrading less-than-honorable discharges, and benefits counseling.

The staff members at the Vet Centers respond to a wide variety of readjustment needs of Vietnam veterans and their families. They go on crisis calls to help a mother whose veteran-son has barricaded himself in the house and threatens to kill her and himself. They respond to calls from wives who fear being harmed by their husbands, who may appear homicidal and/or suicidal. The staffs also respond to requests by police departments to assist them in understanding the Vietnam-related problems of a veteran who has been arrested for a violent act. They assist Vietnam veterans in criminal and domestic legal proceedings; and play advocacy roles to help veterans secure the benefits from adjudication boards to which they are lawfully entitled.

Vet Centers also feature rap groups composed of Vietnam *combat* veterans, often made up of male, and, at times, female veterans. Other men's groups are made up of combat veterans (those who served *in* Vietnam itself) and era veterans (those who served during the Vietnam era in places other than Vietnam or Southeast Asia). These groups offer the veterans the rare, but profoundly important, opportunity to share their mutual experiences in a therapeutic setting that is nonjudgmental, safe, and conducive to trust. For the most part, however, rap groups are comprised solely of Vietnam combat veterans. For these veterans, the groups offer the opportunity to talk and examine emotional issues pertaining to service in Vietnam. Many veterans had been silent about Vietnam for more than 10 years. Now, at the Vet Centers they are able to begin to find meaning, get sanction, and secure respect for their sacrifices. In rap groups, these veterans can share mutual pain, memories, their "bad" dreams, their dangerous startle responses, their violent tendencies, problems in their households, marital difficulties, problems with their children, and so on. These veterans feel understood, respected, and are helped by people who had actually served in Vietnam, or those who did not but who nevertheless demonstrate unusual sensitivity, empathy, and competence.

Vet Centers also feature special groups for female veterans, particularly nurses. Organizing these groups is extremely difficult since few female veterans come to the Centers. Despite this obstacle, some Vet Centers have done noteworthy work with Vietnam nurse veterans. Nurse veteran Rose Sandecki, the Team Leader of the Vet Center in Concord, California, is a glowing example for the successful treatment of female nurse veterans. Vet Center personnel have also helped organize special rap groups for medical personnel in Vietnam—physicians, nurses, and medical corpsmen (usually males). Noteworthy here is the Vet Center in White River Junction, Vermont. Special rap groups for officers, including retired officers who served in Vietnam, are also found at some Vet Centers.

The unique difficulties of the wives and partners of Vietnam veterans are well known to the Vet Center staff, and a variety of women's needs are addressed. Wives and partners of Vietnam veterans engage in mutual sharing and support. As "second generation" survivors, wives and partners of Vietnam veterans live their own hellish existence, and need to learn ways of coping more adaptively with their mates, as well as more appropriate ways to promote their own growth in order to fulfill their potentials as a woman, wife, mother, and human being.

Some Vet Centers hold special rap groups for the children of Vietnam veterans; notable in this regard are the Bronx Vet Center and the Chicago Heights Vet Center. This opportunity offers these children a rare forum in which they can vent their feelings, learn about PTSD and about Vietnam, while allowing them to better understand their own responses to family violence, parental discord, the unhappiness of their fathers, and how to stop blaming themselves for their family's problems. They get the chance to express their fears and feelings of disappointment, despair, anger, and resentment. They often reveal anger and resentment toward their fathers, mothers, and the subject of Vietnam. Some children are not aware of Vietnam as the cause of their parents' current difficulties. Rap groups for children help them to make that link in a manner that takes into account their degree of cognitive and emotional development. We have found that children need to be taught—repeatedly—that they are not to blame for these problems.

The staffs at Vet Centers are involved in the community—civic, political, educational, medical, and economic development, as well as in numerous organizations at federal, state, and local government levels— with issues pertaining to the readjustment of Vietnam veterans and the needs of their families. They make educational and consultative presentations to health and mental health facilities and organizations, and serve as special consultants and trainers to Employee Assistance Program professionals in corporate institutions and organizations that have Vietnam veterans in their employ.

Vet Center staffs are also invited to high schools, where they talk to students about war, peace, the draft, love for country, patriotism, making choices, and readjustment from war. Combat veterans are often quite direct, open, and capable in explaining their own Vietnam experiences to these audiences. Education and consultation are also conducted within the VA Medical Centers throughout the United States, informing, educating, collaborating, sensitizing, and building new bridges over old antagonisms, while linking traditional and nontraditional Vet Center services for the ultimate good of the veteran and his family.

Currently, Vet Centers are staffed by 575 people, with an average of four staff members per Center. They have served over 300,000 veterans since 1979, and have outreached to almost 60,000 veterans during the same period. Family members and partners of veterans have made over 235,930 visits. The staffs have made 550,000 telephone calls on behalf of Vietnam veterans, including telephone counseling for those unable or unwilling to come to the Centers. These figures are astounding for at least two reasons. First, the men and women served do not ordinarily seek mental health services, having found them in the past to be antagonistic to their needs. Second, these veterans are not only an extraordinarily underserved population of Americans, they are also intensely resistive to even the thought of mental health services of any kind.

The questions have been asked, "What makes Operation Outreach so unique and successful in fulfilling its goals?" "What makes staff morale so high that they work, according to recent research, on the national average of 52 hours per week?"[4] That Vet Center staffs donate over 25% additional time "speaks highly of the devotion to the goals of Operation Outreach and the high level of responsibility of employees in accomplishing necessary tasks."[4] Though the answers to these questions are many and complex, we would say that the success of the Vet Centers is inseparably linked to the quality and experience of the staff. Their enthusiasm and motivation have been a balm to the distressed veteran and his family; their feeling of commitment and closeness—as if they were a family—are important ingredients in liking their job and in serving well those they can.

Most of the staff members of Vet Centers served in Vietnam. The others either served elsewhere during the Vietnam era or, if not, had demonstrated sensitivity to Vietnam veterans, their needs, and their search for a new ethos and personal development. Vet Center Program officials recognize the need for continuing education of the staff to refine services to Vietnam veterans. To this end, staff members attend a variety of workshops and training seminars in the areas of traumatic dreams, crisis intervention, family and couples counseling, psychological assessment, interviewing techniques, etc.

Each Vet Center is managed by a Team Leader, who may have formal degrees ranging from a masters in psychology or social work to a doctorate in psychology, social work, or medicine. Other staff includes two or more Veterans Outreach Counselors, with comparable degrees and vast experience working with Vietnam veterans; and an office manager to assist the Team Leader and other staff members with clerical and administrative duties.

Qualified volunteers, inspired by the broad public and professional support of the Vet Center Program, have augmented the work of the existing staff. Professionals and paraprofessionals in mental health and related areas lead or co-lead rap groups, as well as therapy groups designed for the later phases of the treatment.[5] Qualified volunteers assist being group leaders for groups of wives, partners, and children. Vet Center staffs are also assisted by public and private sector-funded Program personnel as well, such as from the Vietnam Veterans Leadership Program and the Disabled Veterans Outreach Program (DVOP). These groups assist Vet Center clients to find jobs and build careers. As of June 1984, DVOP workers spent approximately 2000 hours per week in Vet Centers nationwide! Vet Center staffs, as frequent sponsors of Small Business Administration workshops, lectures, and seminars, have demonstrated that "readjustment counseling" requires a broad spectrum of services to meet the wide array of needs of their clients.

Vet Center staffs also coordinate services with a variety of special service units within local VA Medical Centers and VA Regional Offices. For example, some Vet Center clients may need and are given medication, inpatient care, "Agent Orange" screenings, physical examinations, special inpatient treatment units, special alcoholism treatment programs, etc. The staffs also coordinate their efforts on behalf of the veterans with the VA Regional Offices. Together they secure lawful benefits for Vet Center clients, as well as compensation for service-connected disabilities. Vet Center staffs also explore other possible services at local agencies.

Below is a list of Vet Centers currently in existence. On p. 234–235, the locations of upcoming Vet Centers recently authorized by Congress are given.

ALABAMA

The Birmingham Vet Center
2145 Highland Avenue
Suite 250
Birmingham, AL 35205
(205) 933-0500

The Mobile Vet Center
110 Marine Street
Mobile, AL 36604
(205) 694-4194

ALASKA

The Anchorage Vet Center
4201 Tudor Centre Drive
Suite 115
Anchorage, AK 99508
(907) 277-1501

The Fairbanks Vet Center
712 10th Avenue
Fairbanks, AK 99701
(907) 456-4238

The Kenai Vet Center
905 Cook Street
P.O. Box 1883
Kenai, AK 99611
(907) 283-5205

The Wasilla Vet Center
Box 957 Mile 1/2 Knik Road
Wasilla, AK 99687
(907) 376-4318

ARIZONA

The Phoenix Vet Center
807 North 3rd Street
Phoenix, AZ 85004
(602) 261-4769

The Tucson Vet Center
727 North Swan
Tucson, AZ 85711
(602) 323-3271

ARKANSAS

The Little Rock Vet Center
1311 West 2nd Street
Little Rock, AR 72201
(501) 378-6395

CALIFORNIA

The Anaheim Vet Center
859 South Harbor Blvd.
Anaheim, CA 92805
(714) 776-0161

The Concord Vet Center
1899 Clayton Road
Suite 140
Concord, CA 94520
(415) 680-4529

The Fresno Vet Center
1340 Van Ness Avenue
Fresno, CA 93721
(209) 487-5660

The Los Angeles Vet Center—#606
251 West 85th Place
Los Angeles, CA 90003
(213) 753-1391

The Los Angeles Vet Center—#607
2000 Westwood Blvd.
Los Angeles, CA 90025
(213) 475-9509

The Montabello Vet Center
2449 West Beverly Blvd.
Montabello, CA 90640
(213) 728-9999

The Northridge Vet Center
18924 Roscoe Blvd.
Northridge, CA 91335
(213) 993-8867

The Oakland Vet Center
616 16th Street
Oakland, CA 94612
(415) 763-3904

The Riverside Vet Center
4954 Arlington Avenue
Riverside, CA 92504
(714) 359-8967
The San Diego Vet Center
2900 6th Avenue
San Diego, CA 92103
(619) 294-2040
The San Francisco Vet Center—#619
1708 Waller Street
San Francisco, CA 94117
(415) 386-6727
The San Francisco Vet Center–#620
2989 Mission Street
San Francisco, CA 94110
(415) 824-5111
The San Jose Vet Center—#614
1648 West Santa Clara Street
San Jose, CA 95116
(408) 258-5600
The San Jose Vet Center—#615
361 South Monroe Street
Suite 605
San Jose, CA 95128
(408) 249-1677

COLORADO

The Colorado Springs Vet Center
875 West Morena Avenue
Colorado Springs, CO 80905
(303) 633-2902
The Denver Vet Center
1820 Gilpin Street
Denver, CO 80218
(303) 861-9281

CONNECTICUT

The Hartford Vet Center
370 Market Street
Hartford, CT 06510
(203) 244-3544
The New Haven Vet Center
562 Whalley Avenue
New Haven, CT 06510
(203) 773-2236

DELAWARE

The Wilmington Vet Center
Van Buren Medical Center
1411 N. Van Buren Street
Wilmington, DE 19806
(302) 571-8277

DISTRICT OF COLUMBIA

The Washington, D.C. Vet Center
709 8th Street S.E.
Washington, DC 20003
(202) 745-8400

FLORIDA

The Fort Lauderdale Vet Center
400 E. Prospect Road
Fort Lauderdale, FL 33334
(305) 563-2992
The Jacksonville Vet Center
255 Liberty Street
Jacksonville, FL 32202
(904) 791-3621
The Miami Vet Center
2615 Biscayne Blvd.
Miami, FL 33137
(305) 573-8830

The Orlando Vet Center
333 North Orange
Orlando, FL 32801
(305) 420-6151

The St. Petersburg Vet Center
235 31st Street North
St. Petersburg, FL 33713
(813) 327-3355

The Tampa Vet Center
1507 West Sligh Avenue
Tampa, FL 33604
(813) 228-2621

GEORGIA

The Atlanta Vet Center
65 11th Street, N.E.
Atlanta, GA 31309
(404) 881-7264

HAWAII

The Honolulu Vet Center
1370 Kipiolani Blvd,   Suite 201
Honolulu, HI 96814
(808) 546-3743

IDAHO

The Boise Vet Center
103 West State Street
Boise, ID 83702
(208) 342-3612

ILLINOIS

The Chicago Heights Vet Center
1600 Halsted Street
Chicago Heights, IL 60411
(312) 754-3040

The Chicago Vet Center
547 West Roosevelt Road
Chicago, IL 60607
(312) 829-4400

The Oak Park Vet Center
155 South Oak Park Avenue
Oak Park, IL 60302
(312) 383-3225

The Peoria Vet Center
605 N.E. Monroe
Peoria, IL 61603
(309) 671-7300

INDIANA

The Evansville Vet Center
101 N. Kentucky Avenue
Evansville, IN 47711
(812) 425-0311

The Fort Wayne Vet Center
528 West Berry Street
Fort Wayne, IN 46802
(219) 423-9456

The Indianapolis Vet Center
811 Massachusetts Avenue
Indianapolis, IN 46204
(317) 269-2838

IOWA

The Des Moines Vet Center
3619 6th Avenue
Des Moines, IA 50313
(515) 284-6119

The Sioux City Vet Center
706 Jackson Street
Sioux City, IA 51101
(712) 233-3200

KANSAS

The Wichita Vet Center
310 South Laura Street
Wichita, KS 67211
(316) 265-3260

KENTUCKY

The Lexington Vet Center
249 West Short Street
Lexington, KY 40507
(606) 231-8387
The Louisville Vet Center
736 South 1st Street
Louisville, KY 40203
(502) 589-1981

LOUISIANA

The New Orleans Vet Center
1529 N. Clairborne Avenue
New Orleans, LA 70116
(504) 943-8386

MAINE

The Bangor Vet Center
96 Harlow Street
Bangor, ME 04401
(207) 947-3391
The Portland Vet Center
175 Lancaster Street—Room 213
Portland, ME 04101
(207) 780-3584

MARYLAND

The Baltimore Vet Center—#201
1420 West Patapsco Avenue
Patapsco Plaza
Baltimore, MD 21230
(301) 355-8592

The Baltimore Vet Center—#202
Mondawmin Shopping Center
1153 Mondawmin Concourse
Baltimore, MD 21215
(301) 728-8924

The Elkton Vet Center
7 Elkton Commercial Plaza
Elkton, MD 21921
(301) 398-0171

The Silver Spring Vet Center
8121 Georgia Avenue
Suite 500
Silver Spring, MD 20910
(202) 588-8210

MASSACHUSETTS

The Avon Vet Center
800 North Main Street
Avon, MA 02322
(617) 580-2730

The Boston Vet Center
480 Tremont Street
Boston, MA 02116
(617) 451-0171

The Brighton Vet Center
71 Washington Street
Brighton, MA 02135
(617) 782-1032

The Springfield Vet Center
1985 Main Street
Northgate Plaza
Springfield, MA 01103
(413) 737-5167

MICHIGAN

The Detroit Vet Center
18411 West Seven Mile Road
Detroit, MI 48219
(313) 535-3333
The Grand Rapids Vet Center
1940 Eastern Avenue S.E.
Grand Rapids, MI 49507
(616) 243-0385
The Southgate Vet Center
14405 North Line Street
Southgate, MI 48195
(313) 282-9852

MINNESOTA

The Duluth Vet Center
405 East Superior Street
Duluth, MN 55802
(218) 722-8654
The St. Paul Vet Center
2480 University Avenue
St. Paul, MN 55114
(612) 644-4022

MISSISSIPPI

The Jackson Vet Center
158 East Pascagoula Street
Jackson, MS 39201
(601) 353-4912

MISSOURI

The Kansas City Vet Center
3600 Broadway Street
Suite 19
Kansas City, MO 64111
(816) 753-1866

The St. Louis Vet Center
2345 Pine Street
St. Louis, MO 63103
(314) 231-1260

MONTANA

The Billings Vet Center
2708 Montana Avenue
Billings, MT 59101
(406) 657-6071

NEBRASKA

The Lincoln Vet Center
920 L Street
Lincoln, NE 68508
(402) 553-2068

The Omaha Vet Center
5123 Leavenworth Street
Omaha, NE 68106
(402) 476-9736

NEVADA

The Las Vegas Vet Center
214 South 18th Street
Las Vegas, NV 89101
(702) 385-6368

The Reno Vet Center
341 South Arlington Street
Reno, NV 89501
(702) 323-1294

NEW HAMPSHIRE

The Manchester Vet Center
14 Pearl Street
Manchester, NH 03104
(603) 668-7060

NEW JERSEY

The Jersey City Vet Center
626 Newark Avenue
Jersey City, NJ 07306
(201) 656-6986

The Newark Vet Center
1030 Broad Street
Newark, NJ 07102
(201) 622-6941

The Trenton Vet Center
318 East State Street
Trenton, NJ 08608
(609) 989-2260

NEW MEXICO

The Albuquerque Vet Center
4603 4th Street, N.W.
Albuquerque, NM 87107
(505) 345-8366

The Gallup Vet Center
211 West Mesa Street
Gallup, NM 87301
(505) 722-3821

NEW YORK

The Albany Vet Center
875 Central Avenue
West Mall Office Plaza
Albany, NY 12208
(518) 438-2508

The Babylon Vet Center
116 West Main Street
Babylon, NY 11702
(516) 661-3930

The Bronx Vet Center
226 East Fordham Road—Rooms 216–217
Bronx, NY 10458
(212) 330-2825

The Brooklyn Vet Center
165 Cadman Plaza, East
Brooklyn, NY 11201
(212) 330-2825

The Buffalo Vet Center
351 Lindwood Avenue
Buffalo, NY 14201
(716) 882-0505

The Jamaica Hills Vet Center
148-43 Hillside Avenue
Jamaica Hills, NY 11435
(212) 658-6767

The Manhattan Vet Center
166 West 75th Street
Manhattan, NY 10023
(212) 944-2917

The White Plains Vet Center
200 Hamilton Avenue
White Plains, NY 10601
(914) 684-0570

NORTH CAROLINA

The Charlotte Vet Center
910 North Alexander Street
Suite 210
Charlotte, NC 28206
(704) 333-6107

The Fayetteville Vet Center
4 Market Square
Fayetteville, NC 28301
(919) 323-4908

NORTH DAKOTA

The Fargo Vet Center
1322 Gateway Drive
Fargo, ND 58103
(701) 237-0942
The Minot Vet Center
108 Burdick Expressway
Minot, ND 58701
(701) 852-0177

OHIO

The Cincinnati Vet Center
31 East 12th Street—4th floor
Cincinnati, OH 45202
(513) 241-9420
The Cleveland Vet Center—#405
10605 Carnegie Avenue
Cleveland, OH 44106
(216) 791-9224
The Cleveland Vet Center—#406
11511 Lorain Avenue
Cleveland, OH 44111
(216) 671-8530
The Columbus Vet Center
1751 Cleveland Avenue
Columbus, OH 43211
(614) 291-2227
The Dayton Vet Center
438 Wayne Avenue
Dayton, OH 45410
(513) 461-9150

OKLAHOMA

The Oklahoma City Vet Center
4111 North Lincoln Street
Suite #10
Oklahoma City, OK 73105
(405) 521-9308
The Tulsa Vet Center
1605 South Boulder Street
Tulsa, OK 74119
(918) 581-7105

OREGON

The Eugene Vet Center
1966 Garden Avenue
Eugene, OR 97403
(503) 687-6918
The Portland Vet Center
2450 Southeast Belmont
Portland, OR 97214
(503) 231-1586

PENNSYLVANIA

The Harrisburg Vet Center
127 State Street
Harrisburg, PA 17101
(717) 782-3954
The Monroeville Vet Center
4328 Old William Penn Highway
Monroeville, PA 15146
(412) 372-8627
The Philadelphia Vet Center—#210
1107 Arch Street
Philadelphia, PA 19107
(215) 627-0338

The Philadelphia Vet Center—#219
5601 North Broad Street
Philadelphia, PA 19141
(215) 924-4670
The Pittsburgh Vet Center
954 Penn Avenue
Pittsburgh, PA 15222
(412) 765-1193

PUERTO RICO

The San Juan/Rio Piedras Vet Center
Suite LC-8A/9 Medical Center Plaza
La Riviera
Rio Piedras, PR 00921
(809) 783-8269

RHODE ISLAND

The Pawtucket Vet Center
172 Pine Street
Pawtucket, RI 02860
(401) 774-6674

SOUTH CAROLINA

The Greenville Vet Center
904 Pendleton Street
Greenville, SC 29601
(803) 271-2711
The North Charleston Vet Center
3366 Rivers Avenue
North Charleston, SC 29405
(803)747-8387

SOUTH DAKOTA

The Rapid City Vet Center
610 Kansas City Street
Rapid City, SD 57701
(605) 348-0077

The Sioux Falls Vet Center
100 West 6th Street
Suite 101
Sioux Falls, SD 57102
(605) 332-0856

TENNESSEE

The Knoxville Vet Center
1515 East Magnolia Avenue
Suite 201
Knoxville, TN 37917
(615) 971-5866

The Memphis Vet Center
1 North 3rd Street
Memphis, TN 38103
(901) 521-3506

TEXAS

The Dallas Vet Center
5415 Maple Plaza
Suite 114
Dallas, TX 75235
(214) 634-7024

The El Paso Vet Center
2121 Wyoming Street
El Paso, TX 79903
(915) 921-3733

The Fort Worth Vet Center
Seminary South Office Building
Suite 10
Forth Worth, TX 76115
(817) 921-3733

The Houston Vet Center
4905A San Jacinto Street
Houston, TX 77004
(713) 522-5354

The Laredo Vet Center
717 Corpus Christie
Laredo, TX 78040
(512) 723-4680
            The San Antonio Vet Center
107 Lexington Avenue
San Antonio, TX 78201
(512) 229-4120

U.S. VIRGIN ISLANDS

            The St. Croix Vet Center
United Shopping Plaza
Office #12
4 CND Estate Sion Farms
St. Croix, VI 00820
(809) 776-6201
            The St. Thomas Vet Center
Havensight Mall
St. Thomas, VI 00802
(809) 774-6674

UTAH

            The Salt Lake City Vet Center
216 East 5th Street, South
Salt Lake City, UT 84102
(801) 584-1294

VERMONT

            The White River Junction Vet Center
Building #2, Gilman Office Complex
White River Junction, VT 05501
(802) 295-2908
            The Williston Vet Center
RFD #2, Tafts Corners
Williston, VT 05495
(802) 878-3371

VIRGINIA

The Norfolk Vet Center
7450 1/2 Tidewater Drive
Norfolk, VA 23505
(804) 587-1338
The Richmond Vet Center
Gresham Court Box 83
1030 West Franklin Street
Richmond, VA 23220
(804) 587-1338

WASHINGTON

The Seattle Vet Center
1322 East Pike Street
Seattle, WA 98122
(206) 442-2706
The Spokane Vet Center
North 1611 Division Street
Spokane, WA 99207
(509) 326-6970
The Tacoma Vet Center
4801 Pacific Avenue
Tacoma, WA 98408
(206) 473-0731

WEST VIRGINIA

The Huntington Vet Center
1014 6th Street
Huntington, WV 25701
(304) 523-8387
The Morgantown Vet Center
1191 Pineview Drive
Morgantown, WV 26505
(304) 291-4001

WISCONSIN

The Madison Vet Center
147 South Butler Street
Madison, WI 53703
(608) 264-5343
The Milwaukee Vet Center
3400 Wisconsin
Milwaukee, WI 53208
(414) 344-5504

WYOMING

The Casper Vet Center
641 East Second Street
Casper, WY 82601
(307) 235-8010
The Cheyenne Vet Center
1810 Pioneer Street
Cheyenne WY 82001
(307) 778-2660

The Vet Center Program is beginning a new wave of expansion in late 1984 and early 1985. According to Vet Center Headquarters (Readjustment Counseling Service) in Washington, D.C., new Vet Centers are earmarked for the following locations:

Arizona (Prescott); California (Eureka–Arcadia, Sacramento, Santa Barbara, Santa Cruz, and the Western Imperial County); Colorado (Denver–Boulder); Connecticut (Norwich); Florida (Palm Beach, Pensacola, Sarasota, and Tallahassee); Georgia (Savannah); Idaho (Pocatello); Illinois (Chicago—Northside, Moline–Rock Island, and Springfield); Indiana (Gary); Louisiana (Shreveport); Massachusetts (Lowell, New Bedford, and Worcester); Mississippi (Biloxi); Missouri (St. Louis—East); Montana (Missoula); New Jersey (Southern); New Mexico (Santa Fe); New York (Rochester, Staten Island, and Syracuse); North

Carolina (Greensboro and Rocky Mountain/Jacksonville); Oregon (Salem–Corvallis); Pennsylvania (Erie and Wilkes-Barre); Puerto Rico (Arecibo and Ponce); South Carolina (Columbus); Tennessee (Chattanooga and Johnson City); Texas (Amarillo, Austin, Corpus Christi, Houston, Lubbock, and Odessa—Midland); Utah (Provo); Virginia (Roanoke); and West Virginia (Charleston and Martinsburg).

The reader is alerted to the possibility of changes in this listing of proposed sites. The local VA Medical Center or VA Regional Office may be contacted for information regarding the nearest new Vet Center.

The second service we recommend concerning readjustment care for war-related problems are the Inpatient Specialized Treatment Units (ISTUs) for Vietnam combat veterans, which are now operational in 11 VA Medical Centers around the country.

Each ISTU is a therapeutic program exclusively for men with PTSD. The future promises such units for women. At the present time, certain initiatives are being taken within the Veterans Administration to accommodate the special needs of female veterans. Because of the highly specialized nature of the treatment, ISTU personnel conduct an extensive pretherapeutic series of screening procedures to exclude veterans who have: (1) general mental health problems; (2) psychosis, organic brain syndrome, addictions, or substance abuse problems that might interfere with successful participation in the program; (3) serious legal problems; or (4) ingrained behavioral traits that would interfere with the treatment regime—for himself and for others.

A comprehensive assessment process is begun with each veteran, including a structured interview with a staff member. After the assessment and screening procedures, the veteran is given a number of self-administered tests, as well as psychological testing with a staff member. Every veteran accepted into the ISTU is given a standard workup that includes: (1) medical history, physical examination, and laboratory work; (2) psychiatric history; and (3) social history.

Each ISTU is organized along the lines of a therapeutic community with a sensitive and knowledgeable staff. Specific psychotherapeutic regimes may include psychodynamic, behavioral, cognitive, Gestalt, psychodrama, and transactional analysis. Rules and regulations of the ISTU are explained to the veterans. They are expected to abide by these; if they do not, there are specific consequences of which they are made fully aware.

ISTUs make demands on the veteran patient but also provide excellent care. Among the philosophical goals of the Unit are the following:

1. A safe, predictable, stable, and ideal human-intensive environment. In such an environment, the veteran can risk feeling vulnerable—a very necessary precursor to ultimate healing and recovery—without having to resort to maladaptive survival tactics to "defend" himself. And in such a milieu, unit staff can promote an attitude of trust, while enhancing the veteran's confidence in self and others. He is able to speak openly of his problems without fear of recrimination. Furthermore, this environment provides the necessary stability to help the patient resolve deep-seated fears of rejection, loss, and abandonment.

2. To assist the veteran to overcome arrested psychological development due to the war and its aftermath, while bolstering self-growth and a cohesive identity.

3. To assist the veteran to overcome an intense fear of feeling helpless, fear of authority, and distrust of power. Unit staff teaches self-management, self-relaxation, and self-knowledge, and records in a journal the veteran's traumatic dreams, memories, and general reactions to the treatment. Authority–subordinate role playing and psychodrama is a therapeutic modality which is also beneficial to the veteran. Often a veteran has come to fear power because it is associated with the violence and unchallenged wanton destruction that occurred in Vietnam. Others fear power because they believe it will be misused as it was in Vietnam and since. Conflicts around the issue of authority can escalate quickly, but when Vietnam veterans are in a therapeutic community, within a broader supportive environment, these conflicts are manageable and can be resolved rapidly by means of patient–staff, intrastaff, or hospital–community interactions and meetings. The testing out of power and control issues is likely to continue for a significant portion of the veteran's recovery treatment experience. In the therapeutic millieu, the veteran can learn how to replace destructive power with constructive power—a critical therapeutic task.

4. To assist the veteran to gain feelings of his humanness and vulnerability, along with the self-assurance that he will survive. This may begin with the shedding of tears and grieving for the many losses of friends and others who died in Vietnam. Sometimes it takes many months or even years for some Vietnam veterans to build a trusting relationship that will support them in times of vulnerability and weakness.

5. To assist the veteran to overcome the perceptual sense of inner "badness" and "horror-of-mind." Some men feel "possessed" by an evil force, which has already condemned them to hell. Others believe that they have survived only because of the power of evil—their weapons and their own "corrupt" omnipotence.

6. To assist the veteran to confront the atrocities he participated in by helping him determine his *personal* as well as *shared* responsibility for violence against the Vietnamese.

7. To assist the veteran to handle atrocity-related guilt as well as survivor-related guilt.

8. To assist the veteran to develop a strong network of interpersonal peer contacts.

9. To assist the veteran to reconnect with life, culture, and its processes.

10. To assist the veteran to develop a personal theory of service to others.

Generally, the ISTU treatment process consists of three phases. In the first phase, the veteran is introduced to a variety of therapeutic procedures to assist him in quelling the inner tide of chaos, rage, terror, nightmares, sleeplessness, and depression by using selected behavioral procedures, education about Vietnam and PTSD symptoms, and if needed, medication. Biofeedback and systematic, supervised exercise programs are also used widely during the first phase. Trust building with patients and staff provides a foundation for the second phase, when the veteran is helped to remember his traumatic experiences and how they affect current life problems. He is provided a stable environment and trusted therapists so that he can reveal the most guilt- and grief-ridden memories without fear of reprisal or rejection. In the third phase he is able to begin "owning up" to what is the veteran's and to what is not his, which is essential during this phase. He concentrates on his ability to look at himself honestly, and

learns to ask serious questions about life and how to live it more fully—
in the world of people. The veteran is challenged to engage in humanitarian,
social, political, and community work in an effort to become once again
a contributing member of society, as he significantly broadens his social
and interpersonal base of support. Through the intense group sessions of
the ISTU, a renewal of personal meaning may take place, leading to a
profound desire to reach out to others. The strong subculture of veterans,
with the Vietnam experience as a base, provides a solid foundation upon
which the veteran can now launch a new self-program for his personal and
societal needs.

These ISTUs are located within 11 VA Medical Centers. Several more
ISTUs are planned for the near future including locations in Brockton,
Mass. and Phoenix, Ariz. Some ISTUs are also planning to enlarge their
current bed capacities. Below are those ISTUs currently operational along
with their bed capacities (as of June 1984):

THE MENLO PARK ISTU (California)
(415) 493-5000   90 beds
THE MONTROSE ISTU (New York)
(914) 737-4400   26 beds
THE AUGUSTA ISTU (Georgia)
(404) 724-5116   25 beds
THE NORTH CHICAGO ISTU (Illinois)
(312) 688-1900   25 beds
THE TOPEKA ISTU (Kansas)
(913) 272-3111   24 beds
THE LYONS ISTU (New Jersey)
(201) 647-0180   20 beds
THE BAY PINES ISTU (Florida)
(813) 391-9644   20 beds
THE NORTHAMPTON ISTU (Massachusetts)
(413) 584-4040   19 beds
THE BRECKSVILLE NATIONAL CENTER FOR
STRESS RECOVERY (Cleveland, Ohio)
(216) 526-3030   10+ beds

THE COATESVILLE ISTU (Pennsylvania)
(215) 384-7711   13 beds
THE TOMAH ISTU (Wisconsin)
(608) 372-3971   10 beds

These ISTUs are staffed by a variety of professionals among whom are psychiatrists, psychologists, social workers, psychiatric nurses, recreational therapists, physician's assistants, occupational therapists, and nonpsychiatric nurses and aids. In total, there are 287 beds in the Veterans Administration service delivery system. As thorough as this program is, it is still obviously rather limited in terms of the number of veterans it can accommodate.

The third program featuring readjustment services for Vietnam veterans and their families is the Readjustment Counseling Contracts Program. This program was originally authorized by Congress as part of the same legislation that gave birth to the Vet Center system, discussed earlier. The Readjustment Counseling Contracts Program was intended to augment existing Vet Center capabilities in delivering services to these veterans. Officially called the Readjustment Counseling Contracts Program, this service makes it possible for Vietnam veterans to receive readjustment services from the private sector, paid for by the federal government through the Veterans Administration. Eligibility for these services is service in the United States Armed Forces during the Vietnam era—the period from August 5, 1964 to July 7, 1975. Unlike the Vet Center services, veterans with dishonorable discharges are not eligible for services under this program.* This is also true for the ISTU services. All contracts awarded to private agencies and individual practitioners are for a period of 1 year from the date of award. Family members may also receive services when their problems have been determined to be related to the veteran's readjustment difficulties.

By law, this program is not intended for general mental health problems; rather, it is specifically designed for problems with a clear and distinct relationship to military service. Private therapists must thus engage the veteran in *readjustment counseling,* that is, counseling to help the veteran recover from combat or military experiences that have resulted in severe

---

* Veterans with dishonorable discharges will have to seek upgrading of their "bad paper" in order to use ISTU and Readjustment Counseling Contracts Program services. The nearest VA Medical Center or VA Regional Office as well as the local Vet Center can be helpful in making a referral to a Discharge-Upgrade Center.

problems in living. Included under this provision are: individual, group, and couples and family counseling, employment counseling, benefits counseling, and referral services. Basically, the contractors are expected to provide the same range of services offered by the Vet Centers, but with an emphasis on psychological counseling.

To obtain services from contract providers, the veteran should contact the nearest Vet Center of VA Medical Center. This special service can only be initiated through referral by either the local Vet Center staff or the professional staff of the psychiatry, psychology, and social work departments within the VA Medical Centers.

There are over 540 contract providers nationwide, offering a variety of services to the Vietnam veteran and his family. The interested person should contact the readjustment counseling contracts officer in the VA Medical Center—situated within either the Medical Administration Service or the Supply Service. From statistics compiled by the Vet Center Headquarters in Washington, D.C., the Contracts/Fee Program has given service to 42,000 veterans through private sector providers, with a total of 226,846 veteran visits for the period beginning April 1982 and ending July 1984.

These three services for Vietnam veterans and their families offer the best possible readjustment care for this population at the present time—in the area of war-related mental symptoms and problems. The Vet Centers work cooperatively with ISTUs and with local contract providers. When the Vet Center staff determines that the needs of a veteran can best be met in an ISTU, a referral is made. The Vet Center staff keeps in contact with the veteran; and, together with the ISTU staff, plans are made to refer the veteran to the Vet Center for follow-up and aftercare. Veterans completing an ISTU program are often referred to the Vet Center so that the therapeutic process begun in the ISTU can continue. Together, these programs have moved beyond the rhetoric and debate regarding the nature of PTSDs. They represent a beacon of orientation to the veteran—to help him find his way through the areas of dark clouds in his life; a compass on the uncharted seas of isolation, despondency, fear, and pain. Moreover, these programs have proven helpful in giving the veteran the confidence he needs to live life more fully, and to overcome crippling guilt feelings. As a lifeline, these services provide the veteran with the vision that there *can* be life after death.

REFERENCES

PREFACE

1. Arthur Egendorf, Charles Kadushin, Robert S. Laufer, Georgie Rothbart, and Lee Sloan, *Legacies of Vietnam: Comparative Readjustment of Veterans and Their Peers* (Washington, D.C.: U.S. Government Printing Office, 1981).
2. Jim Goodwin, "The Etiology of Combat-related Posttraumatic Stress Disorders," in: *Posttraumatic Stress Disorders in the Vietnam Veteran,* edited by Tom Williams (Cincinnati: Disabled American Veterans, 1980), p. 10.
3. *Myths and Realities: A Study of Attitudes Toward Vietnam Era Veterans,* Commissioned by the Veterans Administration, Conducted by Louis Harris and Associates, Inc. July, 1980.
4. "Discriminant Analysis of Posttraumatic Stress Disorder Among a Group of Vietnam Veterans," *American Journal of Psychiatry* **139** (1982), pp. 52–56.
5. Nathan R. Denny, Project Officer, National Vietnam Veterans Readjustment Study, October 12, 1984.

6. John Wilson, *Identity, Etiology and Crisis: Vietnam Veterans in Transition, Part I,* Unpublished Manuscript, Cleveland State University, 1977.
7. Ingram Walker, "The Psychological Problems of Vietnam Veterans," *Journal of the American Medical Association* **246** (August 14, 1981), 781–782.
8. Stanley Karnow, *Vietnam: A History* (New York: Viking Press, 1983).

CHAPTER 1

1. Stanley Karnow, *Vietnam: A History* (New York: Viking Press, 1983).
2. Arthur Egendorf, Charles Kadushin, Robert S. Laufer, George Rothbart, and Lee Sloan, *Legacies of Vietnam: Comparative Adjustment of Veterans and Their Peers* (Washington, D.C.: U.S. Government Printing Office, 1981).
3. John P. Wilson, *Forgotten Warrior Project* (Cincinnati: Disabled American Veterans, 1979).
4. Truong Nhu Tang, "The Myth of a Liberation," *The New York Review of Books,* October 21, 1982.
5. Fox Butterfield, "The New Vietnam Scholarship," *The New York Times Magazine,* February 13, 1983.
6. George Will, "U.S. Policy Options Ignored," *Danbury, Ct. News Times,* September 18, 1983.
7. Harry G. Summers, Jr., *On Strategy: A Critical Analysis of the Vietnam War* (San Rafael, Calif.: Presidio Press, 1982).
8. Charles R. Figley, editor, *Stress Disorders Among Vietnam Veterans: Theory, Research, and Treatment Implications* (New York: Brunner/Mazel, Inc., 1978).
9. Terrence Maitland and Stephen Weiss, "Nation within a Nation," in: *The Vietnam Experience: Raising the Stakes,* edited by Robert Manning (Boston: Boston Publishing Co., 1982).
10. William J. Lederer, *Our Own Worst Enemy* (New York: W. W. Norton & Co., Inc., 1968).
11. John Del Vecchio, personal communication (September 1984).
12. Leslie H. Gelb and Richard K. Betts, *The Irony of Vietnam: The System Worked* (Washington D.C.: The Brookings Institution, 1979).
13. Frances Fitzgerald, *Fire In The Lake: The Vietnamese and the Americans in Vietnam* (Boston: Little, Brown & Co., 1972).
14. Chester L. Cooper, *The Lost Crusade* (New York: Dodd, Mead & Co., 1970).
15. Stephen J. Morris, "Vietnam, a Dual-Vision History," *The Wall Street Journal,* December 20, 1983.
16. "The Anti-U.S. Resistance War for National Salvation, 1954–1975: Military Events," *The People's Army of Vietnam,* 1980.

17. "Tonkin Gulf: Untold Story of the 'Phantom Battle' That Led to War," *U.S. News & World Report*, July 23, 1984.
18. Larry Berman, *Planning a Tragedy: The Americanization of the War in Vietnam* (New York: W. W. Norton & Co., Inc., 1982).
19. George C. Herring, *America's Longest War: The United States and Vietnam, 1950–1975.* (New York: John Wiley & Sons, Inc. 1979).

CHAPTER 2

1. E. H. Erikson, *Identity, Youth and Crisis,* (New York: W. W. Norton, 1968).
2. Chaim F. Shatan, "Stress Disorders Among Vietnam Veterans: The Emotional Content of Combat Continues," in: *Stress Disorders Among Vietnam Veterans: Theory, Research, and Treatment Implication,* edited by C. R. Figley New York: Brunner/Mazel, Inc. 1978), pp. 43–52.
3. Thomas Bond, "The Why of Fragging," *American Journal of Psychiatry* 138(11) (1976), pp. 1328–1331.
4. Peter Watson, *War on the Mind: The Military Uses and Abuses of Psychology* (New York: Basic Books, Inc., 1978).
5. Al Santoli, *Everything We Had* (New York: Random House, Inc., 1981).
6. Wallace Terry, "Bringing the War Home," in: *The Vietnam Veteran in Contemporary Society* (Washington, D.C.: Veterans Administration, 1972), pp. 63–72.
7. S. Leventman and P. Camacho, "The 'Gook' Syndrome: The Vietnam War as a Racial Encounter," in: *Strangers at Home: The Vietnam Veteran Since the War,* edited by C. R. Figley and S. Leventman (New York: Praeger, 1980).
8. Martin Binkin and Mark Eitelberg, *Blacks and the Military* (Washington, D.C.: The Brookings Institution, 1982).

CHAPTER 3

1. Mark Baker, *Nam* (New York: William Morrow & Co., Inc., 1981), p. 262.
2. Alfred Schuetz, "The Homecomer," in: *Strangers at Home: The Vietnam Veteran Since the War,* edited by C. R. Figley and S. Leventman (New York: Praeger, 1980), pp. 115–122.
3. William Ryan, *Blaming the Victim* (New York: Random House, Inc., 1971).
4. Erwin R. Parson, "Narcissistic Injury in Vietnam Vets: The Role of Posttraumatic Stress Disorder, 'Agent Orange Anxiety', and the Repatriation Experience," *Stars and Stripes—The National Tribune* November 18, 1982, pp. 1–15.
5. Erwin R. Parson, "The Vietnam Vet: The Inner Battle Rages On," *The Jamaica Times Magazine* 2(4) (1981), pp. 6–9.

6. Erwin R. Parson, "The Reparation of the Self: Clinical and Theoretical Dimensions in the Treatment of Vietnam Combat Veterans," *Journal of Contemporary Psychotherapy* **14** (1984), pp. 4–56.
7. Willard Waller, "The Victors and the Vanquished," in: *Strangers at Home: The Vietnam Veteran Since the War,* edited by C. R. Figley and S. Leventman (New York: Praeger, 1980), pp. 35–53.
8. John Russell Smith, *Vietnam Veterans: Rap Groups and the Stress Recovery Process,* unpublished paper (1980).
9. S. Leventman and P. Camacho, "The 'Gook' Syndrome: The Vietnam War as a Racial Encounter," in: *Strangers at Home: The Vietnam Veteran Since the War,* edited by C. R. Figley and S. Leventman (New York: Praeger, 1980), pp. 56–70.

CHAPTER 4

1. Michael G. Wise, "Posttraumatic Stress Disorder: The Human Reaction to Catastrophe," *Drug Therapy* (March 1983), pp. 97–105.
2. Ernie Pyle, *Here Is Your War* (New York: Henry Holt & Co., 1943), pp. 247–248.
3. Sigmund Freud, "Introduction to Psychoanalysis and the War Neuroses," (1919) in: *Complete Psychological Works, Standard Edition,* edited and translated by J. Strachey (London: Hogarth Press, 1959).
4. Leo Bartmeier, Lawrence S. Kubie, Karl A. Menninger, John Romano, and John C. Whitehorn, "Combat Exhaustion," *Journal of Nervous and Mental Disease* **104** (1946), pp. 358–389.
5. Harry R. Kormos, "The Nature of Combat Stress," in: *Stress Disorders Among Vietnam Veterans: Theory, Research, and Treatment Implications,* edited by C. R. Figley (New York: Brunner/Mazel, Inc., 1978), p. 5.
6. C. R. Hanson, editor "1944 Symposium on Combat Psychiatry," *Bulletin of the United States Army Medical Department* 1949.
7. William C. Menninger, "Modern Concepts of War Neuroses," *Bulletin of the Menninger Clinic* **10** (1946), pp. 196–209.
8. R. R. Greenson, "Practical Approach to the War Neuroses," *Bulletin of the Menninger Clinic* **9** (1945), pp. 192–205.
9. A. Kardiner, *The Traumatic Neuroses of War* (New York: Paul B. Hoeber, 1941).
10. Robert Jay Lifton, "The Survivors of the Hiroshima Disaster and the Survivors of Nazi Persecution," in: *Massive Psychic Trauma,* edited by H. Krystal (New York: International Universities Press, Inc., 1968), pp. 168–189.

11. Peter Watson, *War on the Mind: The Military Uses and Abuses of Psychology* (New York: Basic Books, Inc., 1978).
12. Peter G. Bourne, *Men. Stress and Vietnam* (Boston: Little, Brown & Co., 1970).
13. Robert Jay Lifton, *Home from the War: Vietnam Veterans: Neither Victims nor Executioners* (New York: Simon & Schuster, Inc., 1973).
14. Chaim Shatan, "The Grief of Soldiers: Vietnam Combat Veterans' Self-help Movement," *American Journal of Orthopsychiatry* **43** (1973), pp. 640–653.
15. R. W. Eisenhart, "Flower of the Dragon: An Example of Applied Humanistic Psychology," *Journal of Humanistic Psychology* **17** (1977), pp. 3–24.
16. Presidential Review Memorandum on Vietnam-era Veterans, U.S. House Committee on Veterans Affairs, 96th Congress, First Session, released Oct. 10, 1978 (Washington, D.C.: House Committee print No. 38, 1979).
17. M. Straker, "The Vietnam Veteran: The Task is Reintegration," *Diseases of the Nervous System* **37** (1976), pp. 75–79.
18. J. Yager, "Postcombat Violent Behavior in Psychiatrically Maladjusting Soldiers," *Archives of General Psychiatry* **33** (1976), pp. 1332–1335.
19. *Diagnostic and Statistical Manual of Mental Disorders,* 3rd edition (Washington, D.C.: American Psychiatric Association, 1980).
20. Hans Selye, *The Stress of Life* (New York: McGraw–Hill Book Co., 1956).
21. Mardi J. Horowitz, *Stress Response Syndromes* (New York: Jason Aronson, Inc., 1976).
22. Victor J. DeFazio, "Dynamic Perspectives on the Nature and Effects of Combat Stress," in: *Stress Disorders Among Vietnam Veterans: Theory, Research, and Treatment Implications,* edited by C. R. Figley (New York: Brunner/Mazel, Inc. 1978), pp. 36–37.
23. Herbert Hendin, Ann Pollinger-Haas, Paul Singer, William Houghton, Mark Schwartz, and Vincent Wallen, "The Reliving Experience in Vietnam Veterans with Posttraumatic Stress Disorder," *Comprehensive Psychiatry* **25** (1984), pp. 165–173.
24. Lawrence C. Kolb, "The Post-traumatic Stress Disorders of Combat: A Subgroup with a Conditioned Emotional Response," *Military Medicine* **149** (1984), pp. 237–243.
25. J. O. Brende and I. L. McCann, "Regressive Experiences in Vietnam Veterans: Their Relationship to War, Post-traumatic Symptoms and Recovery," *Journal of Contemporary Psychotherapy* **14** (1984), pp. 57–75.
26. P. D. MacLean, *A Triune Concept of the Brain and Behavior: The Clarence M. Hincks Memorial Lectures, 1969,* edited by D. Campbell and T. J. Boag (Toronto: University of Toronto Press, 1973).

CHAPTER 5

1. E. J. Leed, *No Man's Land: Combat and Identity in World War One* (New York: Cambridge University Press, 1979).
2. Charles R. Figley and Seymour Leventman, editors, *Strangers at Home: The Vietnam Veteran Since the War*, edited by C. R. Figley and S. Leventman (New York: Praeger, 1980), pp. xxi–xxxi.
3. John P. Wilson, "Identity, Ideology and Crisis: The Vietnam Veteran in Transition, Part II," *Psychosocial Attributes of the Veteran Beyond Identity: Patterns of Adjustment and Future Implication*, unpublished monograph, Cleveland State University.
4. John P. Wilson, "Stress and Growth: Effects of War on Psychosocial Development," in: *Strangers at Home: The Vietnam Veteran Since the War*, edited by C. R. Figley and S. Leventman (New York: Praeger, 1980), pp. 123–165.
5. William C. Menninger, "Modern Concepts of War Neuroses," *Bulletin of the Menninger Clinic* 10 (1946), pp. 196–209.
6. Karl A. Menninger, M. Mayman, and Paul Pruyser, *The Vital Balance: The Life Process in Mental Health and Illness* (New York: Viking Press, Inc., 1963), pp. 159–160.
7. Joel O. Brende, "A Psychodynamic View of Character Pathology in Vietnam Combat Veterans," *Bulletin of the Menninger Clinic* 47 (1983), pp. 193–216.
8. Herbert Hendin and Ann Pollinger-Haas, "Combat Adaptations of Vietnam Veterans Without Posttraumatic Stress Disorders," *American Journal of Psychiatry* 141 (1984), pp. 956–960.
9. Peter Marin, "Living in Moral Pain," *Psychology Today* (November 1981), pp. 68–80.
10. John Russell Smith, *Veterans and Combat: Towards A Model of the Stress Recovery Process*, paper prepared for the Veterans Administration Operation Outreach Training Program, (1981).
11. Chaim F. Shatan, "Through the Membrane of Reality: Impacted Grief and Perceptual Dissonance in Vietnam Combat Veterans," *Psychiatric Opinion* 11 (1974), pp. 6–15.
12. Chaim F. Shatan, "Stress Disorders Among Vietnam Veterans: The Emotional Content of Combat Continues," in: *Stress Disorders Among Vietnam Veterans: Theory, Research, and Treatment Implications*, edited by C. R. Figley (New York: Brunner/Mazel, Inc., 1978), p. 49.
13. John M. Del Vecchio, *The 13th Valley* (New York: Bantam Books, Inc., 1982), pp. 566–567.
14. Karl A. Menninger, *Man Against Himself* (New Haven: Harcourt, Brace & World, Inc., 1938).

15. Robert Jay Lifton, *Home from the War: Vietnam Veterans: Neither Victims nor Executioners* (New York: Simon & Schuster, Inc., 1973), pp. 191–216.
16. Robert Frick and Larry Bogart, "Transference and Countertransference in Group Therapy with Vietnam Veterans," *Bulletin of the Menninger Clinic* **46** (1982), pp. 429–444.
17. Sarah Haley, "When the Patient Reports Atrocities," *Archives of General Psychiatry* **30** (1974), pp. 191–196.
18. M. J. Horowitz and G. Solomon, "Delayed Stress Response Syndromes in Vietnam Veterans," in: *Stress Disorders Among Vietnam Veterans: Theory, Research, and Treatment Implications*, edited by C. R. Figley (New York: Brunner/Mazel, Inc., 1978), pp. 268–280.
19. Erwin Randolph Parson, "The Reparation of the Self: Clinical and Theoretical Dimensions in the Treatment of Vietnam Combat Veterans," *Journal of Contemporary Psychotherapy* **14** (1984), pp. 4–56.

CHAPTER 6

1. Charles R. Figley, "Psychological Adjustment Among Vietnam Veterans: An Overview of the Research," in: *Stress Disorders Among Vietnam Veterans: Theory, Research, and Treatment Implications*, edited by C. R. Figley (New York: Brunner/Mazel, Inc., 1978), pp. 57–70.
2. C. R. Figley, M. Robinson, and G. Lester, *The Relation Between Life Change and Family-Related Anxiety among POWs and Veterans*, presented at the 4th Department of Defense Meeting on the POW, San Diego, CA, November 1976.
3. R. Ursano, "The Vietnam Era Prisoner-of-War, Precaptivity Personality and the Development of Psychiatric Illness, *American Journal of Psychiatry* **138** (1981), pp. 315–318.
4. Erwin R. Parson, "The Vietnam Vet: The Inner Battle Rages On," *Jamaica Times Magazine* **2**(4) (1981), pp. 6–9.
5. Arthur Egendorf, "Psychotherapy With Vietnam Veterans: Observation and Suggestions," in: *Stress Disorders Among Vietnam Veterans: Theory, Research, and Treatment Implications*, edited by C. R. Figley (New York: Brunner/Mazel, Inc., 1978), pp. 231–253.
6. Erwin R. Parson, "The Role of Psychodynamic Group Therapy in the Treatment of the Combat Veteran," in *Psychotherapy of the Combat Veteran*, edited by H. J. Schwartz (New York: Spectrum Medical and Scientific Books, 1984), pp. 153–220.

7. Erwin R. Parson, *The CMHC-Based Treatment of the Vietnam Combat Veteran: An Alternative Psychotherapy Model,* paper read at the 32nd Institute on Hospital and Community Psychiatry, Boston, September 1981.

8. Virginia M. Satir, *Conjoint Family Therapy,* revised edition (Palo Alto: Science and Behavior Books, Inc., 1967).

9. Charles Kadushin, Ghislaine Boulanger, and John Martin, *Legacies of Vietnam: Comparative Adjustment of Veterans and Their Peers,* Volume 4: *Long-Term Stress Reactions: Some Causes, Consequences, and Naturally-Occurring Support Systems* (Washington, D.C.: U.S. Government Printing Office, 1981), pp. 478–706.

10. J. O. Brende, "Combined Individual and Group Therapy for Vietnam Veterans," International Journal of Group Psychotherapy **31** (1981), pp. 367–378.

11. Victor J. DeFazio and Nicholas Pascucci: "Return to Ithaca: A Perspective on Marriage and Love in Post-Traumatic Stress Disorder," *Journal of Contemporary Psychotherapy* **14**(1) (1984), pp. 84–85.

12. Erwin R. Parson, "The Gook-Identification and Post-Traumatic Stress Disorders in Black Vietnam Veterans," *Black Psychiatrists of America Quarterly* **13**(2) (1984), pp. 14–18.

13. Sarah Haley, "When the Patient Reports Atrocities," *Archives of General Psychiatry* **30** (1974), pp. 191–196.

14. M. Andolfi, C. Angelo, P. Menghi, and A. Nicolo-Corigliano, *Behind the Family Mask: Therapeutic Change in Rigid Family Systems* (New York: Brunner/Mazel, Inc., 1983).

CHAPTER 7

1. Richard Kolb, "Vietnam Veterans Fact Sheet," *National Vietnam Veterans Review* (November 1982), pp. 30–32, 46.

2. Jeannie Christie, *Women in Vietnam,* paper presented at the National Association of Concerned Veterans (June 19, 1982).

3. Jenny Schnaier, *Women Vietnam Veterans and Mental Health Adjustment: A Study of Their Experiences and Post-Traumatic Stress,* masters thesis (College Park: University of Maryland, 1982). See also Linda Van Devanter, *The Unknown Warriors: Implications of the Experiences of Women in Vietnam,* unpublished paper (1982). We also recommend Judy Marrion, "A Woman Veteran Speaks," in: *The Veteran* Volume 12 (November–December 1982). Myra Macpherson's article, "Vietnam Nurses: These are the Women Who Went to War," published in *Ms. Magazine* taken from her book *Long Time Passing Vietnam and the Haunted Generation* (New York: Doubleday & Co., Inc., 1984), is also highly recommended.

4. *Diagnostic and Statistical Manual of Mental Disorders,* 3rd edition (Washington, D.C.: American Psychiatric Association, 1980).

5. Linda Van Devanter, *Home Before Morning: The Story of an Army Nurse in Vietnam,* (New York: Beaufort Books, 1983).

6. Suzanne Keller, "The Female Role: Constants and Change," in: *Women in Therapy: New Psychotherapies,* edited by V. Franks and V. Burtle (New York: Brunner/Mazel, Inc., 1974), p. 417.

7. John Russell Smith, "Personal Responsibility in Post-Traumatic Stress Reactions," *Psychiatric Annals* **12** (1982), pp. 1021–1030.

8. Robert W. Mullen, *Blacks in America's Wars: The Shift in Attitudes from the Revolutionary War to Vietnam* (New York: Monad Press, 1974).

9. Harold Bryant, "The Black Veteran," *Stars and Stripes—The National Tribune* June 1983, p. 5.

10. Charles Moskos, "Why Men Fight: American Combat Soldiers in Vietnam," in: *The Vietnam Veteran in Contemporary Society* (Washington, D.C.: Veterans Administration, 1971), pp. 8–17. Contrary to the popular belief that the motivated soldier is one who is ideologically inspired, Dr. Moskos believes that the motivation of soldiers to fight comes ultimately from self-concern for survival and the beliefs shared among the fighting men in the unit. We introduce the term "cohesion-for-survival" (COFS) to connote the motivational elements within a group of fighting men. COFS consists of three basic elements: (1) inspirational ideology; (2) instrumental unity ("We unite to save each other as we fight the common enemy"); and (3) shared beliefs and convictions about the specific local conditions and dangers.

11. Charles Moskos, "Surviving the War in Vietnam," in *Strangers at Home: The Vietnam Veteran Since the War,* edited by C. R. Leventman (New York: Praeger, 1980), pp. 71–85.

12. *Report of the National Working Group on Black Vietnam Veterans* (Washington, D.C.: Veterans Administration, 1984), p. 6. This Report is one of several reports on special populations. The Readjustment Counseling Service ("Vet Center" Headquarters) has organized the following Working Groups: The National Working Group on Women Vietnam Veterans; the National Working Group on Hispanic Vietnam Veterans; the National Working Group on Native American Vietnam Veterans; and the National Working Group on Disabled Vietnam Veterans. These reports may be secured by writing to: Dr. Arthur Blank, Director, Readjustment Counseling Service, Veterans Administration Central Office, 810 Vermont Avenue N.W., Washington, D.C. 20420.

13. Martin Binkin and Mark Eitelberg, *Blacks in the Military* (Washington, D.C.: The Brookings Institution, 1982).

14. Erwin R. Parson, "The Intercultural Setting: Encountering the Readjustment Needs of Black Americans Who Served in Vietnam," in: *The Psychiatric Effects of the Vietnam War,* edited by S. Sonnenberg, A. Blank, and J. Talbott (Washington, D.C.: The Psychiatric Press, in press).

15. Erwin R. Parson, "The Gook-Identification and Post-Traumatic Stress Disorders in Black Vietnam Veterans," *Black Psychiatrists of America Quarterly* **13**(2) (1984), pp. 14–18.

16. Thomas Yager, Robert Laufer, and Mark Gallops, "Some Problems Associated with War in Men of the Vietnam Generation," *Archives of General Psychiatry* **41**(1984), pp. 327–333.

17. Wallace Terry, *Bloods: An Oral History of the Vietnam War by Black Veterans* (New York: Random House, Inc., 1984). For a true in-depth understanding of the Vietnam War from the perspective of the black combat veteran, we highly recommend this book. It is the only one of its kind.

18. Lawrence M. Baskir and William A. Strauss, *Chance and Circumstance: The Draft, the War, and the Vietnam Generation* (New York: Vantage Press, Inc., 1978).

19. Charles Kadushin, Ghislaine Boulanger, and John Martin, *Legacies of Vietnam: Comparative Adjustment of Veterans and Their Peers,* Volume 4: *Long-Term Stress Reactions: Some Causes, Consequences, and Naturally-Occurring Support Systems* (Washington, D.C.: U.S. Government Printing Office, 1981), pp. 478–706.

20. Gary Sorenson, "Hispanic Vietnam Veterans," *Vet Center Voice* **4**(6) (1983).

21. Harry Maurer, *Not Working: An Oral History of the Unemployed* (New York: Holt, Rinehart & Winston, Inc., 1979), p. 1.

22. Gary Sorenson, "Trio Addresses Counseling Issues Dealing with Ethnic Minorities," *Vet Center Voice* **3**(3), p. 12 (1983).

23. Tom Holm, "Indian Veterans of the Vietnam War," *Four Winds* Autumn 1982.

24. Edwin Richardson, "Cultural and Historical Perspectives in Counseling American Indians," in: *Counseling the Culturally Different: Theory and Practice,* edited by D. W. Sue (New York: John Wiley & Sons, Inc., 1981), pp. 216–255.

25. Derald W. Sue, editor, *Counseling the Culturally Different: Theory and Practice* (New York: John Wiley & Sons, Inc., 1981).

26. Gustavo Martinez, Presentation made in training film on Hispanic Vietnam veterans, at the Phase V Advanced Clinical Conference for Team Leaders, Providence, R.I., May 1984.

27. George Henderson, "Introduction, Part IV. Japanese Americans," in: *Understanding and Counseling Ethnic Minorities,* edited by G. Henderson (Springfield, Ill.: Charles C. Thomas, 1979), p. 405.

28. Chie Nakane, *Japanese Society* (Berkeley: University of California Press, 1970), pp. 2–3.
29. John W. Connor, "Acculturation and Family Continuities in Three Generations of Japanese American," in: *Understanding and Counseling Ethnic Minorities*, edited by G. Henderson (Springfield, Ill.: Charles C. Thomas, 1979), pp. 416–430.

CHAPTER 8

1. M. Straker, "The Vietnam Veteran: The Task is Re-integration," *Diseases of the Nervous System* 7 (1978), pp. 75–79.
2. Arthur S. Blank, "Apocalypse Terminable and Interminable: Operation Outreach for Vietnam Veterans," *Hospital and Community Psychiatry* 33 (1982), pp. 913–918.
3. Arthur S. Blank, *Vietnam Veterans—Operation Outreach*, Presentation at the First Training Conference for Operation Outreach (St. Louis: Regional Medical Education Center, 1979).
4. Robert B. Shapiro, "Transference, Countertransference, and the Vietnam Veteran," in *Psychotherapy of the Combat Veteran*, edited by H. J. Schwartz (New York, Spectrum Publications, 1984), pp. 85–101.
5. Tom Williams, editor, *Post-traumatic Stress Disorders of the Vietnam Veteran* (Cincinnati: Disabled American Veterans, 1980), p. 25.
6. Stephen Berman, Stephen Price, and Fred Gusman, "An Inpatient Program for Vietnam Combat Veterans in a Veterans Administration Hospital," *Hospital and Community Psychiatry* 33 (1982), pp. 919–922.
7. Chester Paul Adams and Jack McCloskey, "Twice Born Men," in: *Beyond Clinic Walls*, edited by A. B. Tulipan and C. L. Attneave (University: University of Alabama Press, 1974), pp. 46–57.
8. Erwin Randolph Parson, "Narcissistic Injury in Vietnam Vets: The Role Post-traumatic Stress Disorder, 'Agent Orange Anxiety', and the Repatriation Experience," *Stars and Stripes—The National Tribune* November 18, 1982, pp. 1–15.
9. Erwin Randolph Parson, "The Role of Psychodynamic Group Therapy in the Treatment of the Combat Veteran," in: *Psychotherapy of the Combat Veteran*, edited by H. J. Schwartz (New York: Spectrum Medical and Scientific Books, 1984), pp. 153–220.

CHAPTER 9

1. Mardi J. Horowitz, *Stress Response Syndromes* (New York: Jason Aronson, Inc., 1976).

2. Charles R. Figley, editor, *Stress Disorders Among Vietnam Veterans: Theory, Research, and Treatment Implications,* edited by C. R. Figley (New York: Brunner/Mazel, Inc., 1978).

3. John P. Wilson, "Towards an Understanding of Post-traumatic Stress Disorders Among Vietnam Veterans," Testimony before U.S. Senate Subcommittee on Veteran Affairs (May 21, 1980).

4. John Russell Smith, *Veterans and Combat: Towards a Model of the Stress Recovery Process,* paper prepared for the Veterans Administration Operation Outreach Training Program (1981).

5. Robert Jay Lifton, *Home from the War: Vietnam Veterans: Neither Victims nor Executioners* (New York: Simon & Schuster, Inc., 1973), pp. 99–133.

6. Chaim Shatan, "The Grief of Soldiers: Vietnam Combat Veterans' Self-help Movement," *American Journal of Orthopsychiatry* **43** (1973), pp. 640–653.

7. Robert B. Shapiro, "Working Through the War with Vietnam Vets," *Group* **2** (Fall 1978), pp. 156–185.

8. Lawrence C. Kolb, "The Post-traumatic Stress Disorders of Combat: A Subgroup with a Conditioned Emotional Response," *Military Medicine* **149** (1984), pp. 237–243.

9. L. C. Kolb and L. R. Mutalipassi, "The Conditioned Emotional Response a Subclass of the Chronic and Delayed Posttraumatic Stress Disorder," *Psychiatric Annals* **12** (1982), pp. 979–987.

10. Robert Frick, personal communication (April 1983).

11. Joel O. Brende and Bryce D. Benedict, "The Vietnam Combat Delayed Stress Response Syndrome: Hypnotherapy of 'Dissociative Symptoms'," *The American Journal of Clinical Hypnosis* **23** (1980), pp. 34–40.

12. Herbert Hendin and Ann Pollinger-Haas, *The Wounds of War* (New York: Basic Books, Inc., 1984).

13. Arthur S. Blank, *Vietnam Veterans—Operation Outreach,* presentation at the First Training Conference for Operation Outreach," (St. Louis: VA Regional Medical Education Center, 1979).

14. Robert Frick and Larry Bogart, "Transference and Countertransference in Group Therapy with Vietnam Veterans," *Bulletin of the Menninger Clinic* **46** (1982), pp. 429–444.

15. Mardi J. Horowitz, "Stress Response Syndromes," *Archives of General Psychiatry* **31** (1974), pp. 768–781.

16. John A. Fairbank and Terence M. Keane, "Flooding for Combat-related Stress Disorders: Assessment of Anxiety Reduction Across Traumatic Memories," *American Association of Biofeedback Therapy* (1981).

17. John McQueeney, personal communication (June 1984).

18. A. Peter Ziarnowski and Daniel C. Broida, "Therapeutic Implications of the Nightmares of Vietnam Combat Veterans," *VA Practitioner* **1** (1984), pp. 63–68.

19. Mardi J. Horowitz, "Phase Oriented Treatment of Stress Response Syndromes," *American Journal of Psychotherapy* **31** (1977), pp. 38–42

20. Joel O. Brende, "An Educational-Therapeutic Group for Drug and Alcohol Abusing Combat Veterans," *Journal for Contemporary Psychotherapy* **14**, (1984), pp. 122–136.

21. Erwin Randolph Parson, "The Reparation of the Self: Clinical and Theoretical Dimensions in the Treatment of Vietnam Combat Veterans," *Journal of Contemporary Psychotherapy* **14** (1984), pp. 4–56.

22. Joel Osler Brende, "Combined Individual and Group Therapy for Vietnam Veterans," *International Journal of Group Psychotherapy* **31** (1981), pp. 367–378.

23. Erwin Randolph Parson, "The Role of Psychodynamic Group Therapy in the Treatment of the Combat Veteran," in: *Psychotherapy of the Combat Veteran,* edited by H. J. Schwartz (New York: Spectrum Medical and Scientific Books, 1984), pp. 153–220.

24. William Boutelle, Chief, Psychiatry Service VA Medical Center, Northampton, Mass., Personal Communication (August 1983).

25. Roy LaCoursier, Kenneth Godfrey, and Lorne Ruby, "Traumatic Neurosis in the Etiology of Alcoholism: Vietnam Combat and Other Trauma," *American Journal of Psychiatry* **137** (1980), pp. 966–968.

26. John Yost, "The Psychopharmacologic Treatment of the Delayed Stress Syndrome in Vietnam Veterans," in: *Post-traumatic Stress Disorders of the Vietnam Veteran,* edited by T. Williams (Cincinnati: Disabled American Veterans, 1980), pp. 125–130.

27. L. C. Kolb, B. C. Burris, and Susan Griffiths, "Propranolol and Clonidine in Treatment of the Chronic Post-traumatic Stress Disorders of War," in: *Post-traumatic Stress Disorder: Psychological and Biological Seguelae,* edited by B. A. van der Kolk (Washington, D.C.: American Psychiatric Association, 1984).

28. Bessel A. van der Kolk, "Psychopharmacological Issues in Posttraumatic Stress Disorder," *Hospital and Community Psychiatry* **34** (1983), pp. 683–691.

29. G. L. Hogben and R. B. Cornfield, "Treatment of Traumatic War Neurosis with Phenelzine," *Archives of General Psychiatry* **4** (1981), pp. 440–445.

30. David V. Sheehan, James Ballenger, and Gary Jacobsen, "Treatment of Endogenous Anxiety with Phobic, Hysterical, and Hypochondriacal Symptoms," *Archives of General Psychiatry* **37** (1980), pp. 51–59.

31. Joel O. Brende, "Electrodermal Responses in Post-traumatic Syndromes: A Pilot Study of Cerebral Hemisphere Functioning in Vietnam Veterans," *Journal of Nervous and Mental Disease* **170** (1982), pp. 351–361.

32. Claude Chemtob, personal communication (November 1983).

33. J. Breuer and Sigmund Freud, "Studies in Hysteria," in: *Complete Psychological Works, Standard Edition* translated by James Strachey (London: Hogarth Press, 1955).
34. C. J. Jung, "The Therapeutic Value of Abreaction," [from] "The Practice of Psychotherapy," in: *Collected Papers* Volume 16, Part II (New York: Pantheon Books, 1954).
35. William C. Menninger, "Modern Concepts of War Neuroses," *Bulletin of the Menninger Clinic* **10** (1946), pp. 196–209.
36. Sarah Haley, "When the Patient Reports Atrocities," *Archives of General Psychiatry* **30** (1974), pp. 191–196.
37. P. M. Balson and C. R. Dempster, "Treatment of War Neuroses from Vietnam," *Comprehensive Psychiatry* **21** (1980), pp. 167–175.
38. R. R. Grinker and J. F. Spiegel, *Men under Stress* (Philadelphia: Blackstone Co., 1945).
39. David Spiegel, "Vietnam Grief Work using Hypnosis," *American Journal of Clinical Hypnosis* **24** (1981), pp. 33–40.
40. Robert B. Shapiro, "Transference, Countertransference, and the Vietnam Veteran" in: *Psychotherapy of the Combat Veteran,* edited by H. J. Schwartz (New York: Spectrum Medical and Scientific Books, 1984), pp. 85–101.

CHAPTER 10

1. Robert Shapiro, "Working Through the War with Vietnam Vets," *Group* **2** (Fall 1978), pp. 156–185.
2. Erwin R. Parson, "The Reparation of the Self: Clinical and Theoretical Dimensions in the Treatment of Vietnam Combat Veterans," *Journal of Contemporary Psychotherapy* **14** (1984), pp. 4–56.
3. Readjustment Counseling Service (Vet Center Program), Monthly National Program Statistics (Washington, D.C.: Veterans Administration Central Office, July 1984).
4. R. Stille, T. Scarano, and D. Kaliher, "Time Management, Evaluation, and Function of Operation Outreach Vet Centers by Center and Region," paper presented to Operation Outreach at the Regional Managers Quarterly Meeting, Washington, D.C., June 28, 1983.
5. Erwin R. Parson, "The Role of Psychodynamic Group Therapy in the Treatment of the Combat Veteran," in *Psychotherapy of the Combat Veteran,* edited by H. J. Schwartz (New York: Spectrum Medical and Scientific Books, 1984), pp. 153–220.

NAME INDEX

255

SUBJECT INDEX